<User-Centered Web Development>

Jonathan Lazar
Towson University

JONES AND BARTLETT PUBLISHERS
Sudbury, Massachusetts
BOSTON   TORONTO   LONDON   SINGAPORE

World Headquarters
Jones and Bartlett Publishers
40 Tall Pine Drive
Sudbury, MA 01776
978-443-5000
info@jbpub.com
www.jbpub.com

Jones and Bartlett Publishers Canada
2406 Nikanna Road
Mississauga, ON L5C 2W6
CANADA

Jones and Bartlett Publishers International
Barb House, Barb Mews
London W6 7PA
UK

Cover image © Tim Macpherson/Tony Stone

Library of Congress Cataloging-in-Publication Data
Lazar, Jonathan.
    User-centered Web development / Jonathan Lazar.
        p. cm.
    Includes index.
    ISBN 0-7637-1431-3
    1. Web sites—Design and construction. 2. Web site development. I. Title.

    TK5105.888 .L397 2001
    025.04—dc21   00-069027

Senior Acquisitions Editor: Michael Stranz
Development and Product Manager: Amy Rose
Production Assistant: Tara McCormick
Production Coordination: Trillium Project Management
Composition: Jackie Davies
Copyeditor: Roberta Lewis
Text Design: Mary McKeon
Cover Design: Kristin Ohlin
Printing and Binding: Malloy
Cover printing: Malloy

This book was typeset in Quark 4.1 on a Power Macintosh G3. The font families used are
Stone Serif, Rotis Sans Serif, and Trajan. The first printing was printed on 60# Thor D-03
Antique.

Printed in the United States of America
05 04 03 02 01   10 9 8 7 6 5 4 3 2 1

Preface

The World Wide Web has become an integral feature of our every day lives, so that today organizations consider it a necessity to have a web site. Some of these web sites are successful, but just as many of them are failures. To build a successful web site, users should be involved in the development process. This book instructs readers in the process of web development, with a focus on user input. This book is geared towards undergraduate and graduate courses in which students study the process of web site development. In addition, this book can be useful for those in the web development industry who want to include users in the development process but are unfamiliar with the standard processes, tools, and techniques of systems analysis and design or user-centered design.

The idea of writing this book developed as a result of my teaching experience. I teach a course that focuses on web design from a user-centered point of view. In this course, students learn the process and the technical aspects of web design. In the semester-long project for this course, my students build a web site for a non-profit organization. This book is designed to guide the reader through that user-centered web development process. After reading this book, the reader will be able to design a web site, from idea to "going live," incorporating user input, and designing web resources that meet the functionality and usability needs of the users.

User-Centered Web Development

The process of building a web site that meets the needs of the users is known as user-centered web development. User input in the design process of an information system is a well-accepted necessity. Any student of information systems should be familiar with the systems development lifecycle and the value of user involvement in the development process. The user-centered web development process focuses on designing web resources that meet the functionality and usability needs of the end user. Functionality means that a web site must provide resources that users want. Usability means that a web site should be easy to use. The user-centered web development process is playing an important role in businesses, non-profit organizations, and educational institutions.

Case Studies

Case studies are used in this book to show how the user-centered design techniques are applied in a real world setting. This book includes three case studies of actual web sites that were designed or re-designed with user-centered techniques. These three case studies represent three very different organizations: one is a large for-profit corporation, one is a non-profit community organization, and one is a private high school. Although these three organizations differ in size and have very different missions, all three organizations understood the value that the user-centered design processes brought to building or re-designing their web site. Similar development methodologies can be seen in all three cases. The importance of requirements gathering and usability testing is emphasized in all three case studies.

How To Use this Book

This book is structured to follow the user-centered web development process. Chapter 1 provides an introduction to user-centered web development and Chapter 2 describes the lifecycle models for systems development. Chapter 3 describes the first stage of user-centered web development, which is defining the mission of the web site and the target user population. Chapters 4 and 5 discuss requirements gathering. Chapters 6, 7, and 8 instruct the reader in conceptual design. Chapter 9 describes physical design, the actual coding of the web site. Chapter 10 provides information on how to perform usability testing. Chapters 11 and 12 will guide the reader through the implementation, marketing, and the evaluation of a web site.

Web Design Course

A course in web design may be found under a number of names, such as web development, analysis and design for web sites, web site development, web usability, interface design, and web technology. In these courses, it would be appropriate to go through one chapter a week. A few weeks should be left for discussing physical design of web sites, focusing on either programming, such as HTML and JavaScript, or a web development application, such as FrontPage or DreamWeaver.

Systems Analysis and Design Course

Those in systems analysis and design courses will undoubtedly be interested in Chapter 3, on defining the site mission and target user population. Chapters 4 and 5, on requirements gathering, offer information on web-based methods of requirements gathering, which are not available in most analysis and design textbooks. Chapter 10 offers information on web-based usability testing, and Chapter 12 discusses maintenance and evaluation, which are important topics in analysis and design courses.

Human–Computer Interaction Course

Those in human-computer interaction courses will probably be most interested in Chapters 6–8, which focus on conceptual design of the user interface. Chapter 10 focuses on usability testing and offers methods of web-based usability testing. Chapter 12 concludes our discussion of the web development process with a look at evaluation tools. This material includes many items that are fresh from the research literature.

Resources Available

At the end of every chapter, discussion questions are available to stimulate conversation in the course. Book-related resources are available at the Jones and Bartlett web site <http://www.webdesign.jbpub.com>. For instructors, a sample syllabus is available for download, to help in course planning. A peer-reviewed paper provides suggestions for having students successfully complete web design projects for local community organizations. For students, links to related resources are provided.

Acknowledgments

First, and most importantly, I want to thank the people who are closest to me, who have helped me become the person that I am today. My parents, Drs. Libby Kumin and Martin Lazar, and my grandparents, Berniece and

Herbert Kumin, and Mollie and Aaron Lazar have always provided love and support, and made sure that I grew up appreciating everything that life has to offer, and my responsibilities to the world, as well.

I would like to thank Drs. James Clements, Doris Lidtke, Chao Lu, Anthony Norcio, and Jenny Preece for all of their professional advice and support. I could not ask for a better group of colleagues to work with. Thanks also to the Center for Applied Information Technology at Towson University for their financial support. My student assistant, Jason Kemp, was an invaluable asset throughout the writing process. He deserves a hearty thank you for tracking down many references and screen shots.

Thanks to all of the wonderful people at Jones and Bartlett Publishers. Michael Stranz, Amy Rose, and Tara McCormick were an enjoyable team to work with. They were always available with suggestions and support. I would also like to thank Bobbie Lewis for her copyediting assistance. Although she did not directly work on the book project, Christine Tridente was always very encouraging.

Thanks to the following people who took the time to review the manuscript: Dr. Kevin Crowston, Syracuse University; Dr. Anthony Norcio, University of Maryland; Dr. Ruth Small, Syracuse University.

I would like to thank some of the many people who have influenced me in my life: Mark Broderick, Fr. John Brunett, Dr. Freeman Hrabowski, Dr. Joel and Sandra Lazar, Barbara Morris, Phyllis and Milton Shuch, and the entire Wolsey family.

The case studies that illustrate the user-centered web development techniques in real-world settings are a major component of this book. Kudos to MyVan Baranoski, Fuliscia Black-Morrison, Darin Daubert, Keven Lehmann, and Brett Johnson, from the Institute of Notre Dame case study; Josephine Barton, Keith Kaplan, Seitaro Matsui, Malik Oussalah, and Bill Sandison, from the Best Buddies Maryland case study; and Jack Yu, from the Eastman Kodak Company case study. Not only are these the individuals who wrote the case studies, but they were also the ones responsible for managing the actual web development projects. Dick Horst provided the usability lab pictures, and Sam Houston provided the web site logs. I am grateful to both of them.

No thank you list would be complete without mentioning Meg Richards, who introduced me to the field of information systems many, many years back. Thank you for introducing me to the field that I love.

Jonathan Lazar

Contents

Introduction to User–Centered Design for the Web

The Internet and the World Wide Web have become an integral part of our world. In approximately a decade, the Web has grown from a theoretical concept to a daily part of our lives. Most for-profit companies, nonprofit organizations, and schools and universities either currently have web sites or plan to create them. And more information is being made available on the Web every single day. The number of web users is now so large it is impossible to precisely count. The Web has truly become a presence at all levels of society.

When a technology such as the Web is first introduced, the primary concern is making sure that the technology works. But as we get more experience with designing web sites, the problem is no longer designing the technical infrastructure of the web site, but rather, how to make a *good* web site, one that is easy to use, and meets the needs of the users.

► 1.1 FOCUS ON THE USER

The purpose of this book is to guide the web developer through the process of designing a web site while incorporating the input of the user. It is well-accepted that an information system needs to be developed around the needs of the user.[1] An information system that has not included the user in the design process will most likely not be successful. Such a system will leave users frustrated and possibly unable to achieve their goals.[2] A web site is a type of information system and as such needs to be designed to meet the needs of the user. It must offer content that users want and be designed so the users can easily access it in order for the web site to be a success.

Unlike traditional informational systems, the Web has a short history. It has not been around for very long. The theoretical concept of a "web" of information was first introduced by Vannevar Bush in the classic 1945 paper "As We May Think."[3] The technical foundation of the Internet, on which web traffic travels, has been around since the early 1970s (although, not in its current form) and the technical infrastructure for the Web (including the standards for HTML and HTTP) has existed for approximately a decade. The Web has seen widespread acceptance only within the last five or six years. As the Web grows and matures, we see more of a focus on the user in designing web sites.

► 1.2 USER–CENTERED WEB DEVELOPMENT

User-centered web development refers to a design process for designing a web site that meets the needs of the user. That is, users should be included in the design process for web sites. Another related term that is becoming popular in the media is *web usability*, a term that refers to web sites that are easy to use. Not only are new web sites being developed using the user-centered process, but many organizations are reevaluating their existing web sites. Many are realizing that their current web sites are not meeting the needs of the users, and these organizations are redesigning their web sites using the user-centered approach. Research on both user-centered web design and web usability is also increasing. However, user-centered web development is not merely an interesting process that is limited to those doing research. Companies, nonprofit organizations, and governmental agencies are also starting to adopt the user-centered approach to web design. Why? Users will be satisfied when web sites are easy to use and when they can complete their tasks with relative ease. Users will return to these sites.

Corporate Examples

In many cases, user-centered web development comes down to the issue of money. Companies realize that bad web design means lost revenue. For example, the e-commerce web site of IBM was very hard to use, and IBM realized that the two most-used features on the web site were the "search" function, and the "help" button; users could not understand how to use the e-commerce site.[4] After a redesign effort that cost millions of dollars, sales increased 400 percent, while use of the "help" button decreased 84 percent.[4] The functionality of the IBM web site stayed the same—users could perform the same tasks as before, but the redesign effort made the web site easier to use. And with that redesign effort, users were more satisfied. Other companies and organizations, such as Eastman Kodak and Indiana University, have also employed the user-centered design process to redesign their web sites.[5,6] Governmental agencies, too, are increasingly realizing the importance of considering the user in web development.[7]

Applying a User-Centered Design

Considering the user in the design process has a number of ramifications. For instance, many sites are designed in a specific manner because the web designer thought that it would be "cool." Other sites are designed to "be noticed." However, we know from research that users are not interested in either of these goals. The Technology Acceptance Model is a validated model from the research literature. The TAM has discovered that the two factors that most influence the use of computer technology are the ease of use and the usefulness of the technology.[8]

These factors also apply to the users of a web site.[9] Users want a site that is easy to use, that has a minimum download time, and that allows them to complete their tasks in a minimal amount of time with a minimal amount of frustration. Users equally want a site that provides some type of meaningful information or interaction to meet the user's task goals, whether those goals are to trade stocks, purchase books, learn more about golfing, or find out about an organization in the community. These standards apply to all types of web sites, including those featuring information, e-commerce, or entertainment. For instance, a user will not purchase from an e-commerce web site that does not offer good prices or quick delivery of products.[10] Nor will a user purchase from a web site that is complicated and frustrating to use.[10,11]

Web developers should not substitute their own personal preferences for the principles of user-centered design. What a web developer might consider to be "cool," a user might consider to be annoying. A web developer's perceptions and knowledge base can thus be quite different from those of the targeted users of the technology.

▶ 1.3 COGNITIVE FOUNDATIONS

Web site designers face new challenges in designing information systems. The web environment is a paradigm shift from past software development. In the near past, software applications were designed either for a set group of users within an organization (such as a custom payroll system) or for the mass market (such as a word processing application). For a set group of users within an organization, it was possible to determine exactly who these users were, and their exact computing environments. For mass market software, the software could have minimum requirements (such as 8 MB RAM, 50 MB free hard drive space, and so on), and the software was sold to work only with one platform (such as IBM PC). Web sites, however, are totally different because they can be accessed by anyone, anywhere, with any technological environment, using any platform, any browser, and any browser version. A web site therefore has to work under hundreds or thousands of possible technological environments.

Training for a Web Environment

When users utilize a traditional software application (such as a spreadsheet or custom student records database), they receive training and/or documentation.[12,13,14] Users may feel comfortable only after having received the training sessions, handouts, or books on the software application. If users move from one brand of software to another (such as moving from Corel WordPerfect to Microsoft Word), they must be retrained, or at least receive documentation on the new software application. The web environment is fundamentally different. The users can access many different web sites, but they cannot receive training on how to use specific web sites themselves. The users of major software applications that happen to be delivered via the web browser interface (through an intranet) are an exception. These applications are more similar to the traditional software application and the users can receive documentation and training. Users will access these applications on a daily basis. But most web users will visit numerous web sites and spend only a small amount of time on each site. It is impossible to provide training on how to use the many sites each user will potentially visit. Instead, users may receive training on how the web environment as a whole works, and specific training on how the web browser works.[15,16,17] Users will then expect that the many different web sites will operate in a similar manner. For instance, if most web sites use blue text as hyperlinks, then users will expect that blue text indicates a hyperlink.[18] If most e-commerce web sites use the metaphors of a "shopping cart" and a "checkout," then users will expect these terms, and may be confused when other terminology is used.[11] Conformity of web sites can actually facilitate users' performance of their tasks.

Predictability Means Ease of Use

Much as uniformity of software applications (such as Word, Excel, and Access) was a successful strategy for Microsoft Office Suite, similarity among different web sites is also beneficial because it allows users to carry over their knowledge from one web site to the next. Think about it—if Microsoft Word acted differently every time that a user accessed it, wouldn't that user become frustrated pretty quickly? The same result can occur with web sites. In fact, due to the nature of the Web itself (a distributed network with numerous components that are all susceptible to failure), the web experience is inherently unpredictable.[19,16] Errors occur frequently, and many of these errors are not due to the actions of the users. Therefore, it is very important to make the web browsing experience as predictable as possible. A predictable web site, a web site that is quickly understood by a user, is a web site that is easy to use.

▶ 1.4 THE PROCESS

The web development person or team must follow an orderly process to achieve a successful web site.

Define the Users

A web site that is "easy to use" can have different meanings, depending on who your users are. Some people have claimed that, on the web, it is hard to design a site based on the needs of the users, because the web has no defined population of users.[20] This is not really the case. There might be a few web sites that are designed for everyone, all ages, both genders, and from all geographic locations—such as web sites for the New York Times or CNN. However, most web sites have a defined population of target users. For instance, a web site about Pokemon would have a defined user base, namely, children, and much is known about designing technology for children.[21]

Other web sites might be targeted towards college students, senior citizens, miniature train enthusiasts, or fans of Carly Simon. So the first step, then, for the web development team is to define the user population.

Gather Requirements

By doing a *requirements gathering*, the web development team can learn more about the targeted user population, and this knowledge will influence the web design. Do the targeted users tend to have slow connections to the Web? Are the targeted users experienced computer users or novices? What type of content would the targeted users be interested in? What plug-in technologies do the targeted users have? The development team may be interested in a range of questions. For instance, do college students tend to have high-speed connections to the Web? Do Carly Simon fans tend not to have plug-in applications installed? What type of content would Carly Simon fans be interested in seeing on the web, anyway? Concert dates, Carly Simon trivia, and/or pictures of Carly Simon?

Involve the User

The movie *Field of Dreams* introduced the phrase, "Build it, and they will come." Although this is an optimistic phrase, it does not apply to building web sites. If you design a web site that does not have content that the users are interested in, and present a web site that is too technologically advanced or confusing, the users will *not* come. Maybe a better phrase would be: "If you build it, and it offers the users something they want, and it's easy to use, then they will come." Not as poetic, but more realistic.

Design the Site

Once we know who the targeted users are and have gathered the requirements, we then conceptually design the web site. Now we handle issues such as navigation design and page design. The next step is to physically design the web site, which means either coding HTML, JavaScript, and other languages by hand, or using a web design application (such as Microsoft FrontPage) to assist us.

Testing and Beyond

After designing a web site, usability testing is required to make sure that the users do not find the web site difficult to use. After testing, the site should be unveiled and marketed to the user population. Then the web site needs to be updated with new content, and periodically evaluated to ensure that it continues to meet the users' needs. A web site has been created and implemented, through a process that is somewhat similar to that of the systems development lifecycle.[12]

Later chapters will discuss techniques for communicating with users and getting them involved in the design process. In addition, later chapters will describe the web development lifecycle in greater detail. The differences between designing a new web site and re-designing a currently existing web site will be discussed, presenting a full picture of the web development process.

► 1.5 CASE STUDIES

Throughout the book, case studies will examine the development or re-design of three different web sites:

- The Institute of Notre Dame is a private, Catholic high school located in Baltimore, Maryland. The Institute of Notre Dame had a web site, but was interested in doing a site redesign using the user-centered design process.

- Best Buddies Maryland helps form partnerships between people with mental disabilities and the greater community, and is affiliated with the national Best Buddies organization. Best Buddies Maryland did not have a web site, and the case study will follow the development of their first web site.

- Eastman Kodak Company is a large-scale corporation, providing photographic and electronic equipment and services. Eastman Kodak Company had an existing web site and wanted to redesign their web site using the user-centered design process.

Although these are three different organizations (a school, a nonprofit organization, and a for-profit corporation), similar threads of user-centered design and usability appear in all three cases.

SUMMARY

When designing any type of informational system, such as a web site, it is important to get the user involved in the design process. User-centered web development methods can assist in making a web site that users find both useful and easy to use. This book is geared toward developing these web sites by a user-centered web development process; it is primarily focused on small to medium size informational web sites. Some web sites have hundreds of thousands of web pages (such as the Library of Congress), but the majority of web sites are much smaller. There are also web sites that offer entertainment (such as a soap opera), but a majority of web sites are informational. These informational web sites are the focus of our discussion. However, the techniques for user-centered design (such as the requirements gathering and the usability testing) can be used to incorporate user feedback into designing any web site, of any size, with any purpose. Just remember . . . the user is the most important part of developing a web site!

Discussion Questions

1. How is web site design different from traditional software design?
2. Why is user-centered design for the web so important?
3. What two factors greatly influence the users to use a new technology?

REFERENCES

1. Norman, D., & Draper, S. (1986). *User-Centered System Design*. Hillsdale, NJ: Lawrence Erlbaum Associates.
2. Preece, J., Rogers, Y., Sharp, H., Benyon, D., Holland, S., & Carey, T. (1994). *Human-Computer Interaction*. Wokingham, England: Addison-Wesley.
3. Bush, V. (1945). As we may think. *The Atlantic Monthly*, 176, 101–108.
4. Tedeschi, B. (1999). Good web site design can lead to healthy sales. *The New York Times*, August 30, 1999.
5. Corry, M., Frick, T., & Hansen, L. (1997). User-centered design and usability testing of a web site: An illustrative case study. *Educational Technology Research and Development*, *45*(4), 65–76.
6. Yu, J., Prabhu, P., & Neale, W. (1998). *A user-centered approach to designing a new top-level structure for a large and diverse corporate web site*. Proceedings of the 1998 Human Factors and the Web Conference. Available at: http://www.research.att.com/conf/hfweb/
7. Lohrmann, D. (2000). Government web sites must focus more on the user. *Government Computer News*, June 19, 2000. Available at http:///www.gcn.com
8. Davis, F. (1989). Perceived usefulness, perceived ease of use, and user acceptance of information technology. *MIS Quarterly*, *13*(3), 319–340.
9. Lederer, A., Maupin, D., Sena, M., & Zhuang, Y. (1998). *The role of ease of use, usefulness, and attitude in the prediction of world wide web usage*. Proceedings of the Conference on Computer Personnel Research, 195–204.
10. Lazar, J., & Norcio, A. (2001, in press). User Considerations in E-commerce Transactions. In Q. Chen (Ed.), *Human-Computer Interaction: Issues and Challenges*. Hershey, PA: Idea Group Publishing, 185–199.
11. Nielsen, J. (2000). *Why Doc Searls Doesn't Sell Any Books*. Available at: http://www.useit.com
12. Hoffer, J., George, J., & Valacich, J. (1999). *Modern Systems Analysis and Design*. Reading, MA: Addison-Wesley.

13. Martin, E., DeHayes, D., Hoffer, J., & Perkins, W. (1994). *Managing Information Technology: What Managers Need to Know.* New York: Macmillan.

14. Whitten, I., & Bentley, L. (1997). *Systems Analysis and Design Methods.* Boston: Irwin McGraw-Hill.

15. Lazar, J., & Norcio, A. (1999). *A framework for training novice users in appropriate responses to errors.* Proceedings of the International Association for Computer Information Systems Conference, 128–134.

16. Lazar, J., & Norcio, A. (2000). System and Training Design for End-User Error. In S. Clarke & B. Lehaney (Eds.), *Human-Centered Methods in Information Systems: Current Research and Practice* (pp. 76–90). Hershey, PA: Idea Group Publishing.

17. Lazar, J., & Norcio, A. (2000). Training novice users in developing strategies for responding to errors when browsing the web. Paper under review.

18. Nielsen, J. (2000). *Designing Web Usability: The Practice of Simplicity.* Indianapolis: New Riders Publishing.

19. Lazar, J., & Norcio, A. (1999). *To err or not to err, that is the question: Novice user perception of errors while surfing the web.* Proceedings of the Information Resource Management Association 1999 International Conference, 321–325.

20. Head, A. (1999). *Design Wise: A Guide for Evaluating the Interface Design of Information Resources.* Medford, NJ: Information Today.

21. Druin, A. (Ed.). (1998). *The Design of Children's Technology.* San Francisco: Morgan Kaufmann Publishers.

User–Centered Web Development Lifecycle

The World Wide Web poses new challenges for those seeking to manage an information systems project. Issues such as browser compatibility and download time were not problems when software applications were being designed for mainframe computers. The complexity of the web environment only increases the need for a good development process with a strong requirements-gathering component. It is a frequent but incorrect assumption that designing a web site begins with HTML. Frequently in business, timelines are pushed up to have a "live site" in a short period of time. Many times, the end-user of the web site is forgotten, and instead, web sites are designed to "make a statement." However, when designing any type of information system, it is important to design the system around the needs of the user. Lifecycle models such as the Systems Development Life Cycle assist in managing large information systems development projects. These models address issues such as requirements determination, conceptual design, and testing. Using a lifecycle model helps to make sure that important aspects of systems development are not forgotten.

► 2.1 TRADITIONAL LIFECYCLE MODEL OF SYSTEMS DEVELOPMENT

In traditional systems development, information systems are developed using a Systems Development Life Cycle (SDLC), also called the *waterfall model*. Although the exact lifecycle steps differ depending on the source, overall all lifecycle models are similar in the steps they describe. The lifecycle models ensure that users are included in the design process, and that there is appropriate planning and testing. This can be seen by examining the SDLC models presented in two of the most popular textbooks for Systems Analysis and Design.

Lifecycle Models and Their Steps

Compare the following two lifecycle models:

► The Hoffer, George, and Valacich SDLC[1]

1. Project identification and selection—An organization's overall IS needs are analyzed.
2. Project initiation and planning—A potential IS project is presented and a detailed plan developed.
3. Analysis—The current system is studied and replacement systems are proposed.
4. Logical design—All functional features of a potential system are described.
5. Physical design—The logical design is turned into technology-specific details.
6. Implementation—IS is developed, tested, and implemented in the organization.
7. Maintenance—The IS is tested, repaired, and improved.

► The Whitten and Bentley SDLC[2]

1. Planning—Identify the scope of the problem, and plan the overall strategy.
2. Analysis—Study the problems and identify system requirements.
3. Design—Design the system solution, if necessary.
4. Implementation—Document and implement the solution.
5. Support—Find errors; seek and make improvements.

In these models of the SDLC, the steps are not necessarily sequential; some of the steps take place simultaneously. Besides these two well-known lifecycle models there are other models in the literature for developing information systems. These other models tend to address issues that are crucial for specialized types of information systems projects. For instance, the *evolutionary model* (also called the spiral model) is used in projects where there are a large number of risk factors.[1,3] Both the lifecycle and evolutionary models address system development by involving the user in some stages.

User Input in the Lifecycle

User input is traditionally included during the requirements gathering, testing, and implementation phases. A number of design models have been presented that focus more on user input into the system design.[5] For instance, some user-centered design approaches, such as participatory design and the star lifecycle, focus on including users in all phases of design.[5] In participatory design, users become members of the actual development team.[4] In the star lifecycle, users get to evaluate each stage of development.[5] The usability engineering lifecycle focuses on usability at all stages of development.[6] Regardless of how users are included in the development of an information system, it is necessary to include user input when developing an information system.[7] After all, the purpose of an information system is to "serve the user".[7] Without a thorough analysis of who the users are and what their tasks are, it is impossible to design a truly useful system.[7]

► 2.2 NEW CHALLENGES FOR WEB DEVELOPMENT PROJECTS

Web development projects must face obstacles that were not a consideration in traditional information systems projects. Web sites must be designed so that they are accessible from a number of different browsers (e.g., Internet Explorer, Netscape Navigator, AOL) and a number of different browser versions (e.g., versions 2.0, 3.0, 4.0, and 5.0).[8] The same HTML code (as well as JavaScript) can appear differently depending on the browser in which it is displayed. Therefore, thorough testing must be done to ensure that web pages will appear appropriately (or appear at all!) in a number of different browsers. Web designers must also consider that users will be accessing web sites using monitors of different sizes (from 21-inch monitors to laptop computers and smaller), and may also have slow connections (e.g., below 56 kbps) to the web. All of these factors influence the usability of the web site.

The Usability Challenge

Usability is even more of a concern in developing web sites than in traditional information systems. In many traditional information systems (such as transactional systems), the information system is designed for daily use by the user. The user will be interacting with the information system on a frequent basis and will learn about and possibly "get used to" any parts of the interface that might be confusing. Because the user may be accessing a web site on an infrequent basis,[6] the site must be easy to use. Users may be intermittent users—they access a specific web site on an infrequent basis;[11] web sites should not require that those users remember any information from their previous visit to the web site.[6] In general, users will not spend a lot of time trying to learn the interface of the web site. If previous knowledge is required, or if the interface is confusing, or if the user cannot find the necessary information or has to ask for outside assistance, he or she might just access another web site, since there are virtually no costs involved in switching web sites.[9,10,11]

User Input in Web Development

Web site development does not start at coding. Instead, when you are developing web sites, a structured process needs to be followed in a manner somewhat similar to software engineering.[10] In some cases, it can be challenging to first define your user population and determine how to include the users in the development process. However, leaving the user out of your web site design can be a recipe for failure. If you do not include users in the design process for your web site, there is no way to know whether your web site provides the type of content that the users are looking for, or whether your users find the site easy to use.[13]

A number of examples exist of web development projects that have employed user input in the process. The Indiana University web site was redesigned with a user-centered approach.[13] User input was included in the design process at two phases: in the requirements gathering stage, and in usability testing on the web site.[13] IBM redesigned their web sites using a user-centered approach, incorporating user feedback, requirements gathering, and usability testing.[15,16]

Ideally, user-centered design for the Web would include requirements gathering with the users.[17] At a minimum, user-centered design for the Web would need to include usability testing with users.[18] For some web sites that were originally designed without users in mind, the designers (or the organization that sponsors the web site) have realized that the current web sites are not meeting the needs of the users and a number of redesign projects are featuring a user-centered approach. Regardless of whether a web site is being redesigned or whether it is being designed for the first time, it is important to understand and consider users throughout the design process.

The Role of Clients

Clients are not equivalent to users. Clients are the people and the organizations that ask you (or hire you) to develop or redevelop a web site.[19] Users are the people who will actually be using the web site. Clients will give their perceptions of what the users want and the users need, but only the targeted users can actually tell you what they want and need. Sometimes, the wants of the clients and of the users will conflict.[13] For instance, the users might be interested in a quick download time, but the clients want to see a large number of graphics on their site.[13] There might be other conflicts between what the users have indicated that they want, and what the clients have indicated that they want. This presents a tricky tightrope for you to walk as a web developer. You don't want to counter your client's request nor do you want to ignore the wishes of the users. The best hope is to *show* the clients the results of your requirements gathering with users. At a later stage, you can show the clients the results of the usability testing. This way, you can convince the client that you have the client's best interests at heart, since you are trying to satisfy the client's users. Another possibility is to allow the client to see users actually attempting to navigate through their web site, and struggling. This is one of the most effective ways of convincing the clients of the importance of satisfying the users.[20]

After your client sees the importance of including users in the development process of a web site, the question is how can users best be included in the process? Let's examine the development lifecycles that have been presented for developing web sites and compare their approaches.

► 2.3 CURRENT LIFECYCLE MODELS FOR MANAGING WEB DEVELOPMENT PROJECTS

Although the lifecycle models for systems development presented earlier in this chapter can be used for many types of information systems, a few development lifecycles have been presented that address the specific needs of web sites.

▶ Lynch and Horton Model[21]
1. Site definition and planning—Define the overall goals for the web site.
2. Information architecture—Focus on content and organization for the web site.

3. Site design—Focus on page design and overall graphical design.
4. Site construction—Code, fill pages with content, and test for errors
5. Site marketing—Publicize site through advertisements and search engines.
6. Tracking, evaluation, and maintenance—Monitor, update, and improve the web site.

▶ Fleming Model[22]

1. Information gathering—Define project goals, mission, and target audience.
2. Strategy—Brainstorm, plan, and identify problems.
3. Prototyping—Create a conceptual plan for site design.
4. Implementation—Technical development and content design.
5. Launch—Test for errors and consistency, and market the site.
6. Maintenance and growth—Introduce new content, keep site updated, and evaluate success.

▶ Burdman Model[19]

1. Strategy—Determine the objectives and requirements for the web site.
2. Design—Create the preliminary design of the interfaces and content.
3. Production—Create final design and functionality of the web site.
4. Testing—Test the web site; fix problems; introduce the site.

TABLE 2-1	A comparison of web development lifecycle models	
Lynch and Horton Model	**Fleming Model**	**Burdman Model**
Site definition and planning	Information gathering	Strategy
Information architecture	Strategy	Strategy
Site design	Prototyping	Design
Site construction	Implementation	Production
Site marketing	Launch	Testing
Tracking, evaluation, and maintenance	Maintenance and growth	Testing

From the table, you can see that the three lifecycle models for web development are quite similar. The stages themselves have similar goals and have similar names. Another similarity between these three models is that user input in the lifecycle is limited. None of these models addresses gathering requirements from actual users. Additionally, the Lynch and Horton and Burdman lifecycle models mention testing, but do not focus on user testing. Instead, the testing focuses on the functionality of the web site. But usability from a user standpoint is becoming an increasing concern as companies realize that users avoid web sites that are hard to use.[23,24] Without usability testing with actual users, designers can only guess at what the user would find easy and what the user would find confusing.

Modifications to the Lifecycle Models

In their book on web site engineering, Powell, Jones, and Cutts suggest using existing systems development lifecycle models, with minor modifications, for designing web sites.[12] For instance, they suggest that a large amount of time should first be spent on continuous iterations of the problem definition and the requirements analysis (two separate stages in the waterfall model) before any conceptual web site design takes place.[12] Powell, Jones, and Cutts also suggest that Joint Application Development (JAD), a newer systems-development lifecycle model, could be used for developing web sites.[12] JAD is where a series of intense structured meetings, lasting one day to a week, helps to determine requirements. The main weakness of Joint Application Development is that it requires continuous communication and meetings between users, clients, and developers, a collaborative effort that may not always be possible.[12] Without this continuous communication, there is a high likelihood for failure. Therefore, JAD might be a more appropriate technique for developing web sites for internal corporate use, where the users, clients, and developers are by nature in continuous communication.[12]

Although ideally, users would be involved with every stage of the web site development, there are two major stages for user involvement in the web site development process. The first stage of user involvement is in the requirements gathering. The second stage of user involvement is in the usability testing. However, if the users are involved in additional stages of the lifecycle, this would certainly be beneficial. This would all depend on how much access the site designers have to the user population, and how much time the users can donate to the development process.

► 2.4 USER NEEDS AT THE CENTER OF A LIFECYCLE MODEL

Following is a lifecycle model that is centered around the needs of the user population. This model was developed by Jonathan Lazar and models the development processes actually used in industry. It is a modified version of the SDLC and the web lifecycle models presented earlier in this chapter.

It can be conceptualized as having seven stages.

1. *Define the mission of the web site and the user population*

The first stage is to decide the mission and user population of your web site. What is the goal of this web site? Is this web site expected to advertise a product, provide information on upcoming events, or collect names to add to a mailing list? A popular quote is, "If you don't know where you are going, you are never going to get there." As this quote is applied to web site development, if you don't know why you are developing a web site, chances are you will not meet your goal. A parallel decision is to decide who the target users of your web site will be. Are the targeted users from a certain geographic area? A certain age group? A certain area of interest? A certain cultural group? Defining your target user population will have ramifications for the requirements gathering (see Step 2 below) and the web usability needs.

2. *Collect the user requirements for the web site*

The second stage is to collect requirements from the targeted population of users. There are a number of important requirements at this stage to be discussed. What are the technological characteristics of the users? What browsers are they using? What connection speeds? What type of web site would they like to use? What content and information would the users be interested in? What qualities would cause users to keep coming back to your web site, and what qualities would keep users away from your site? Are there any preferences that they have in terms of web site design?

3. *Create the conceptual design of the web site*

At this stage, the development team must determine the conceptual design of the web site. For instance, how will navigation be provided to the user? What page layout will be used? What color schemes would be appropriate for the users? Will there be any graphics on the web site? What content will need to be developed? At the conceptual design stage, the development team must decide what the web site will "look like" to create detailed specifications for the web programmers.

4. *Create the physical design of the web site*

This stage covers coding and technical development of the web site. In this stage, the developers actually create the code for the web site. They may use hand-coding of the HTML and JavaScript, or a web development application (such as FrontPage or DreamWeaver). Frequently, designers use a web development application to get a "head-start," then edit the code and fine-tune it to meet their needs. In addition, they can turn to a number of web sites that provide assistance with web development, in terms of creating buttons and downloading graphics and scripts. At this stage, functionality testing should be performed to make sure that code is correct and that scripts and applets work properly.

5. *Perform usability testing on the web site*

At this stage, testing is performed on the web site. First, designers need to briefly test to make sure that all of the pages are accessible, that any scripts are working appropriately, and that the navigation scheme is working. Then, people from the target population of users get a chance to test the web site and evaluate whether it is easy to use or whether it is confusing. These users provide feedback on the web site, point out problem areas, and possibly provide suggestions for improvements to the site. As part of the usability testing, the web site needs to be tested using numerous browsers, monitor sizes, and connection speeds. In addition, the development team might have usability experts look at the web site and offer their suggestions.

6. *Implement and market the web site*

At this stage, the web site "goes live," and users all around the world are able to access the web site. Any decisions about where the site will be housed need to have been made. The web site needs to be marketed through traditional marketing (tote bags, fliers) or electronic marketing (search engines, web rings).

7. *Evaluate and improve the web site*

Periodic evaluations of the effectiveness of the web site should be performed. User feedback should be considered as to whether the web site is meeting their needs, or whether it might be time to redesign or improve the web site. Content should always be kept up to date.

▶ **The Lazar User-Centered Web Development Lifecycle**

- Define the mission of the web site and the user population.
- Collect the user requirements for the web site.

- Create the conceptual design of the web site.
- Create the physical design of the web site.
- Perform usability testing on the web site.
- Implement and market the web site.
- Evaluate and improve the web site.

► 2.5 PROJECT MANAGEMENT TECHNIQUES

It is important to note that traditional project management techniques are still very appropriate in the user-centered web development lifecycle.

Clear Objectives

At the beginning of the web development project, there should be a clear objective (see web site mission and targeted users in Chapter 3), as well as an estimated timeline and cost for the web development project.[25] The client should be clear about these objectives and timelines, and there should be a written agreement to these facts, because if the client changes the objectives or missions of the project, the time needed for completion of the web development will most certainly increase.[19] With this clarification, both the client and the web development team will be "on the same page," and any initial confusion can be limited.[19]

Specific Responsibilities

Responsibilities for the web development project should be broken down, with specific tasks assigned to specific members of the web development team.[25] Web developers must also expect and prepare for political situations within the client organization. For instance, the web development team may hear different viewpoints stated as "fact" from different members of the client organization, which may cloud an understanding of responsibilities.

Documentation

As in any type of systems development, as well as any type of project, all stages of the process should be well-documented. Nothing can be more frustrating than trying to remember what occurred or what was decided at an earlier stage of development, and not being able to remember, or to find the documentation. Documentation of the user requirements is especially important if there are any conflicts between what the client wants and what the user wants. When completing one stage of the lifecycle, the clients should be presented with the documentation, and should be asked to "sign-off" on that stage.[19]

Progress Reports

Regular scheduled progress reports are also a useful technique to inform the client of the progress towards the project goal.[25] If the client later says that "this isn't what we wanted!" or that the time frame for development isn't what they expected, the development team can show the client the documentation, as well as the signature. Thorough documentation and timely progress reports can assist in clarifying what was agreed to, and what was performed, and can help guide changes in the scope or direction of the web development project.

▶ **Project Management Techniques Useful in Web Development**
- Set a clear project objective and timeline.
- Clearly assign tasks to members of the web development team.
- Document everything!
- Send the client periodic status reports.
- Understand the politics of the client organization

SUMMARY

With the user-centered approach to web design, the needs of the users are carefully considered in the entire process of the development of the web site. The final web site is more likely to meet the needs of the users, both in terms of content and usability. The user-centered approach to web design is appropriate for creating a new site, or for redesigning a currently existing web site. But regardless of whether a web site is being developed from scratch or whether a currently existing web site is being redesigned, the stages of development are the same. For a currently existing web site, the user population is already well-defined, and there is data existing on the current usage patterns for the web site. This data can make the process flow more easily and increase the effectiveness of the requirements gathering process.[14]

The user-centered lifecycle approach is similar to a traditional information system, in which a change or improvement is made to a system after going through a series of lifecycle stages.[1] In the rest of the book, we will present each of the steps in the web development lifecycle in greater detail.

Discussion Questions

1. How is web development similar to developing a system using the traditional Systems Development Life Cycle (SDLC)?
2. What are some of the challenges in web development that make it more difficult than development of a traditional information system?
3. At what stages are users involved in the traditional SDLC? At what stages are users involved in the user-centered web development?
4. Why is it important to define your target user population?
5. What project management techniques can help designers in managing web development projects?

References

1. Hoffer, J., George, J., & Valacich, J. (1999). *Modern systems analysis and design.* Reading, MA: Addison-Wesley.
2. Whitten, I., & Bentley, L. (1997). *Systems Analysis and Design Methods.* Boston: Irwin McGraw-Hill.
3. Boehm, B. (1988). A spiral model of software development and enhancement. *IEEE Computer, 21*(5), 61–72.
4. Druin, A. (Ed.) (1998). *The Design of Children's Technology.* San Francisco: Morgan Kaufmann Publishers.
5. Preece, J., Rogers, Y., Sharp, H., Benyon, D., Holland, S., & Carey, T. (1994). *Human-Computer Interaction.* Wokingham, England: Addison-Wesley.
6. Mayhew, D. (1999). *The Usability Engineering Lifecycle.* San Francisco: Morgan Kaufmann Publishers.
7. Norman, D. (1986). Cognitive Engineering. In D. Norman & S. Draper (Eds.), *User-Centered System Design* (pp. 31–61). Hillsdale, NJ: Lawrence Erlbaum Associates.
8. Niederst, J. (1999). *Web Design in a Nutshell.* Sebastopol, CA: O'Reilly and Associates.
9. Kanter, J. (2000). Have we forgotten the fundamental IT enabler: Ease of use. *Information Systems Management,* 70–77.
10. Fuccella, J., & Pittolato, J. (1999). Giving people what they want: How to involve users in site design. *IBM DeveloperWorks.* Available at: http://www-4.ibm.com/software/developer/library/design-by-feedback/expectations.html
11. Nielsen, J., & Norman, D. (2000). Usability on the web isn't a luxury. *Informationweek,* February 14, 2000, 65–73.
12. Powell, T., Jones, D., & Cutts, D. (1998). *Web Site Engineering: Beyond Web Page Design.* Upper Saddle River, NJ: Prentice Hall.
13. Corry, M., Frick, T., & Hansen, L. (1997). User-centered design and usability testing of a web site: An illustrative case study. *Educational Technology Research and Development, 45*(4), 65–76.
14. Yu, J., Prabhu, P., & Neale, W. (1998). *A user-centered approach to designing a new top-level structure for a large and diverse corporate web site.* Proceedings of the 1998 Human Factors and the Web Conference. Available at: http://www.research.att.com/conf/hfweb/
15. Fuccella, J. (1997). *Using user-centered design methods to create and design usable web sites.* Proceedings of the 1997 ACM Conference on Systems Documentation, 69–77.

16. Lisle, L., Dong, J., & Isensee, S. (1998). *Case study of development of an ease of use web site.* Proceedings of the 1998 Human Factors and the Web Conference. Available at: http://www.re-search.att.com/conf/hfweb/

17. Scoresby, K. (2000). Win consumers with better usability. *E-Business Advisor,* June 2000, 16–22.

18. Head, A. (1999). Web redemption and the promise of usability. *Online Magazine,* November/December 1999, 21–32.

19. Burdman, J. (1999). *Collaborative Web Development.* Reading, MA: Addison-Wesley.

20. Nielsen, J. (1994). *Usability Engineering.* Boston: Academic Press.

21. Lynch, P., & Horton, S. (1999). *Web Style Guide: Basic Design Principles for Creating Web Sites.* New Haven, CT: Yale University Press.

22. Fleming, J. (1998). *Web Navigation: Designing the User Experience.* Sebastopol, CA: O'Reilly and Associates.

23. Spool, J., Scanlon, T., Schroeder, W., Snyder, C., & DeAngelo, T. (1999). *Web Site Usability: A Designer's Guide.* San Francisco: Morgan Kaufmann Publishers.

24. Tedeschi, B. (1999). Good web site design can lead to healthy sales. *The New York Times,* August 30, 1999.

25. Gido, J., & Clements, J. (1999). *Successful Project Management.* Cincinnati, OH: South-Western College Publishing.

Defining the Site Mission and the Target User Population

I t all starts here. The web development lifecycle begins when you are contacted about designing or redesigning a web site. You might be a member of a consulting firm that has been formally hired to develop a web site. You might be an individual who has been asked by a colleague or friend to develop a small web site. You might be an employee in the information technology division (or MIS shop, or user services, or web development team) of the client organization and have been asked to design or redesign a web site for the client organization. You might have been asked to develop a site for a community organization. You might be required to develop a web site as part of a class project. Or, you might have personally thought, "Hey, I would really like to design a web site on my favorite hobby, underwater basket weaving." In any event, you are about to design a web site, either on your own or as a part of a development team.

▶ 3.1 ESTABLISHING THE MISSION AND THE TARGET USER POPULATION

The first steps in developing a web site are to determine the mission of the web site and determine the target user population. Only if you know the specific mission of the web site and the user population for which it is created will your user-centered design be successful. One by one we consider the questions that should be asked and answered.

▶ 3.2 WHO DECIDES THE MISSION OF THE WEB SITE?

The mission of the web site should be defined by the client. When the client asks for a web site to be designed, they have an idea of what the web site should do for them. Even though the client might not have a clear vision of exactly what the web site should do, the client should have a basic idea of its purpose. Should the web site provide information? Should it provide entertainment? Should it allow users to purchase products? How will the web site support the organizational mission?[1] The literature shows that a large majority of sites now in existence are either informational or e-commerce related[2,3] so your web site is likely to be one or the other of these types.

Once the general mission of the web site is stated by the client, you or your development team can then use that as a guide to determine exactly what type of content the users want. An essential task for the development team is to understand the mission of the client organization, the history of the client organization, as well as current issues the client organization is grappling with. If the team is not too familiar with the client organization itself, this would be a good time to read as much as possible about the client organization. It would also be helpful to examine any organizational documentation such as press releases, brochures, catalogs, and annual reports. As background information you might even ask if there were any previous plans to develop a web site, and if so, why those plans did not come to fruition. Such information can help to highlight problems to avoid in the current web development effort.

▶ 3.3 WHY MUST THE MISSION OF THE WEB SITE BE ESTABLISHED?

Information on the mission of the web site is essential because without it, requirements gathering with users would have no boundaries. When you discuss the mission of the web site with a client, a project scope should be decided, so that you both know what the mission of the web site is and what it is not.[4] Without a defined scope, a project can easily lose focus, attempting to do everything without any limits on time and cost.[5] Most web development projects will not be large-scale e-commerce projects, with tens of thousands of pages, offering entertainment, information, chat rooms, products for sale, and so on. A web development project for a local church, synagogue, or mosque is not equivalent to developing a competitor web site for amazon.com or yahoo.com. One of the quickest ways for a project to fail is to allow the project to include anything and everything under the sun.[5] Therefore, a clear web site mission must be established early on.

Characterizing web sites

Most web sites do fall under one of these three categories: informational, e-commerce, or entertainment. But a web site mission is not necessarily limited to only one of these goals. Many web sites have multiple missions. Or web sites may be classified by the number of web pages in the site.[6]

A web site mission can be described in terms of its various goals; a number of different taxonomies have been presented in the literature. These describe different approaches for determining the overall goal of the web site, and in the following pages we present two of these taxonomies—those of Shneiderman (Table 3.1) and Navarro and Khan (Table 3.2).

TABLE 3-1	Shneiderman's taxonomy of web site missions[6]
Goal	**Examples**
Sell products	Publishers, airlines, department stores
Advertise products	Auto dealers, real estate agents, movie studios
Inform and announce	Universities, museums, cities
Provide access	Libraries, newspapers, scientific organizations
Offer services	Governments, public utilities
Create discussions	Public interest groups, magazines
Nurture communities	Political groups, professional organizations

TABLE 3-2	Navarro and Khan's taxonomy of web site missions[8]
Goal	**Examples**
Inform or educate	Universities, schools, charitable foundations, nonprofit organizations, government, businesses, political organizations, personal home pages
Entertain	Magazines, e-zines, galleries, museums, media clubs, organizations, personal home pages
Market, sell, or persuade	Businesses, political organizations, nonprofit organizations, universities, schools, personal resumes

A web site mission can be any of these listed goals, as well as a combination of those listed. For many smaller-to-medium size web sites, the web site is simply informational.

► 3.4 HOW IS THE WEB SITE MISSION DEFINED?

Since the mission of the web site is determined by the client, an important question is "How?" When the development team first meets with the client, the client may have a definite idea of exactly what the mission of the web site should be. More likely, the client will have some inkling of what the web site should do, but will need some assistance in clarifying the web site mission. The web site mission may be then determined through a series of interviews, focus groups, or meetings with upper-level management in the client organization.

A Written Statement

Having a written mission statement for a web site is a very good idea.[4] For instance, "Company X will develop a web site to advertise our products, with the goal of increased sales" or "Community group Y will develop a web site to help keep our community members informed, with the hope that the attendance at community meetings will increase" or "Organization Z will develop a web site to help increase awareness about the need for recycling in our community." Perhaps there are a number of different missions, related to different target user populations. If there are several separate targeted user populations, there might be a different mission for each targeted user population and you should have each mission described in the written statement.

Clarifying the User Interaction

An important question at this point is to ask the client what they want the users to do when they access the web site.[8] Does the client want the user to purchase a product? Provide address information to be added to a mailing list? Complete an online survey? Or just read the information to stay informed?[8] It is important for the client to determine just what interaction they hope for from the user. Again, if the client does not know what interaction they want with the user, this should raise a red flag for the web development team. The web development project should go no further until a clear web site mission is established.

Evaluation Goals

When developing the web site mission, evaluation goals can and should be considered. For instance, a good question to ask the client would be: "A year after the web site has gone live, what do you want to say that the web site has done to improve your organization?" Make sure the client can say how success will be measured. By page visits? By products sold? By satisfied customers? By larger turnouts at organizational meetings? By a higher public recognition of the organization? Although evaluation of the success of a web site will not come until after the web site has actually been implemented, this is a good time to define what criteria will be used for evaluation and how "success" can be measured.[4]

The Centrality of Mission

It is important to note that there should be a site mission. If the clients and web development team cannot determine a clear site mission, it might mean that the web site is not actually needed. It is also possible that the web site is being developed only because the competitors already have one, or the client just wants to quickly have a presence on the web.[7] If a "preliminary" web site is placed on the web without sufficient planning, users will likely get frustrated and not return to the web site in the future.[9] A preliminary web site without consideration for user needs will hurt the client organization in the long run.[9]

▶ Important Questions to Ask:
1. What is the mission of the web site?
2. What type of interaction with users does the client want?
3. How will success be measured?

▶ 3.5 TARGETED USER POPULATION

Once the mission of the web site is defined, the next important question is: Who are the users to whom the site is targeted? This determination of the target user population is sometimes known as "audience definition."[10] Only a few specific types of web sites, such as search engines (Altavista, Yahoo, and so forth), and news services (such as CNN, MSNBC, and the Washington Post) are targeted to the entire population of web users.[11] Most other web sites have a very specific targeted population of users. These are known sets of users, with demographic information available about them, and potential access to them for requirements gathering. Web sites and their targeted user population can be widely diverse:

- The Association for Information Systems <http://www.aisnet.org> web site is targeted towards researchers, teachers, and students who study information systems.

- The Hava Nashira <http://www.uahcweb.org/hanashir> web site is targeted towards Jewish song leaders and educators.

- The AARP <http://www.aarp.org/> web site is targeted towards people who are current or prospective members of AARP, the American Association of Retired People, who are 50 years or age or older.

- The INFORMS <http://www.informs.org/> web site is targeted towards people who are interested in operations research and management science.

- The National Academic Quiz Tournaments <http://www.naqt.com/> web site is targeted towards high school students and college students who play a sport called quiz bowl.

- The St. John's Lutheran Church of Blenheim <http://www.stjohnslcms.org/> web site is targeted towards current church members, as well as potential members of the church near Baltimore, MD.

Advantages of Knowing a Targeted Population

Without defining your targeted user population, there will be no way to develop a successful site, because if you don't know who the targeted users are, how can you meet their needs?[4] As discussed in Chapters 1 and 2, if you don't know who you want to use the web site, how can you make a site that it both easy to use and useful?[12] As stated earlier, the focus in information systems is on designing for functionality (the ability to perform tasks that are needed) and usability (ease of use).[13] If you don't know who your users are, it is impossible to determine what their functionality and usability needs are.[14]

You might think of a web site as a consumer product. If you don't know who your targeted users are, how will you advertise the existence of your web site? How will you evaluate whether it is successful? Powell, Jones, and Cutts point out that most companies would not develop a product without first determining who the target consumers of that product are.[7] Products are not developed with the idea that someone will eventually purchase it. Business plans must specify who the target consumers will be for the products or services sold by the business. These same techniques should apply to web sites.

Targeting Different User Groups

A targeted population does not need to be only one group of people. It is possible that a web site is targeted to three or four specific groups. If there are different user groups that would constitute the target population, it is best to determine them at the beginning of the web site development. For example, most university web sites are targeted to a few different groups of people: current students, former students (alumni), potential students, and faculty and staff.[15] These groups together formed a well-defined target population for whom the Indiana University web site was redesigned.[15] Each of these user groups may be interested in different information. For instance, alumni might want to know about alumni events, sports, and general university news. Current students will probably want to know about courses, registration, and campus organizations and events. Faculty and staff might want to know about campus events, health insurance, and reserving rooms and equipment. Prospective students might want to know about dorms, tuition costs, and campus organizations. Some of the informational needs might be the same, some might be different. Another consideration is the technology: students, faculty, and staff on-campus might have fast connections to the WWW, but prospective students and alumni (who are off-campus) may have slow dial-up speeds. All of these different groups and their respective needs must be taken into consideration.

In situations where there are different user groups within the target user population, it is necessary to do user requirements gathering with all of the different sets of users. In the book *The Usability Engineering Lifestyle,* Mayhew suggests developing user profiles for each user group in the target user population.[16] These profiles should contain as much information as is currently known about each user group.[16] That will also assist in determining what information about the characteristics of the users will still need to be collected during requirements gathering.

Audience-Splitting

Planning at this stage can have major implications for later stages of web design. If there are different groups of users within the target population for a web site, information on the web site can be presented for these different user groups using a technique called audience-splitting.[1] An example of audience-splitting can be seen in Fig. 3.1. Right on the home page, the proverbial "front door" to the web site, there are different links for current students, prospective students, alumni, and faculty and staff. These links will immediately take the different user groups to web pages that are specifically tailored to their interests. Figure 3.1 is a screen shot of the Towson University web site, showing audience-splitting in use.

Separate Requirements Gathering

If there are different user groups within the target population of users, then it will be necessary to do requirements gathering with all of those groups. If requirements gathering is done with only one of the user groups that make up the target population, then the results of the requirements gathering will be biased and will not be representative of the target population.

Figure 3.1

An example of
audience-splitting

▶ Important Questions to Ask:
1. To whom is this web site targeted?
2. Are there different user groups within the target population?
3. Can we develop separate user profiles?
4. Can we contact all of these different user groups?

▶ 3.6 ADDITIONAL CONSIDERATIONS FOR WEB SITE REDESIGN

When designing a web site from scratch, there are a number of issues that need to be decided, such as the target user population and the mission of the web site. However, redesigning a web site with the user-centered approach is a little bit different than designing a new site. If you are redesigning a currently existing web site, the site mission and the target population should be well-established. The client should easily be able to identify the mission of the web site, as well as who the target user population is. It is possible that with a site redesign, the client might be interested in changing the mission of the web site (providing new types of services), as well as broadening the target user population. It is also possible that the client wants to keep the site mission and user population the same, and is only interested in changing the design to increase the usability.

Broadening the Target User Population

The IBM Ease of Use web site provides a great example of site redesign. In 1996, the web site was developed with software designers and developers in mind, and in fact was called the HCI (Human-Computer Interaction) web site.[17] However, as the web site grew, the target user population was broadened. The name of the web site was changed to the "Ease of Use" web site and the target user population was expanded to include human factors professionals, students, professors, and the media.[17] With this redesign, new considerations for these populations needed to be taken into account.

Web Site Logs

For a site redesign, the web site logs are a good resource for examining who the users of the web site have been in the recent past. Web site logs track information about those who have requested pages from your web site.[18] These web site logs are usually stored on the web server.[8] The web site logs can hold information such as which web pages are viewed most often, which domains request web pages from your site, and what path users follow through your web site.[8] As you analyze web site logs, you might discover that the target population of users and the users who have actually been accessing the web site are two different groups of people. Or, if you are redesigning an existing web site you might also look at the logs from the search engine, and any comments left in the web site "guest book," if either of these existed on the previous web site.[20] There are a number of statistical packages that can be used to assist in doing data analysis on web site logs. More information about web site logs is available in Chapter 12. In addition, more information on web site logs is available in *Web Site Stats*,[18] in Chapter 4 of *Advertising on the Internet*[19] and in pages 235–244 of *Effective Web Design*.[8]

Research Any Prior Relationships

When you redesign a currently existing web site, it is important to examine who developed the site in the first place (whether a consulting firm or an in-house MIS shop) to determine whether or not the relationship between the client organization and the original web site developer is still positive. If the relationship between the client organization and the original site designer(s) is good, it might be useful to ask that designer for any past documentation from their original development of the web site. In some cases, the client organization might be very unhappy with the web site that was originally developed; that, in fact, might be the reason for the redesign. In that case, the relationship might be less than positive, and it might be best not to get in contact with the original site designers. In extreme cases, the person or firm that developed the original web site might still have password access to the HTML files, causing a particularly awkward situation. Political organizational issues might arise, and as part of the new development team, it is best to work through your client organization.

▶ Important Questions to Ask:
(if the web site is being redesigned)

1. Should the target user population stay the same or change?
2. Should the mission of the web site stay the same or change?
3. Should the interface design stay the same or change?
4. Does documentation exist from the original web site design?
5. Can the original design team be contacted?
6. Are there any political or organizational issues that could affect the successful development and implementation of the web site?

SUMMARY

Before any web site development takes place, two decisions must be clear: (1) the mission of the web site, and (2) the targeted user population (or populations) for the web site. Unless the client has defined these two issues, the rest of the web development process will be fruitless. Without knowing who the users are and what the web site should do, it will be impossible to collect user requirements (because you don't know who your users are), impossible to design a web site that meets their functionality or usability needs (because you don't know what they want), impossible to test your web site (because you wouldn't know with whom to test), and impossible to advertise your web site (because you wouldn't know whom to target). This first step in web site development is an important step that will ensure that the other phases of the web development lifecycle are not fruitless.

Deliverables

At this point, you should have:
1. Determined the mission of the web site
2. Determined what type of user interaction the client is interested in
3. Determined how "success" will be measured
4. Determined who the targeted user populations are
5. Created user profiles (as detailed as possible) for all target user groups within the target population

Discussion Questions

1. Who should you talk with to determine the mission of the web site?
2. What are the three main types of web sites?
3. What type of documentation can be useful in determining the mission of the web site?
4. What is audience-splitting?
5. What is a web site mission statement, and how does it relate to evaluation goals?
6. What is a user profile, and why might it be useful?
7. Give an example of a web site that has multiple targeted user populations.
8. When you are redesigning a currently existing web site, can the targeted user population change from that of its previous site?
9. What techniques for gathering information can be used for redesigning currently existing web sites that cannot be used for designing new web sites?

REFERENCES

1. Lynch, P., & Horton, S. (1999). *Web Style Guide: Basic Design Principles for Creating Web Sites.* New Haven: Yale University Press.

2. Lazar, J., & Norcio, A. (2001, in press). User Considerations in E-commerce Transactions. In Q. Chen (Ed.), *Human-Computer Interaction: Issues and Challenges.* Hershey, PA: Idea Group Publishing, 185–195.

3. Niederst, J. (1999). *Web Design in a Nutshell.* Sebastopol, CA: O'Reilly and Associates.

4. Burdman, J. (1999). *Collaborative Web Development.* Reading, MA: Addison-Wesley.

5. Gido, J., & Clements, J. (1999). *Successful Project Management.* Cincinnati, OH: South-Western College Publishing.

6. Shneiderman, B. (1998). *Designing the User Interface: Strategies for Effective Human-Computer Interaction* (3rd ed.). Reading, MA: Addison-Wesley.

7. Powell, T., Jones, D., & Cutts, D. (1998). *Web Site Engineering: Beyond Web Page Design.* Upper Saddle River, NJ: Prentice Hall.

8. Navarro, A., & Khan, T. (1998). *Effective Web Design.* San Francisco: Sybex.

9. Nielsen, J. (2000). The Mud-Throwing Theory of Usability. Available at http://www.useit.com/alertbox/20000402.html, April 2, 2000.

10. Fuccella, J. (1997). *Using user-centered design methods to create and design usable web sites.* Proceedings of the 1997 ACM Conference on Systems Documentation, 69–77.

11. Fleming, J. (1998). *Web Navigation: Designing the User Experience.* Sebastopol, CA: O'Reilly and Associates.

12. Fuccella, J., & Pittolato, J. (1999). Giving people what they want: How to involve users in site design. *IBM DeveloperWorks.* Available at: http://www-4.ibm.com/software/developer/library/design-by-feedback/expectations.html

13. Goodwin, N. (1987). Functionality and usability. *Communications of the ACM, 30*(3), 229–233.

14. Kanter, J. (2000). Have we forgotten the fundamental IT enabler: Ease of use. *Information Systems Management,* 70–77.

15. Corry, M., Frick, T., & Hansen, L. (1997). User-centered design and usability testing of a web site: An illustrative case study. *Educational Technology Research and Development, 45*(4), 65–76.

16. Mayhew, D. (1999). *The Usability Engineering Lifecycle.* San Francisco: Morgan Kaufmann Publishers.

17. Lisle, L., Dong, J., & Isensee, S. (1998). *Case study of development of an ease of use web site.* Proceedings of the 1998 Human Factors and the Web Conference. Available at: http://www.research.att.com/conf/hfweb/

18. Stout, R. (1997). *Web Site Stats.* Berkeley, CA: Osborne McGraw Hill.

19. Zeff, R., & Aronson, B. (1999). *Advertising on the Internet.* New York: John Wiley & Sons.

20. Yu, J., Prabhu, P., & Neale, W. (1998). *A user-centered approach to designing a new top-level structure for a large and diverse corporate web site.* Proceedings of the 1998 Human Factors and the Web Conference. Available at: http://www.research.att.com/conf/hfweb/

CASE STUDY #1

▲ Best Buddies Maryland

(Note: This case study was written and developed by Josephine Barton, Keith Kaplan, Seitaro Matsui, Malik Oussalah, and Bill Sandison.)

Best Buddies Maryland is the local chapter of Best Buddies International, Inc., a non-profit organization founded by Anthony Kennedy Shriver in January of 1989. Best Buddies is dedicated to enhancing the lives of people with mental retardation by providing opportunities for socialization and employment. The focus of Best Buddies is to foster friendships between people with mental retardation and students from middle school through college and other community members. In Maryland, Best Buddies partners with three middle schools, 24 high schools, 25 colleges, and one community group to provide these friendships. It is the goal of the organization that someday people with mental retardation will be so well integrated into society that support groups such as Best Buddies will no longer be necessary.

The development team first visited the Best Buddies Maryland offices in downtown Baltimore. As a first step in building the web site, the development team met with client contacts Michelle Bicocchi, Program Manager, and Carrie Cerri, State Director. The purpose of this informal meeting was to allow the client and the development team to get to know each other, to create a friendly atmosphere at the beginning of the project, and to learn more about the web site mission and targeted users of the web site. The client provided information packets for each team member, detailing the mission of the organization. Additionally, the client enthusiastically agreed to provide access to the three other Best Buddies Maryland employees and several other people who participate in their program.

Best Buddies Maryland has never had a web site. The international organization has a web site (www.bestbuddies.org) that provides background information about the group and links to the few state organizations that have a web site. During the first meeting, the client expressed several reasons for developing a web site:

1. Best Buddies does receive some government grants, but the program relies heavily on private contributions. The client sees a web site as a way to make Best Buddies Maryland more visible to people interested in contributing both time and money to an organization such as theirs.

2. Second, the client would like to use the web site as a means for providing information to their members about upcoming events.

3. The client would like to use the web site to provide people with mental retardation and their families information about the Best Buddies program.

4. The client would like to provide contact information and links to the international organization and the local community and to school partners in Maryland that have web sites.

Currently, Best Buddies has a large amount of printed information about their organization and its structure. Additionally, they have photographs of people who participate in their program and have access to a scanner. In the initial meeting, the client volunteered that they have no preconceived notion of how the web site should look, and they are interested in seeing a variety of ways of presenting information on the World Wide Web. The client agreed to make time available for filling out surveys, participating in interviews, providing any information that will be needed, and taking part in the testing of the web site.

CASE STUDY #2

▲ Institute of Notre Dame

(Note: This case study was written and developed by MyVan Baranoski, Fuliscia Black-Morrison, Darin Daubert, Keven Lehmann, and Brett Johnson.)

Figure 3.2
IND web site before redesign

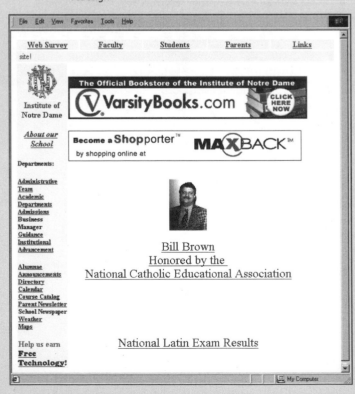

The Institute of Notre Dame High School is a Catholic girls' high school, located in downtown Baltimore, Maryland. The Institute of Notre Dame (known as IND) was founded in 1847 when five School Sisters of Notre Dame (SSND) left Germany and came to Baltimore. According to the IND web site, the mission of the school is to provide "a nurturing environment in which girls can grow into young women of moral character and academic competence."

IND was interested in redesigning their web site. The IND web site (at http://www.indofmd.org) was considered to be difficult to use by many users, and the school thought that it would be useful to redesign the web site so that information would be easier to find. In addition, there were many web pages on the IND web site that were listed as "under construction," so new content would need to be developed for the user population. At the beginning of this development project, the amount of content on the web site was limited. The previous IND web site is displayed in Fig. 3.2.

The contact person for the web development at IND was Fred Germano, the director of educational technology at the school. Through e-mail communication, it was determined that there were a number of distinct user groups that made up the user population of IND's web site:

1. Faculty and staff at IND
2. Current students at IND
3. Parents of current students at IND
4. Alumni (former students) of IND
5. Prospective students of IND

Although a similar design could be appropriate for all of these many user populations, it was very possible that each user group would be interested in different types of content. However, with this site redesign, the target user population would stay the same, and the mission of the web site (to provide information about events, classes, and people at IND) would also stay the same. The changes to the web site would specifically relate to making the site easier to use, and increasing the amount of content that is available for users.

CASE STUDY #3

▲ Eastman Kodak Company

This case study was written and developed by Jack Yu, Senior User Interaction Designer, Kodak.

Background

Kodak is the world's largest manufacturer and marketer of imaging products and has one of the world's most recognized and respected brand names.

We make photographic films and papers for a wide range of consumer, entertainment, professional, business, and health-related uses. We develop, manufacture, and market traditional and digital cameras, photographic plates and chemicals, processing and audiovisual equipment, as well as document management products, applications software, printers, and other business equipment. We also provide photographic processing and repair and maintenance services.

Kodak products are sold throughout the world.[1]

kodak.com, the Web site of Eastman Kodak Company, caters to a very diverse audience. Besides serving a broad consumer market for photographic products, Kodak develops, manufactures, and delivers products and services for a variety of business, commercial, and work-related applications, and the content served on kodak.com is appropriately varied.

---

[1] From the Prospectus of Eastman Kodak Share Program—http://www.kodak.com/US/en/corp/investorCenter/sharesProspectus.shtml.

From 1995 to 1997, the kodak.com *top level*—including the home page and the pages to which it linked directly—retained essentially the same standard page layout, visual design motif, and information architecture. Figure 3.3 below shows the design of the Kodak home page during this time. The two-year period was one of tremendous growth for kodak.com; traffic to the site grew to roughly a quarter of a million page views daily, and many new types of content were added to the site. At the beginning of 1997, it became evident that the top level of kodak.com needed to be redesigned to accommodate this tremendous growth. From the outset, our goal was to drive the redesign with an understanding of the needs and desires of kodak.com's diverse user population and the business goals of the company.

Figure 3.3

The design of the Kodak home page from 1995 to 1997

Mission of the Web Site

In 1997, Kodak utilized its Web site in primarily a marketing and communications capacity. The most abundant content on kodak.com included marketing and technical support information for Kodak products, educational materials on photography, and corporate information.

The primary function of the kodak.com home page was to act as a gateway to the tens of thousands of pages in the site. We wanted the redesigned version to play this role effectively, in addition to meeting the following internal requirements:

1. Have the flexibility to change in appearance, content, and emphasis depending on company or user needs and priorities. If Kodak's business audiences changed, or a new product was launched, or an important announcement was made, or if we found that a certain area of the site just didn't work well, we wanted to be able to easily modify the home page. The previous home page did not allow for easy modification.

2. Present a compelling "teaser" for featured information on a regular basis.

3. Showcase outstanding photography. Kodak is the world leader in imaging; we wanted the home page to convey this message through the display of dazzling imagery.

4. Convey the following attributes:

    - Kodak is consumer-friendly.
    - Kodak is an imaging technology leader.
    - Kodak has a worldwide presence.
    - Beyond the general consumer, Kodak also has a stake in professional, business, and government interests.
    - Kodak wants to build a community of people who repeatedly visit our Web site.
    - Kodak is selling products/services on the Web.
    - kodak.com has new and informative content that is continually updated.
    - kodak.com's content is diverse, i.e., interesting for a broad range of individuals.

Target User Population

There were a number of different user groups within the target user population for the Kodak Web site. We wanted the home page design to cater to the following audiences, segmented by *information interest*:

1. **The consumer-imaging visitor:** one who is interested in imaging products and information for personal use. This represents a very broad segment of visitors, including any of the ones listed below:

    - A serious amateur photographer looking for advanced photography tips and technical information about films and cameras
    - A "point-and-shooter" looking for information on how to correct problem photographs, creative and innovative ways to share pictures

- A "browser" seeking a new and compelling experience (such as KODAK Picture This postcards, Kodak Photonet online)
- Anyone who is looking to learn about new technologies or Kodak's progress and participation in them (such as digital photography)

2. **The "commercial-imaging" visitor:** one who is interested in imaging products, services, and solutions in the context of their work or profession. Efficient access to content, minimizing obstacles and "fluff," is key to this segment. This segment includes business professionals, professional photographers, motion picture professionals, health professionals, government contractors, law enforcement personnel, printers, publishers, and teachers, among others.

3. **The corporate visitor:** one who is interested in some aspect of Kodak as a company (as opposed to imaging information). This might include any of the following:

   - A reporter looking for corporate officer biographies, information about major corporate decisions and actions
   - A job-seeker looking for employment opportunities
   - An investor interested in Kodak stock who wants to learn about the company's financial outlook and plans for growth in the future
   - A community leader looking for information on community events and sponsorships by Kodak
   - A person interested in environmental issues looking for information on Kodak's work processes and how they affect the environment

4. **The Kodak partner:** a person or company that has a relationship with or somehow works together with Kodak to provide solutions for others. Examples include:

   - A retailer or corporate reseller who sells Kodak products
   - A software developer who creates solutions that use and/or interact with Kodak products and technology

5. **The surfer:** those who come to the Kodak site without any particular, specific information interest. They may be in search of generally fun and cool stuff or simply curious as to what Kodak is doing on the Web.

We wanted the redesigned kodak.com top level to meet the needs of all of these different types of users; consequently, requirements for the design needed to include input from various user groups.

Requirements Gathering from Users

The next phase of the web development lifecycle is requirements gathering. In the requirements gathering phase you learn about your target users. You learn who they are, you learn what they want, and you learn about their computer experience and their computing environment. The discussion of the requirements gathering stage will take place in two chapters. This chapter will discuss the types of information that need to be collected from the users, and the next chapter will discuss methods for collecting that information. There are a number of different types of information that need to be collected from users, including general demographic information, domain knowledge, user computing experience, user computing environment, content, and benchmarking. In the next sections, each type of information will be discussed in detail.

▶ 4.1 GENERAL DEMOGRAPHIC INFORMATION

The process begins with gathering general demographic information about your users. For instance, what are the respective ages of your target population? Is your target population mostly male or female? What is the respective educational level of your target users?

Some basic demographic information may have been provided by the client organization. This information can then be compared to the responses collected in the requirements gathering phase. The purpose of this comparison is to determine if the responses you gathered truly represent the target population. If your target population is 15- to 21-year-old males and most of the responses you received were from females, then your inquiries might not represent the target population and your collected information might be biased.[1] Or perhaps your web site is not targeted to a specific gender, but all of your information gathering responses came from men; you might suspect that your responses do not accurately represent the target population.[1]

Other demographic questions might relate to current employment status, job position, and salary.[2] The salary question might be more appropriate for sites that attempt to sell products or solicit donations; otherwise, it is questionable whether users would be comfortable responding with their salaries.

▶ Some Questions to Ask:
1. What is your age?
2. What is your gender?
3. What is your educational experience?
4. What is your current job?

▶ 4.2 DOMAIN KNOWLEDGE

When we are involved in jobs or tasks, or other responsibilities, there is a certain amount of previous knowledge and experience that we bring to a task and that is required to effectively complete a task—that previous knowledge is known as domain knowledge. For instance, most adults would know how to complete a task at the bank (adults being familiar with checks, credit cards, bank accounts, and the processes involved), but most children under the age of 13 would not. Many job openings require that the employees have previous job experience; this prior experience would serve as knowledge of the job domain.

It is possible that there is previous domain knowledge that is required in order to effectively use a web site. This might be the case if there is highly specialized information on the web site, and the target population tends to be specialized. For instance, a web site about anesthesiology would likely include a lot of medical terminology, but this would be fine if the target population is anesthesiologists. However, technical terminology about anesthesiology would be inappropriate if the web site was targeted to children who want to learn about anesthesiology. Here's another example of domain knowledge from the web: The acronyms NAQT, CBI, and ACF on a web site might mean a lot to people who play a sport called Quiz Bowl, but they might not mean much to people who are not experienced with Quiz Bowl.[3]

If any domain knowledge is required for effective use of a web site, the web development team should query the targeted user population to determine what level of domain knowledge the users actually have. It would be wrong for the clients to assume that "everyone knows about X and Y." Assuming that "everyone already knows all about X and Y" would be as silly as saying, "We don't need to provide driving directions on our web site . . . everyone already knows how to get to our organizational headquarters." A web site with a lot of technical jargon may limit effective use to those users with a large amount of domain knowledge. If there might be any limitations to user domain knowledge that could affect how material is presented on the web site, this needs to be discovered at an early stage in the development process.

▶ 4.3 USER COMPUTING EXPERIENCE

The amount of computing experience of the users can have a great impact on the successful interaction with the web site. In human–computer interaction research, we talk about the novice–expert continuum of users.[4,5,6] Although definitions of novices and experts can differ, novice users can be considered to be users who do not know much about the interface and the computer system and may use an interface infrequently, whereas experts use an interface frequently and are very familiar with the interaction required to complete their tasks.[7] A newer category is the intermittent user, who may have broad knowledge of interface concepts, but who may use an interface irregularly or may use a number of different interface systems.[7] When traditional information systems are designed, one of the most important considerations is the computing knowledge level of the target users.

It would be inappropriate to force novice users to use a command language such as UNIX, which requires detailed knowledge to perform tasks.[8] On the other hand, UNIX may be a natural choice for computer scientists or engineers. Novice users and expert users have different experiences, and therefore have different needs.

Levels of Computing Experience

When gathering information from our users, we are also interested in finding out the exact level of their computing experience. It is possible that a user could be experienced in using word processing, but not much else. It is possible that a user could use the web often, but only check his or her three favorite web sites every time, and not use any other computer applications. It is possible that a user in the targeted user population could have never used a computer before. As web developers, we are interested in knowing all of this information, because the more detailed a user profile we can create, the better.[9]

It is important to understand the level of experience that the user has with computers in general, the level of user experience with software applications such as those that make up the *Microsoft Office Suite*, the level of user experience with browsing the web, and the extent of user experience with different types of web sites. Within these categories, important questions could relate to the frequency of use (how many hours per week, or how many weeks between usage), and the satisfaction of use. It might also be useful to ask users whether they use a computer in their workplace, and if so, whether that experience is enjoyable.[9] Typing skill might be important to ascertain.[9] If it is expected that the target user population is not too experienced with using computers, you might ask how the users feel about working with computers: whether they strongly like computers, like computers, dislike computers, or strongly dislike computers.[9] This information might alert the web development team (as well as the client organization) as to whether they might face resistance from their targeted user population to using the web site. If there are several user groups within the target user population, the information collected related to user computing experience can help you gain a better understanding of how these user groups differ.

Adapting Metaphors

Novice web developers might ask, "Why is it important to find out all of this information from users? What difference does it make if our users are familiar with spreadsheets? We are designing a web site, not a spreadsheet." More information about your users is always better than less information. For instance, if all of the user population is familiar with spreadsheets, you might be able to adapt spreadsheeting concepts or terminology in the design of your web site. The more you know about the users, the more you can use that information to design an interface that the users can relate to. If you find that most or all of your users are familiar with other software applications or real-world tasks, those concepts can be included into the interface design of the web site. For instance, in many e-commerce sites, the metaphors of a shopping cart and a check-out are used.[10] This object (the shopping cart) in the interface relates to objects in the user's real-world experience. Amazon.com has successfully adapted the shopping cart concept of the real world to their web site (see Fig. 4.1).

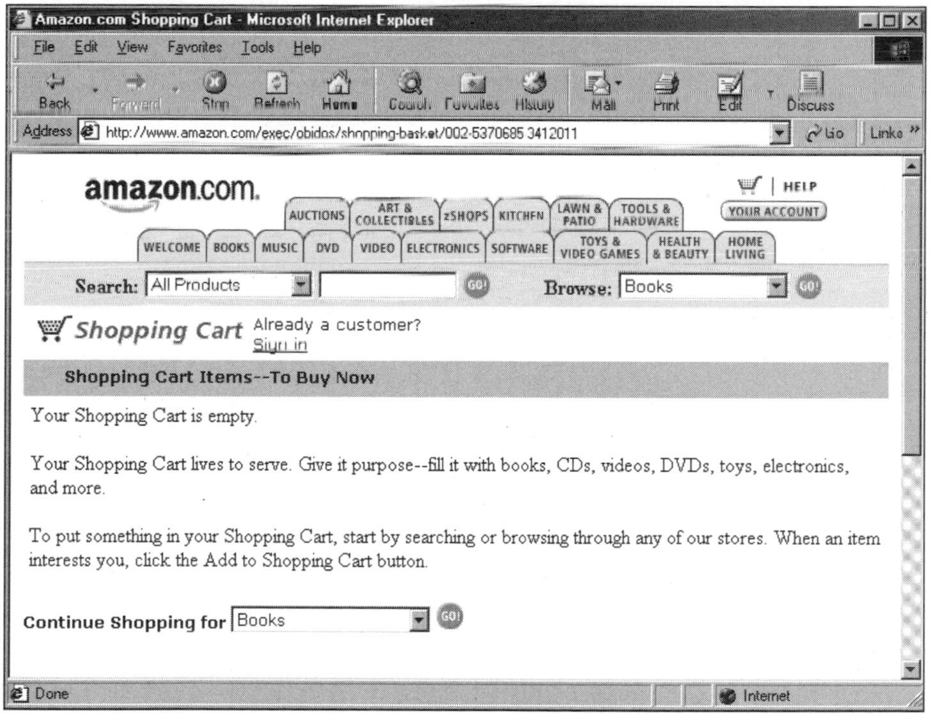

Figure 4.1

The shopping cart metaphor in use at Amazon.com

Besides the shopping cart, other metaphors can assist the user in understanding the required interaction with the computer. Another example of a metaphor for novice users is the file folder. In the real world, file folders store information, and usually each folder represents a different topic or person. File folders are objects in the user's real-world setting that they can relate to and understand. Some web sites use the metaphor of a file folder to provide navigation. Each file folder tab represents different information that is available to the user. See the web site of the Towson University leadership program (Fig. 4.2) for an example of use of the file folder metaphor.

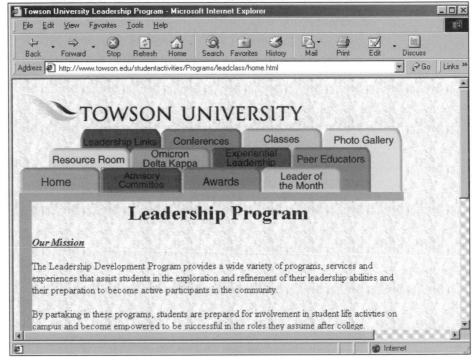

Figure 4.2

The file folder metaphor in use at the web site of the Towson University leadership program

Adapting to Past User Experiences

Other information about the users' computing experience can be used to help tailor the web site to the users. For instance, if most of the users have never browsed the web before, then it would be inappropriate to require plug-in applications (such as Adobe Acrobat) to view some documents on the web site. The web site for ISWORLD (http://www.isworld.org) requires using Adobe Acrobat to view some documents, but this is acceptable since ISWORLD is a resource used by teachers, researchers, and students of information systems, all of whom would be familiar with using Adobe Acrobat. On the other hand, if the target population for a web site is preschool teachers, it might be unreasonable to assume that all preschool teachers are familiar and comfortable with using Adobe Acrobat.

Asking questions about the users' satisfaction with their previous computing experiences might give some pointers as to what problems have persisted for the target user population in the past, which can point to pitfalls to avoid in developing the web site. For instance, if the most frequent frustration for a large number of users has been a slow download speed, then a primary design goal for the web site should be a quick download time, which means avoiding all graphics and any large documents. If a sore point for users has been the use of confusing terminology, then extra care should be made to ensure that the terminology used in the web site is clear and easy to understand. Finding out about the positive and negative computing experiences of the users can be very useful, because the web development team can learn what mistakes to avoid from the previous experiences of the users.[2]

▶ Important Questions to Ask:

1. Have your users ever used a computer before?
2. How often do the users use a computer?
3. What software applications do the users use?
4. Have the users ever browsed the web before?
5. How often do the users browse the web?

▶ 4.4 USER COMPUTING ENVIRONMENT

In the traditional computing environment, systems designers generally knew in advance what type of computer, what type of monitor, and what type of operating system the end users would be using. Although this is still true for those designing for a corporate intranet,[11] in the Internet/WWW environment, web designers' knowledge is at the other end of the spectrum.[12] For these web designers, it is difficult to determine what browser, what version, what screen size, or what processor the user will be using. While the ramifications of this uncertainty will be discussed in later chapters, the need for collecting as much information as possible about the user's computing environment will be discussed here.

Viewing the Web Page

A web page can be viewed by anyone connected to the Internet who is running a web browser. For designers, this means that they need to design web pages that can be successfully viewed by almost anyone. Web pages can appear differently depending on what browser and what version of that browser the user is using. Depending on the connection speed and processor speed, web pages can take differing amounts of time to appear. In addition, some web pages can appear inappropriately on smaller screens, and it can be a problem if a document requires the use of a plug-in (such as Adobe Acrobat or RealAudio) that the user does not have installed. Although it will be impossible to determine in advance what equipment every user has, the important consideration is what computing environment the *target* users have. If the targeted users tend towards a certain common hindrance (older browser version, slow connection speed, textual browsing), then that consideration (small file sizes, compatibility with older versions of browsers, compatibility with text based browsers) should become even more important during the design phases. It is especially true that for web sites that are not targeted towards high-end users (such as computer professionals, engineers, and so on), designers need to consider that a large percentage of their users might be accessing the web site through a slow connection and a small monitor.[11,12]

Computing Environment Affects Usability

The user computing environment can affect usability, so understanding the user computing environment can assist in requirements gathering for usability.[13] This is true for designing new web sites, as well as redesigning currently existing web sites. For instance, when redesigning the Kodak web site, web site developers determined during requirements gathering that textual navigation and fast download times were necessary usability requirements.[14] Usability requirements such as these should be documented because they can be helpful if there is a disagreement between the client organization and the development team as to the usability requirements.[15] It can sometimes be difficult to convince a client organization of the need for usability, and the more documentation on usability needs that exists, the better.[16] Since no complete database of web users exists, it is impossible to make any statements about the computing environment of all web users. A number of studies have been published;[17,18,19] however, all of the studies suffer from the same limitation, which is that there is no centralized database of all Internet or Web users.[1] Therefore, it is impossible to make statements such as "69% of all web users are running IE 4.0 or higher."

▶ Important Questions to Ask:

1. What browser are you using? (Internet Explorer, Netscape Navigator, AOL, Lynx)
2. What version of the browser are you using? (Version 3, 4, 5, etc.)
3. What size monitor do you use? (15 inch, 17 inch, 21 inch, or other)
4. What processor speed do you have?
5. What is your connection speed to the Internet? (28.8, 56k, cable modem, T1, etc.)
6. What plug-ins do you have? (Abobe Acrobat, RealAudio, RealVideo)

▶ 4.5 CONTENT

An important consideration in requirements gathering is determining what type of content the users are interested in.[2] If the web site does not offer content that the users are interested in, users might not visit the web site at all. The different user groups that make up a target user population might have different ideas regarding what content might be useful to them; this should be taken into consideration.

Determining Content Preferences

Web development teams should try to determine whether users are interested in news about the client organization, a list of phone numbers, pictures of events, or something else, like a "spotlight of the month." Other possibilities include FAQs, success stories, and file downloads.[2] Would the users like to purchase certain products? Would users be interested in video clips of events? What about educational materials? The content should also draw users to the web site. For instance, placing an electronic version of a paper brochure on the web will probably not be sufficient to draw users to the web site.

Determining the content that users are interested in can be a challenge. The web development team can discuss this with the client, and try to come up with a list of possibilities. However, coming up with the list of possible content can be tricky. The web development team and the client may not always be able to guess at what the users are interested in. It might be necessary to do an exploratory study first, using interviews with users, or possibly a focus group (see the next chapter for more information on focus groups) or a survey, to determine what types of resources the users would be interested in. Another possible source of content ideas can be found if the client organization describes some problems that they have recently had. For instance, if the client organization describes a large number of requests for a certain document, maybe that document can be made available via the web. Or if the organization has to repeatedly give the same explanation over the phone, this information would be a good candidate for content development for the web site. In addition, benchmarking can also provide possible ideas for content by examining the benchmark web sites (see the section later in this chapter on "benchmarking").[2]

Although the client has a good understanding of what they want the web site to do, the users are the ones who actually use the web site, so their comments on content are very important. The users can be given a list of possible resources, and asked to rank these using a scale (1=most interested, 9=least interested). Or users can be asked to select whether the content is needed, wanted, or not wanted, or rank each choice in terms of importance (1=first most important content, 2=second most important content, etc.). Users should also be encouraged to suggest new ideas for content.

It is possible that there might be a disagreement between what the users want on the web site and what the client wants on the web site. In the case of a disagreement, the best strategy is to show the clients the responses from the users. If a web site does not have any users, it is essentially meaningless. Therefore, clients must consider the users in their decision-making processes.

An Indirect Approach

Another possibility is to indirectly collect content requirements from the users. When Indiana University redesigned their web site, they consulted 35 departments on campus.[15] Each department was queried as to what questions were asked of the department most frequently.[15] These questions came through phone calls, visits, mail, and e-mail.[15] A list of these questions and appropriate responses was developed and included as part of the content on the web site. Although the users were not contacted directly, their feedback and content needs were considered in the design process.

Assessing Currently Existing Content

When the needed user content is defined, it is important to determine whether any of this content already exists in paper or electronic form.[21] Other resources might already exist in photo, artwork, or video format.[20] The web development team should ascertain whether some of the content needs to be developed from scratch, or whether the resources already exist in a format that can be easily transformed into a web page. It is useful to examine currently existing materials (such as brochures, reports, advertisements, press releases, newsletters, and forms) to see if there is any useful content that could be included on the web pages.[21] This is not to say that all currently existing content should be placed on the web, without regard to whether it is useful for users, or even appropriate to the electronic medium.[11] As Powell, Jones, and Cutts say, "The real goal is to give the users what they want and need, which may not be what you currently have."[11]

In one community-based organization (a local church), all of the content that was to be placed on the web already existed in word processing files stored at the client organization. In this circumstance, the content was already developed but not publicly distributed; the only task related to content was to copy the content onto web pages and do the necessary formatting. However, this is a rare situation. In many cases, some of the needed content (such as frequently asked questions) may already exist in paper format. But many of the other content resources will need to be developed.

Responsibility for Developing Content

It is the client organization's responsibility to develop and provide the content. The client organization is the entity with the expertise to develop the needed content. Although the web development team might be responsible for determining what content is needed, and then adding that content to the web site, the web development team does not usually have expertise in the content areas. Therefore, the responsibility of developing and providing the content (in paper, electronic, or other format) should be the responsibility of the client organization. Of course, it doesn't always work out perfectly. If the web development team becomes responsible for any content development, the time required to do so should be considered when discussing project timelines.[11] Even if the client agrees to develop the content completely, a project timeline might have to be reworked if the client organization does not provide the promised content in the promised timeframe.

▶ Sources of Ideas for Content:
- User responses to requirements gathering
- Questions that users commonly ask the client organization
- The client organization itself
- Currently existing content
- Benchmark web sites

▶ 4.6 BENCHMARKING

The final part of requirements gathering is determining benchmark sites that can serve as a comparison to the site that you are developing. Ask the target users what web sites they currently go to, and which sites might be related to your web site. This is useful information for a number of reasons. If you find out what other web sites the target user population is interested in, you can create a set of benchmarks to compare the new web site to. The site under development can be compared to other sites that have a similar mission; you might find good suggestions for the new web site under development, as well as ideas of what not to do. In addition, if you are developing an informational web site, you might be able to provide a list of external links to those web sites. In return, those web sites can provide links to your new web site. This can assist in marketing your web site (see the chapter on marketing your web site). For an e-commerce web site, you would not want to provide links to your competitor's web sites, and it would be expected that your competitors would not want to provide a link to your web site. However, for developing an e-commerce site, determining your benchmark web sites can assist in figuring out who your main competition is. Using a search engine to find web sites on related topics can also be helpful.[21]

External Links

If you ask targeted users generally what type of web sites they are interested in, the web development team and the client organization will gain an understanding of what external links would be useful. In addition, the web development team and the client organization might be able to find web sites that would be of interest to the users, even though the users are not aware of those web sites. A final possibility is that the web development team or the client organization might also be a source for benchmark web sites. For instance, if you are designing a web site for a Lutheran Church, it might be useful to look at the web sites for other Lutheran Churches in that geographic area to see what types of resources they are offering. This way it can be ensured that the web site developed does not provide the exact same content as an already-existing web site.

▶ Important Questions to Ask:

1. What other web sites do you frequently use?
2. What other types of web sites would you be interested in?

▶ 4.7 ADDITIONAL CONSIDERATIONS FOR WEB SITE REDESIGN

For those web developers who are redesigning a currently existing web site, there is more information available to assist in requirements gathering than is available to web developers who are creating a new web site from scratch. Information on who has visited the web site in the past can assist in requirements gathering.

It is possible that there might have been information previously collected about visitors to the web site, using a form of some type. This demographic data might have been collected in the process of other data collection. This data could assist with determining demographic information, domain knowledge, and user computing experience.

For content, there might be a number of resources available for knowing what content users are interested in. Users sometimes leave messages in web site guest books; these messages can suggest possible directions for new content.[14]

If a web site has already existed and is being redesigned, the web site logs are very important informational tools. The web site logs can provide information on what site the users visited before coming to the web site. This may help in establishing benchmark web sites. Also, the web site logs can provide some information about the user computing environment. For instance, logs can provide information on what browser and what browser version the user is using to request the web page. Also, if most of the web page requests are coming from a specific domain on the Internet (such as a school or organization), it might be possible to determine what the connection speeds, processor speeds, and monitor sizes are at that organization. The web site logs can assist in identifying which parts of the web site are the most frequently visited, and which parts of the web site are visited less frequently.[14] More information on web site logs is available in Chapter 12.

It is also possible that usability testing has previously been performed on the currently existing web site. The results of the usability tests can point out possible usability pitfalls to avoid. In addition, if usability testing has not been performed on a currently existing web site, usability testing with a few users might be useful to uncover usability problems that currently exist. Users may not be able to describe the usability problems in a survey, but these problems may be clear when the web development team watches users attempting to find information on a web site and failing miserably. See Chapter 10 for more information about performing usability tests.

SUMMARY

When collecting user requirements, there are a number of different types of information that are important to collect. It is important for the web development team to learn more about general demographic information, domain knowledge, user computing experience, user computing environment, content, and benchmarking. These types of information can assist the web development team in determining what the users need. There are a number of techniques for gathering these requirements, such as paper surveys, electronic surveys, focus groups, and interviews, and these will be discussed in detail in the next chapter.

Deliverables

At this point, you should have decided:
1. What categories of information need to be collected from the users?
2. Which data is most important to collect?
3. What other web sites would be good benchmarks?

Discussion Questions

1. Why it is important to find out what domain knowledge the users have?
2. What question related to user computing experience might be important?
3. What are metaphors, and how are they used in web sites?
4. What are five important factors in the user computing environment related to usability?
5. Why is it impossible to make statistical statements about the entire population of web users?
6. What are seven examples of content?
7. What are some different sources for possible content ideas? What are the advantages and disadvantages of each?
8. Where does the content physically come from?
9. What is benchmarking, and how is it different for informational web sites versus e-commerce web sites?
10. What are three requirements gathering areas that can be utilized for currently existing web sites?
11. How and when does usability testing fit into the requirements-gathering process for currently existing web sites?

REFERENCES

1. Lazar, J., & Preece, J. (2001, in press). Using Electronic Surveys to Evaluate Networked Resources: From Idea to Implementation. In C. McClure & J. Bertot (Eds.), *Evaluating Networked Information Services: Techniques, Policy, and Issues*. Medford, NJ: Information Today.

2. Fuccella, J., & Pittolato, J. (1999). Giving people what they want: How to involve users in site design. *IBM DeveloperWorks*. Available at: http://www-4.ibm.com/software/developer/library/design-by-feedback/expectations.html

3. Lazar, J., Tsao, R., & Preece, J. (1999). One foot in cyberspace and the other on the ground: A case study of analysis and design issues in a hybrid virtual and physical community. *WebNet Journal: Internet Internet Technologies, Applications, and Issues, 1*(3), 49–57.

4. Allwood, C. (1986). Novices on the computer: A review of the literature. *International Journal of Man-Machine Studies, 25*(6), 633–658.

5. Barfield, W. (1986). Expert–novice differences for software: Implications for problem-solving and knowledge acquisition. *Behaviour and Information Technology, 5*(1), 15–29.

6. Preece, J., Rogers, Y., Sharp, H., Benyon, D., Holland, S., & Carey, T. (1994). *Human-Computer Interaction*. Wokingham, England: Addison-Wesley.

7. Shneiderman, B. (1998). *Designing the User Interface: Strategies for Effective Human-Computer Interaction* (3rd ed.). Reading, MA: Addison-Wesley.

8. Whitten, I., & Bentley, L. (1997). *Systems Analysis and Design Methods*. Boston: Irwin McGraw-Hill.

9. Mayhew, D. (1999). *The Usability Engineering Lifecycle*. San Francisco: Morgan Kaufmann Publishers.

10. Lazar, J., & Norcio, A. (2001, in press). User Considerations in E-commerce Transactions. In Q. Chen (Ed.), *Human-Computer Interaction: Issues and Challenges*. Hershey, PA: Idea Group Publishing, 185–195.

11. Powell, T., Jones, D., & Cutts, D. (1998). *Web Site Engineering: Beyond Web Page Design*. Upper Saddle River, NJ: Prentice Hall.

12. Niederst, J. (1999). *Web Design in a Nutshell*. Sebastopol, CA: O'Reilly and Associates.

13. Fuccella, J. (1997). *Using user-centered design methods to create and design usable web sites*. Proceedings of the 1997 ACM Conference on Systems Documentation, 69–77.

14. Yu, J., Prabhu, P., & Neale, W. (1998). *A user-centered approach to designing a new top-level structure for a large and diverse corporate web site*. Proceedings of the 1998 Human Factors and the Web Conference. Available at: http://www.research.att.com/conf/hfweb/

15. Corry, M., Frick, T., & Hansen, L. (1997). User-centered design and usability testing of a web site: An illustrative case study. *Educational Technology Research and Development, 45*(4), 65–76.

16. Nielsen, J. (1994). *Usability Engineering*. Boston: Academic Press.

17. Pitkow, J., & Kehoe, C. (1996). Emerging trends in the WWW population. *Communications of the ACM, 39*(6), 106–110.

18. Feinberg, S., & Johnson, P. (1998). *Designing and developing surveys on WWW sites*. Proceedings of the Special Interest Group on Computer Documentation, 38–42.

10. Bikson, T, & Panis, C. (1997). Computers and Connectivity: Current Trends. In S. Kiesler (Ed.), *Culture of the Internet* (pp. 407–430). Mahwah, NJ: Lawrence Erlbaum Associates.

20. Lynch, P., & Horton, S. (1999). *Web Style Guide: Basic Design Principles for Creating Web Sites.* New Haven, CT: Yale University Press.

21. Navarro, A., & Khan, T. (1998). *Effective Web Design.* San Francisco: Sybex.

Methods for Gathering Requirements

Once it is determined what type of information should be collected from the users of a web site, the next step is to actually collect that information. There are a number of different techniques for collecting information, including paper surveys, electronic surveys, focus groups, interviews, electronic focus groups, with the resulting information evaluated through more interviews and card sorting. The method (or methods) chosen depend on what type of access to users the web development team has. This chapter will discuss methods of collecting requirements, when those different methods are appropriate, and how to implement the technical portion of the data collection method.

It is important to note that each method of requirements gathering (surveys, focus groups, interviews, and so on) can be considered a subfield of its own. Each also has its own terminology, such as a respondent (for a survey), an interviewee (for an interview), and a participant (for a focus group). Each of these terms is really referring to the same type of person: a member of the target user population. During the process of requirements gathering, it is also possible that a specific user could have participated in a number of different activities, and therefore could have more than one of these terms attached to them, depending on which method for gathering requirements is being described.

► 5.1 DETERMINING THE ACCESS TO USERS

One of the deciding factors regarding which information gathering methods to use is what type of access you have to the target users. Are all of the targeted users in a specific geographic location, or are they geographically dispersed? Do you have e-mail addresses for the users? Do you have postal addresses for the users? Do the users check out the web frequently? Are there frequent face-to-face meetings of the users? The client organization should be able to provide this information to you. In addition, the client organization should have defined the target users in earlier stages of the lifecycle and should be able to provide ideas of how you can have access to them.

Access Affects the Information Gathering Techniques Used

The type of access that you have to targeted users will, in part, determine what type of information gathering techniques you can use. For instance, if there are face-to-face meetings of potential users, the web development team can visit those meetings and lead focus groups, perform interviews, or pass out paper surveys. If you have a list of home or work postal addresses for potential users, the web development team can send out paper surveys to those addresses. If there are no face-to-face meetings with potential users, who are geographically distributed, but there is a list of e-mail addresses, the web development team can send out electronic surveys. Each type of requirements gathering technique can collect different types of information. Surveys are good at getting shallow data from large numbers of respondents. Interviews are good at getting deep data from a small number of respondents. The methodologies for collecting user requirements are endless, and there are no right-or-wrong methods. There is also no limit on the number of information gathering techniques that can be used together. If it is feasible, you can use paper surveys together with electronic surveys and focus groups and interviews and card sorting. The more information collected, the better. However, it is unlikely that the web development team will be able to use all of these techniques, as the user's time is limited.

► 5.2 CHOOSING AN INFORMATION GATHERING TECHNIQUE

Various combinations of methods can be used. For example, if the target population of users consists of a number of different user groups, it is important to get a representative sampling of responses from each group.

The web development team collecting user requirements for a Quiz Bowl web site, for instance, discovered that there were some face-to-face meetings of potential users (at tournaments); however, the people who attended the face-to-face meetings made up only a small portion of those potentially interested in the web site (who were geographically distributed).[1] There were also a number of targeted users who did not come to any of the face-to-face meetings. Therefore, web-based surveys were used to collect requirements from those who were geographically distributed, and paper versions of the survey were passed out at face-to-face meetings.[1] By using this hybrid approach, potential users who responded to the survey were representative of those (1) who attended face-to-face tournaments as well as those who did not, and (2) of users who were located across the country.[1]

Another example is the development of the web site for the Down Syndrome Online Advocacy Group.[2] It was determined that the only way to access the targeted users (who were geographically distributed) was through a list of e-mail addresses.[2] Therefore, an e-mail survey was sent out to targeted users.[3] For the web site for St. John's Lutheran Church of Blenheim, the target users were mainly current members of the church.[3] It was determined that the best way to access these users was by visiting the Sunday services and passing out paper surveys. After the surveys had been collected and analyzed, the development team led focus groups to help clarify the information collected.

Guidelines for Choosing Techniques

In general, the following guidelines apply: When the web development team has access to users face-to-face (at a workplace, meeting, or monthly gathering), interviews and focus groups are appropriate. If there are a large number of users at these meetings, surveys are also useful. If the web development team has access to postal addresses for targeted users, paper surveys would be appropriate. If the web development team has access to phone numbers of the targeted user base, phone surveys might be appropriate. If the web development team has e-mail addresses for targeted users, or it is known that all targeted users are reachable via some type of electronic forum (such as a listserver, USENET newsgroup, or groupware package), e-mail surveys might be appropriate. If a web site already exists, it may be appropriate to place a web-based survey on the web site.

► 5.3 SURVEYS

A popular technique for gathering information from people is the survey. Surveys allow data to be collected from large numbers of people in a brief time.[4] Surveys can consist of closed-ended questions (those requiring that respondents choose from a list of choices), open-ended questions (where respondents answer however they like), and other types of questions, such as ranking and likert scales.[4] The boxed material in Fig. 5.1 illustrates these types of survey questions. Someone who responds to a survey is called a respondent. For the purposes of this book, a targeted user has the same meaning as a respondent.

Different Types of Survey Questions

Closed–Ended Question
Have you ever visited the Three Stooges web site?
(Please select only one answer)
A. Yes   B. No

Open–Ended Question
What types of resources would you like to see available on the web site?

_____

_____

I would purchase products from the Sneaker Incorporated web site if:

_____

_____

Ranking Question
Please rank the following web resources in order of importance (5=most important)
___ Calendar of events
___ Online phone directory
___ History of the company
___ Merchandise available
___ Pictures from previous events

A Likert Scale Question
Finding information on the Towson University web site is:
Enjoyable   Painful
1   2   3   4   5   6   7   8   9   NA

Figure 5.1
Various types of survey questions

There are some commonalities that apply to all surveys, including paper surveys, e-mail surveys, web-based surveys, and phone surveys. Questions must be well-written and unambiguous.[4,5] It is important to test your survey questions with a few users (respondents) before unleashing the survey on the general population of respondents. This test is called a pretest or a pilot study.[5,6] A pilot study can ensure that the questions are well-written, unbiased, and appropriate, and that the respondents are able to understand the questions. Respondents (or people whom you hope will respond to the survey) need to be aware of the purpose of the survey. The survey team (in this instance, the web development team) should attempt to get as high a response rate as possible. The same issues relate to all types of surveys (paper, phone, e-mail, web-based).

Paper Surveys

A traditional technique for collecting information is the paper survey. Paper surveys have been used in the requirements gathering stage of systems analysis and design for many years.[7] These surveys are distributed to the targeted population of users, either in person, or via postal mail, and hopefully, a large percentage of the targeted users will fill out the survey and return the survey. Paper surveys can include the types of requirements gathering questions that were discussed in Chapter 4.

As in any type of survey, the survey questions must be pilot-tested with a few users before being used with the target user population. With paper surveys, there are a number of time-tested techniques for increasing the response rate. An introductory letter should be sent out prior to the survey, letting respondents know (1) the purpose of the survey, (2) the importance of the survey, and (3) the qualifications of those performing the survey, in this case the web development team. Without such an advanced notice, users will be unlikely to respond, because they do not know why the survey is being performed, nor do they know or trust those who are performing the survey. During the survey period, the targeted users should be reminded about turning in the survey. Reminders can be handled through announcements at meetings or through postcards in the mail. Once surveys have been collected, the data should be entered into a spreadsheet or database for easy data analysis.

Electronic Surveys

There are many advantages to using electronic surveys. It is possible that targeted users will respond more quickly to electronic surveys than to paper surveys (because the user does not have to worry about finding a stamp or a postal drop).[6,8] Web developers using electronic surveys do not have to worry about the costs of copying and printing the surveys.[6,8] In many cases, it is possible to configure an electronic survey to directly enter responses into a spreadsheet or database program, eliminating the need for data entry and possibly eliminating the errors that can occur during data entry.[6,8,9] However, using exclusively electronic surveys is appropriate only if the entire targeted user population can be easily reached through electronic means. Otherwise, the web development team should pass out paper surveys in addition to electronic surveys.[6,8] Since it is very possible that there are web users who just are not using the web site that currently exists,[1] it can be a challenge to reach these potential users.

E-Mail vs. Web-Based Electronic Surveys

There are two different types of electronic surveys: e-mail surveys and web-based surveys.[6,8] E-mail surveys are sent as part of an e-mail message, or are sent as a file attachment.[8] Web-based surveys are surveys that exist as a web page, and users can answer the questions online.[6,8] Web-based surveys and e-mail surveys each have their advantages and disadvantages. E-mail surveys require that users have an e-mail account that they check; users do not need to have an e-mail account to respond to a web-based survey.[8] If a web site is being redesigned, web-based surveys can be used on the site itself, so that users can respond to the survey while browsing the web site.[8] Web-based surveys can provide assistance to the user in filling out the survey, with help screens or additional information.[6,8] This is not possible with an e-mail survey.[8] One odd fact is that users who receive an e-mail survey can actually change the wording of the survey instrument if they are not happy with the questions.[10] Users cannot modify the survey instrument on a web-based survey.[8] An e-mail survey, through the e-mail address, may possibly provide more identification of the user who responded to the survey.[8] Although web-based survey respondents may choose to identify themselves, this does not occur automatically, as is the case with e-mail surveys. E-mail addresses (or other identification information) can assist in determining whether the survey responses are representative of the target user population.[8]

The nature of the population of interest may affect the decision to use an e-mail survey instead of a web-based survey. For instance, if there is a well-defined population and corresponding e-mail addresses available (such as in a professional organization), it may make more sense to utilize an e-mail survey.

Implementing Any Electronic Survey

Regardless of whether an electronic survey is an e-mail survey or a web-based survey, there are a number of preliminary steps that must first take place before the survey can be distributed. The survey should first be designed on paper.[6] As in any other type of survey, questions must be clear, easy to understand, and unbiased. After writing the survey questions, they need to be pretested with a few respondents that represent the target user population.

After the written survey instrument has been created, it can then be turned into an electronic survey. If the web development team has decided to utilize an e-mail survey, this stage is simple. The team needs only to copy and paste the survey into an e-mail message. Alternatively, the survey could be attached to an e-mail message in MS-Word, WordPerfect, or RichTextFormat; this approach could help in maintaining survey formatting and allowing for clarity. It is important to note that recent research has found that users are more likely to fill out a survey that is embedded in an e-mail message than they are to fill out a survey that is sent as a file attachment.[11] Users might not want to respond to a survey as a file attachment because they are worried about viruses, because they may not have a word processor that can read the file, or because answering a file attachment involves more steps than answering an embedded e-mail survey.[11]

Creating a Web-Based Survey

Alternatively, the web development team can turn the paper survey into a web-based survey. There are a number of different possibilities for creating this type of survey. The process requires a basic knowledge of web programming. The web development team can use the form controls in HTML (Hypertext Markup Language),[12] a relatively simple task. What is harder is creating the code to *do something* when the user hits the Submit button to respond the survey. The web development team can use a Common Gateway Interface (CGI) script that can process the form and send an e-mail response to the web development team. CGI scripts can be written in different programming languages, such as Perl and C++.[12] However, the web development team does not necessarily need to write a CGI script from scratch. A number of web sites offer free, downloadable CGI scripts that can easily be modified and used to activate an HTML form. For instance, it is possible to download, customize, and install the FormMail script from Matt's Script Archive in approximately 15–20 minutes. (This web site also provides instructions on how to download and install the script.) The FormMail script will process the HTML form and send the survey responses to an e-mail address. The following is a list of several web sites that offer free CGI scripts.

▶ **Sites that Offer CGI Scripts for Download**

CGI Resource Index	http://cgi.resourceindex.com/
Developer's Daily	http://www.devdaily.com/
FreeCode	http://www.freecode.com/
Freescripts.com	http://www.freescripts.com/
Free-Scripts.net	http://www.free-scripts.net/
Matt's Script Archive	http://www.worldwidemart.com/scripts/

It is also important to check with the Internet service provider that is being used. Some Internet service providers will not allow users to run CGI scripts. Other Internet service providers already provide a set of commonly needed CGI scripts for use by their customers; downloading and modifying a CGI script might be unnecessary.

A second possibility for creating a web-based survey is to use a web site that allows developers to create surveys without doing any coding. A number of web sites will guide the user through developing a web survey, host the survey at no cost, and then tabulate results. It is important to note that the more popular term for web surveys is a poll, so many of the web sites that offer free surveys refer to them that way. The following is a list of several sites that offer free web-based surveys.

▶ **Sites that Offer Free Web–Based Surveys**

Alxnet.com	http://www.alxnet.com/
Extreme Polling	http://www.extremepolling.com/
FreePolls	http://www.freepolls.com/
GigaPoll	http://www.gigapoll.com/
NetVotes	http://www.netvotes.com/
Pollcat	http://www.pollcat.com/

Web development software such as Microsoft FrontPage offers tools for developing surveys (in some cases called forms). Usually, these applications require only a minimum of programming by hand. (See Chapter 9 for more information on web development software.) It is also possible to purchase a software package tailored to the needs of web-based surveys (such as SurveySolutions, <http://www.perseusdevelopment.com/fromsurv.htm>). For advanced survey needs, it might be necessary to hire a consulting firm that specializes in this area (such as Virtual Surveys, <http://www.virtualsurveys.com/>). However, most web-based surveys are relatively simple and can be developed in a short period of time.

Usability Testing of the Web-Based Survey

Once the electronic survey is developed, usability testing must be performed.[6,8] Usability testing is different from the pretesting of a survey. Pretesting focuses on whether the questions are well-written and easy to understand, whereas usability testing focuses on whether the interface is easy for the user to understand. In the case of a web-based survey, usability means issues such as whether the text is large enough to read, whether the page layout is easy to follow, whether the color scheme is appropriate, whether the graphics overwhelm the user, and whether the navigation of the survey instrument is easy to understand. A list of usability heuristics for web-based surveys is listed below. For instance, it would hurt usability if the survey was divided into five logical sections, and the users had to hit a submit button for each one of the five sections.

▶ Usability Guidelines[6]

- *Make the survey error-proof.* If one question requires an answer, while another question has an optional answer, those rules should be enforced. If there *must* be a response to a specific question, then the user should not be allowed to submit a web-based survey without answering that question. If the web development team wants only a numerical answer, that rule should be enforced. The user should receive an error message if he or she has not filled out the form correctly. However, it is not a good idea to require that the user respond to all questions, as the user may be reluctant to do this, and this requirement would decrease the likelihood that the user would respond to the survey at all.

- *Make the survey accessible from all common browsers.* The web development team should test to make sure that the web-based survey appears correctly in Internet Explorer, Netscape Navigator, and Lynx, as well as in different versions of those browsers.

- *Test the survey with different monitor sizes*. The web development team should make sure that the web-based survey does not appear hard to use on a smaller monitor size.

There are a number of different approaches to usability testing.[13] However, for the design of a web-based survey, the most appropriate method is to ask a few of the targeted users (possibly 3–5) to attempt to fill out the web-based survey. Those users should be encouraged to comment openly about any problems or confusing aspects of the interface, either by speaking aloud or by writing those comments on paper or in an e-mail. In addition, the web development team can ask specific questions of the users related to the interface design. Feedback from the users should be used to clarify and improve the web-based survey before the majority of users get to respond to it. If time is a critical factor, the pretesting of the survey questions can be combined with the usability testing of the web-based survey—as long as the web development team makes sure that both areas get attention.

Informing Users about the Electronic Survey

After designing and testing the electronic survey, the next step is to inform the target users about the existence of the survey. For an e-mail survey, this step simply consists of sending the e-mail that includes the survey to the targeted users.[8] For a web-based survey, informing the targeted users can be more of a challenge. The web development team must contemplate how they can contact the targeted users, and use whatever means are available to them. This might mean distributing fliers; making phone calls; announcing the URL at face-to-face meetings; posting an announcement to a related newsgroup, bulletin board, or listserver; adding a login script (if users are required to log in to a system somewhere); or creating a link to the survey on web pages that are frequently visited by targeted users.[8,14] In addition, if there is a list of e-mail addresses available, but a web-based survey is being used, the target user population can simply be e-mailed, asking them to access the web-based survey.[15] Targeted e-mail lists can be purchased from marketing companies.[15] The target user population can also be informed about the web-based survey through the use of banner advertisements on web sites that those users frequent.[16] Periodic reminders (with a deadline date by which all surveys must be received) can then be sent via the same medium used to advertise the web-based survey, with the eventual goal of maximizing the number of respondents to the survey. For web sites that are being redesigned, web-based surveys can simply be included on the current web site, with a notice on the home page requesting that users fill out the web-based survey. For example, when Kodak was redesigning their web site, they utilized a web-based survey, which allowed them to collect important information about user demographics.[17]

▶ Steps in Implementing an Electronic Survey
1. Create the survey on paper.
2. Pretest the survey questions.
3. Turn the paper survey into an electronic survey.
4. Perform usability testing on the electronic survey.
5. Inform the target user population about the survey.

▶ Getting a Good Response to Surveys
1. Have trusted people introduce the survey.
2. Advertise the existence of the survey.
3. Send periodic reminders to targeted users.

▶ 5.4 INTERVIEWS

Interviews are useful tools for collecting information. If targeted users are available, face-to-face interviews can be used, and in traditional requirements gathering they are used heavily.[18] These interviews involve an interviewer and an interviewee; the level of structure varies.[7] Some interviews are highly structured, and a specific set of questions are asked of the interviewee. Other interviews can be unstructured; there is a general goal for the interview, but there is no set of definitive questions, and the interview is more exploratory.[7] In reality, most interviews fall somewhere in the middle, and are semi-structured. Interview questions can also be open-ended ("What do you think the web site needs?") or closed-ended ("Does the web site need a schedule of events?"). However, caution should be taken to ensure that the questions asked are not loaded so that the response of the interviewee is influenced. Interviews were used in redesigning the Kodak web site, to help understand the needs of different user groups within the target user population.[17]

Advantages and Disadvantages

Face-to-face interviews are very useful when there is little information available to the web development team, and the team needs a foundation of understanding before going any further in the requirements gathering. Interviews can also assist in clarifying responses given by users in other requirements gathering activities (such as surveys) that might have been unclear. The interviewer can change the course of the discussion if it appears that there is an area of questioning that needs more attention. It is possible that, based on the responses from the interviewee, the interviewer can explore different directions or can ask for more in-depth information about a certain area. This "drill-down" of information is not available when using a survey. Interviews also allow for in-depth discussion of issues, and can be good for collecting a lot of data.

There are a number of disadvantages to using interviews, however. Interviews can be very time-consuming for both the interviewer and the interviewee.[7] Another disadvantage is that the quality of the information collected is directly related to the interviewer's experience in performing interviews.[7] In the interview it is important that the interviewer make the interviewee feel at ease by being friendly, never threatening, and by being able to explain the nature and purpose of the interview.[18] It is possible that in some cases, the interviewee may not feel comfortable revealing some information face-to-face, and would prefer anonymity.[7]

Planning

Planning is very important for a successful interview. In advance, the interviewer should check whether tape recording of the meeting is permissible.[18] If it is not, then it is imperative to take detailed notes. There should be a general outline of how the interview will be performed.[18] The interviewer should know what type of information is important to collect, and should have a list of possible questions to ask. The interviewee should be prepared on the topic of the meeting and the approximate time that the interview will take.[18] After the interview, the interviewee should be thanked for his or her time, especially if a follow-up interview might be necessary.

Phone Interviews

In a phone interview, researchers (i.e., the web development team) call targeted users and ask them standardized questions. Some researchers call this technique a "phone survey." It is debatable whether this should be categorized as an interview or a survey, but one way of looking at it is that if the interviewer does not deviate from a prepared list of questions, it could be considered a survey. If the interviewer changes the questions or the depth of the questions based on responses from the interviewer, it could be considered an interview.

When Are Phone Interviews Appropriate?

Phone interviews can be used if a list of phone numbers of targeted users is available. Conducting phone interviews can be tricky, however; many people do not respond to any interviews over the phone, or to any unsolicited phone calls. Therefore, phone interviews might be appropriate only if the targeted users comprise a small, focused population, are well aware of the development of the web site, and are supportive of the web site development. For instance, phone interviews were used in the requirements gathering phase for an online community for the neighborhoods of Lake Linganore, a planned community in Frederick County, MD. Phone interviews took place with chairpeople of the villages in Lake Linganore (the clients) and citizens of Lake Linganore (the users). The web development team felt that it was important to talk with a number of individual users, but because of time constraints, it was not possible to meet with the users face-to-face. The web development effort was sponsored in part by the community association, and community members (the users) were in favor of building a web site, so people responded to the phone interviews. If there had not been a high of level of support for the web site effort, the phone interviews might not have been successful. For more information on the Lake Linganore Development, please see <http://www.ifsm.umbc.edu/onlinecommunities/>.

► 5.5 FOCUS GROUPS

Focus groups are an additional technique for collecting user requirements. A focus group is a discussion among a group of people with similar interests. (In the case of requirements gathering, all participants are a part of the target user population.) The discussion usually takes place in a room with all participants present together. Although it is also possible to have a one-way mirror through which researchers can watch the focus group, this is not necessary, nor is this common practice. A focus group usually consists of 4 to 12 people. In a group of 15 or more, communication can become confusing, and the group can break down into subgroups.[19]

Multiple Focus Groups

Usually, a series of focus groups take place, which allows for diverse views to be heard but no single group's views to dominate. Some focus groups can have a "personality," either quiet, outspoken, or warlike.[19] Just as the survey response from one person isn't statistically significant, the response from one focus group can possibly be biased.[19] Therefore, when it is possible, it is preferable to hold a series of focus groups with different participants. For example, when the Kodak web site was developed, three focus groups were held in different cities to help better determine what type of content (such as product information and photography tips) the users wanted.[17]

Focus Groups vs. Interviews

In comparison to an interview, in which specific, closed-ended questions might be used, in a focus group, the questions are nondirective.[19] There are no specific answers, nor a list of possible answers. The focus group participants are asked a number of general questions, and discussion among the participants is encouraged without any limitations to the possible responses.[19] A specific facet of the focus group is the creation of a permissive environment in which participants are encouraged to openly share their feelings.[19] This is one of the main advantages of focus groups; participants get to interact with each other, share their thoughts, and in the process, stimulate new ideas and comments that would not have not come to the forefront in one-on-one interviews. Hoffer, George, and Valacich have described this aspect of a focus group as a synergy. Because of synergy, focus group participants might be reminded of additional examples or problems. As these topics come to the forefront for discussion, the development team can observe whether there is majority agreement among participants, and they can ascertain the strength of any disagreement.[18]

The Moderator's Role

Successful focus groups require an experienced focus group moderator who asks questions and helps manage the group. The moderator must make sure that there is an environment of openness in which participants are encouraged to share their thoughts. A focus group moderator should not be someone who has power or influence with the participants in the focus group in any area outside of the focus group, such as in the workplace.[19] The moderator should encourage participation, stimulate discussion, and help the group stay on task when the participants start digressing onto unrelated topics.[19] The moderator might also have to help keep in check any participant who dominates the discussion and does not allow others to speak, or who mocks the statements of others. The moderator should not be concerned with taking notes during the focus group. Instead, the focus group should be taped (either in audio or video), or additional people from the web development team who are familiar with the project should be present at the focus group, taking detailed notes.

Challenges of Working with Focus Groups

There are a number of problems that can occur with focus groups. Some participants may hesitate to talk at all, while other participants might dominate the discussion and fail to allow others to speak.[19] An experienced moderator can try to ameliorate this situation by saying something like, "John Doe has already given us a lot of wonderful feedback; who wants to add to his comments?" It is also possible that outside influences will affect candor in the focus group. If the participants know each other outside of the focus group, they probably have some type of shared experience or history, and there might be issues among them that would hinder the effectiveness of the focus group. For instance, if a church group was taking part in a focus group, participants might hesitate to speak up until they heard the views of the priest, pastor, or deacon. The same might hold true for a group of people from the same workplace; the participants might hold back on their comments until they heard the viewpoints of their superiors. Because the participants might be likely to echo the views of their superiors, and not discuss their true feelings, it is better to hold a focus group of participants who do not work together or know each other well.

Electronic Focus Groups

An electronic focus group is similar in structure to a traditional focus group, in that there are a number of people involved, the focus group participants interact with each other, improving the discussion of ideas, and there is a moderator. However, focus groups need not be limited to a group of people sitting around a room. There can also be electronic focus groups of geographically dispersed individuals.

GDSS and other Electronic Technologies

One possibility would be to hold a focus group using a technology called a group decision support system (GDSS), in which the discussion takes place over a set of computers located in a room, and all comments and discussions are anonymous.[20] There is a projection screen in the front of the room, for all participants to see, and idea generation, idea ranking, and categorization are supported. In addition, since all of the communication is electronic, there is automatic recording of all comments made. The idea behind a GDSS is that since the originator of the comments and ideas is not identified, then only the idea will be considered, and the status of the person presenting the idea is not considered.[20] By using a GDSS, information gathering can be improved, because group hierarchy and political issues are "taken out of the equation."[20] However, installing GDSS software, or a GDSS room, is expensive and is feasible only for situations where the client organization can afford to pay for the installation. This is usually not possible. It's one of those "it would be wonderful if we had unlimited money, but we don't" situations.

Another possibility would be to have an electronic focus group in cases in which the target users are distributed geographically. The focus group discussion could take place using groupware software that could provide chat areas and shared tools, such as drawing tools.[15,21] The electronic focus group could also take place using standard chat room software.[22]

Electronic vs. Traditional Focus Groups

With an electronic focus group, the same types of group discussion could occur as with a traditional focus group, with the moderator playing the same role. Electronic focus groups might be less expensive, since there are no travel costs incurred for participants to come to the focus group location.[22] A drawback to the electronic approach is that the moderator and the participants might feel less at ease, since they could not see each other, and therefore would have less communication feedback (whether people are smiling, frowning, look bored, angry, or otherwise). Another challenge of electronic focus groups is that all users must have access to the specific chat room technology (some web sites require that you download chat room software) or groupware technology, and be experienced using it. And all participants must be available at the same time, even if they are physically located in different time zones. So, while electronic focus groups look promising, they are not appropriate in many cases.

▶ 5.6 OTHER CONSIDERATIONS

After requirements have been gathered—whether by using surveys, interviews, or focus groups—the data now needs to be collected and interpreted.

Card Sorting

Once the general web site requirements have been collected, the technique of card sorting can be used to better understand the information that users have supplied.[15] Card sorting helps influence the navigation structure of the web site because it reveals the users' mental models of how the information is organized.[23] In card sorting, names of the different content areas are placed on index cards. For instance, items such as a schedule of events, personnel lists, membership benefits, and so on can be listed. The names on these index cards should match the web site content needs (also called pages or objects) that were discovered during the main requirements gathering. The cards are give to the users in a random order. Targeted users (5–10 users would be more than sufficient) are given these cards and asked to organize them.[23] By doing a card sorting activity, it is possible to see how the users view the content, and what their mental model is of how the content should be organized. One of the more frustrating situations is for a user to want content, for the content to be on the web site, but for the user not to look in the right place for that content. Users should be encouraged to describe why they organized the cards in that manner, and also suggest names for each group of cards. If there is a consensus between a few users of how the content should be organized, the web development team can use this organizational scheme on the web site itself. Card sorting has been used as part of requirements gathering at a number of organizations, including IBM and Indiana University.[15,24] This technique tends to be used more frequently when a web site already exists and the web development team is looking for a better way to organize the currently existing content.

Preserving Anonymity

In all of the requirements gathering techniques, targeted users should be notified that their responses will not be attributed to any of them personally. If users are worried that their identities will be displayed with their responses, they may hesitate to be open or as truthful as they might otherwise be. Users might worry that the web development team will reveal that it was Joe Smith who said that "the system is hard to use and whoever designed it is a moron." Anonymity encourages the targeted users to be open and honest and to provide useful comments and suggestions.

Accepting Limits

In a perfect world, the web development team would be able to learn everything there is to know about the users and their needs. However, in reality, it is impossible to find out everything about the targeted users. A full-scale survey might reach 10 pages, which most users would hesitate to fill out. Gathering user requirements from all users, on all possible topics, using all of the methods discussed is simply not feasible; it is therefore necessary to compromise. The web development team should select and ask those questions that are most important to the development of the web site. The team should examine the methods that are most appropriate for collecting the requirements, and proceed with those methods. Targeted users are not going to be willing to respond to two surveys, come in for an interview, take part in a focus group, and answer a phone survey. The user will feel intruded upon and could possibly develop some negative feelings towards the web development team! In addition, even though a large number of users should take part in the requirements gathering, unless the target user population is very small (20–30 people), it will be impossible to collect information from all users, or even a majority. It is therefore important to gather requirements from a representative sample of users.

SUMMARY

Requirements gathering can be a long and detailed process; however, is central to the concept of user-centered design. It is through gathering user requirements that the web development team discovers whether a system or web site will ever meet the needs of the users. Requirements gathering is more of an art than a science. There is not "one right way" to do requirements gathering. The methods chosen are influenced by how much access and what type of access the web development team has to the targeted users. Surveys, interviews, focus groups, and card sorting can all be used to help gather and sort user requirements. Obviously, the more information that can be gathered, the better. It is unrealistic, however, to assume that all methods of requirements gathering will be used, just as it is unrealistic to assume that all users will be queried. The web development team needs to decide when they have gathered enough information to understand the user requirements, and only at that time should the requirements gathering stage end.

Deliverables

At this point, you should have:
1. Determined how you will have access to the users
2. Chosen an appropriate method (or methods) of collecting requirements
3. Developed, acquired, or purchased any software, HTML forms, or equipment that will needed for requirements gathering
4. Developed and pilot tested survey forms, interview scripts, and so on
5. Implemented the requirements gathering
6. Begun data analysis of the requirements gathering

Discussion Questions

1. Why is access to users an important consideration in how to do requirements gathering?
2. What are the different types of surveys? How do they differ, and in what situations would they be appropriate?
3. Imagine developing a new web site for a restaurant chain called Veggieland. Create five different types of survey questions related to the requirements gathering for the Veggieland web site.
4. How is pretesting a survey different from usability testing a survey?
5. When might an interview be appropriate for requirements gathering? What are some steps involved in planning for an interview?
6. Name three challenges in implementing a successful focus group.
7. Create a situation in which an electronic focus group might be appropriate. Describe the users involved and the technology used to implement the electronic focus group.
8. Why is card sorting used frequently when redesigning already existing web sites?

REFERENCES

1. Lazar, J., Tsao, R., & Preece, J. (1999). One foot in cyberspace and the other on the ground: a case study of analysis and design issues in a hybrid virtual and physical community. *WebNet Journal: Internet Technologies, Applications, and Issues, 1*(3), 49–57.
2. Lazar, J., Hanst, E., Buchwalter, J., & Preece, J. (2000, in press). Requirements Gathering in a Virtual Population: A Case Study. *WebNet Journal: Internet Technologies, Applications, and Issues, 2*(4), 46–53.
3. Lazar, J. (2000, in press). Teaching web design though community service projects. *Journal of Informatics Education and Research, 2*(2), 69–73.
4. Fowler, F. (1993). *Survey Research Methods* (2nd ed.). Newbury Park, California: Sage Publications.
5. Oppenheim, A. (1992). *Questionnaire Design, Interviewing, and Attitude Measurement.* London: Pinter Publishers.
6. Lazar, J., & Preece, J. (1999). Designing and implementing web-based surveys. *Journal of Computer Information Systems, 39*(4), 63–67.
7. Whitten, I., & Bentley, L. (1997). *Systems Analysis and Design Methods.* Boston: Irwin McGraw-Hill.
8. Lazar, J., & Preece, J. (2001, in press). Using Electronic Surveys to Evaluate Networked Resources: From Idea to Implementation. In C. McClure & J. Bertot (Eds.), *Evaluating Networked Information Services: Techniques, Policy, and Issues.* Medford, NJ: Information Today.
9. Bertot, J., & McClure, C. (1996). *Electronic surveys: Methodological implications for using the World Wide Web to collect survey data.* Proceedings of the 59th Annual Meeting of the American Society for Information Science, 173–185.

10. Witmer, D., Colman, R., & Katzman, S. (1999). From Paper-and-Pencil to Screen-and-Keyboard: Toward a Methodology for Survey Research on the Internet. In S. Jones (Ed.), *Doing Internet Research: Critical Issues and Methods for Examining the Net* (pp. 145–161). Thousand Oaks, California: Sage Publications.

11. Dommeyer, C., & Moriarty, E. (2000). Comparing two forms of an e-mail survey: Embedded vs. attached. *International Journal of Market Research, 42*(1), 39–50.

12. Niederst, J. (1999). *Web Design in a Nutshell.* Sebastopol, CA: O'Reilly and Associates.

13. Nielsen, J. (1994). *Usability Engineering.* Boston: Academic Press.

14. Schmidt, W. (1997). World Wide Web survey research: Benefits, potential problems, and solutions. *Behavior Research Methods, Instruments, & Computers, 29*(2), 274–279.

15. Fuccella, J., & Pittolato, J. (1999). Giving people what they want: How to involve users in site design. *IBM DeveloperWorks.* Available at: http://www-4.ibm.com/software/developer/library/design-by-feedback/expectations.html

16. Tuten, T., Bosnjak, M., & Bandilla, W. (2000). Banner-advertised web surveys. *Marketing Research, 11*(4), 17–21.

17. Yu, J., Prabhu, P., & Neale, W. (1998). *A user-centered approach to designing a new top-level structure for a large and diverse corporate web site.* Proceedings of the 1998 Human Factors and the Web Conference. Available at: http://www.research.att.com/conf/hfweb/

18. Hoffer, J., George, J., & Valacich, J. (1999). *Modern systems analysis and design.* Reading, MA: Addison-Wesley.

19. Krueger, R. (1994). *Focus Groups: A practical guide for applied research.* Thousand Oaks, California: Sage Publications.

20. Turban, E. (1995). *Decision Support and Expert Systems: Management Support Systems.* Englewood Cliffs, NJ: Prentice Hall.

21. Dix, A., Finlay, J., Abowd, G., & Beale, R. (1998). *Human-Computer Interaction.* (2nd ed.). London: Prentice Hall England.

22. Collins, C. (2000). Focus groups go online to measure the appeal of web sites. *The New York Times,* July 6, 2000.

23. Lisle, L., Dong, J., & Isensee, S. (1998). *Case study of development of an ease of use web site.* Proceedings of the 1998 Human Factors and the Web Conference. Available at: http://www.research.att.com/conf/hfweb/

24. Corry, M., Frick, T., & Hansen, L. (1997). User-centered design and usability testing of a web site: An illustrative case study. *Educational Technology Research and Development, 45*(4), 65–76.

CASE STUDY #1

▲ Best Buddies Maryland

The web development team for Best Buddies Maryland concluded that in order to produce a superior web site, the information gathered would have to reflect the needs of
all of the potential users of the site. The team recognized that this would be an extremely difficult task to fulfill. Best Buddies works with students from the middle-school
level through the college level and also with adult members of the community. These future users of the web site will likely have a wide range of skills, information needs, and
tastes. They will also use a variety of computer hardware and software to access the site.
In order to best accommodate this diverse population, the development team decided to
collect information in three general categories: Personal Information, Computer
Information, and Web Preferences.

Personal Information

The first information category, Personal Information, focused on the user's age, highest
level of education, gender, whether or not they had a computer at home, if they were
involved in any other type of volunteer work, and whether or not English was their native language. This information would give the development team a better picture of
who the web site's users would be. The team believed that, whenever information is presented, the audience is the key consideration. The development team therefore would
match the wording of text on the site with the educational level and age of the site's
users. When users have computers at home they can spend relaxed, quality time looking at web sites. If they access the web at work, at the library, or at some other location, they are likely to feel rushed, so the team wanted to know about the users' place
of access. The development team also felt that it would be good to know if users were
doing other volunteer work in addition to Best Buddies, so more could be discovered
about the values of the user population.

Computer Information

The second information category, Computer Information, focused on computer hardware
and software used by the future visitors to the Best Buddies site. Users were asked about
the type of computer they used, their Internet service provider, their connection type and
speed, the age of their computer, and their computer's operating system, monitor size,
and resolution. These hardware and software factors play a role in how well, and how
quickly, users will be able to view a web site. If a majority of users have older computers and slower Internet connections, it would be unwise to design a graphics-intensive
web site. The size and resolution of the users' monitors directly impact the layout of the
web site. Particularly in the case of the web site's homepage, the development team
used this data to ensure that the most important information and the site navigation
are visible on users' screens without the use of the scroll bars. The computer informa-

tion would guide the development of the content on the web site. Gathering information about the Internet service providers used by viewers of the web site and their browsers of preference provided a minimum standard for testing how well the web site performed on various web browsers.

Web Preferences

Finally, the development team felt it was necessary to gather information in the category of Web Preferences. Users' views on frames, their opinions on the use of animation, how long they have been using the web, how often they use the web, where they browse the web, their browser of choice, their favorite search engines, the type of information they would like to see on the Best Buddies web site, and their purposes for using the web would be collected. Their responses related to frames and animation would directly affect the design of the Best Buddies web site. For instance, a general disapproval of frames from the user population would necessitate the use of a different navigational strategy. Rather than provide a definition of frames, the development team decided to allow a response that would indicate that the user did not know what frames are. This question allowed the team to collect feelings about frames while also gaining more insight into how web-savvy the user population is. Should users respond that they did not care for large amounts of animation, a more conservative approach to graphics on the web site would be taken.

The questions pertaining to how often users access the web, how long they have been using the web, and where they do most of their browsing from all would provide insight into users' familiarity and comfort level with the web. The question about users' search engine preferences would provide information that was useful in the marketing of the web site. Lastly, and perhaps most importantly, the development team intended to learn what type of content (e.g., calendars of events, ways to donate time and money, or other information) on the Best Buddies Maryland web site would make our users want to visit it frequently. The information collected would be vital in determining the type of web site that was designed.

Requirements Gathering Begins

The initial meeting with the client was held at the offices of Best Buddies Maryland in downtown Baltimore. The development team met with the primary contacts at Best Buddies, Michelle Bicocchi and Carrie Cerri. Although the purpose of the meeting was to allow the team and the client to get to know each other, some general information gathering was also completed. To facilitate this information gathering, the team formulated a list of questions to bring to the meeting (see Best Buddies Maryland Form A, Fig. 5.2). The information collected in the initial meeting formed the foundation of further requirements gathering.

During the initial meeting, the client agreed to allow the development team to tape record future client interviews. The client also agreed to help provide users for information gathering and web site testing, which subsequently was handled through e-mail messages and phone calls with the client. The differences between the Maryland chapter of Best Buddies and the international organization were examined during the meeting, and the client provided the development team with an organizational chart. The client identified some of the primary users of the proposed web site as volunteers, and people outside of the organization looking for an avenue to donate time or money to the group. In general, the client said they would like the web site to include a calendar of events, contact information, and general information about the organization. Although the international organization had a web site, the Maryland chapter had never had one and they were looking for guidance on the subject of web site hosting and domain names.

Questionnaires

The development team decided to use questionnaires as one method for collecting user requirements. Questionnaires were designed to collect information and opinions from the client, the volunteers of Best Buddies Maryland, and the potential users of the web site. Best Buddies volunteers are distributed across 3 middle schools, 24 high schools, and 25 colleges around Maryland. The employees of the client are located in the home office in Baltimore and also in a branch office in Silver Spring, some 40 miles away. With this large, widely dispersed population, a questionnaire represented the best chance to reach the largest number of target users. A single member of the development team could distribute a large number of questionnaires more quickly than one-on-one interviews or focus groups could be implemented. Questionnaires also would allow participants to answer anonymously and at their own convenience.

The potential questionnaire respondents included the employees of Best Buddies Maryland, volunteers from middle schools, high schools, colleges, and community organizations, and people who were not currently involved with Best Buddies Maryland. This last group was included to get an understanding of the kind of information the wider Internet audience required. As Best Buddies wished to use the web site as a vehicle for growing the organization, the information on the site had to appeal to a wider audience than the current employees and volunteers.

The development team's goal was for the questionnaire to reach a total of 100 users. Distribution of the questionnaires was divided up between the members of the development team, with each of the five team members being responsible for 20 questionnaires. When possible, in order to save time and lower distribution costs, the questionnaires would be sent out and collected via e-mail, with the questions sent as an actual part of the message rather than as an attachment. The instructions for the questionnaires sent via e-mail differed from those distributed by hand in that e-mail respondents were instructed to delete all of the responses other than the one that was their choice. The development team also would use a fax machine, whenever that proved to be the easiest method for sending and receiving questionnaires from some of the users.

The questionnaires contained all three information categories: Personal Information, Computer Information, and Web Preferences. The questionnaire was comprised mostly of fixed-format questions that required a specific response from the individual providing the answers. When offering the user a multiple-choice question, the development team provided the response "Don't Know" to discourage guessing. Additionally, because the wide variety of hardware and software sold in the United States could not be adequately reflected in the responses to some questions, the team provided an "Other" response and prompted the user to provide more detailed information. Some questions asked the user to rate answers on a scale of 1 (not important) to 5 (very important). Some of these questions were expanded upon and used during structured interviews. See Best Buddies Maryland Form B (Fig. 5.3) for the full user questionnaire.

Pretesting the questionnaire allowed the development team to rewrite, add, or delete any questions on the questionnaire that might be unclear or unnecessary. A small sample of the users were given the questionnaire ahead of time in order to gather their suggestions for improvement. The development team decided to give the questionnaire to one employee of Best Buddies, one middle-school volunteer, one high school volunteer, one college volunteer, and one person who was not currently involved with the organization. After completing the questionnaire, each member of the test population was asked whether any of the questions were unclear and if he or she had any suggestions for making improvements.

Structured Interviews

The questionnaire is one of the most popular methods for collecting user requirements because it enables a development team to collect information quickly, inexpensively, and efficiently from a large number of geographically dispersed people. However, a questionnaire does not provide individual contact between the development team and the end user. In gathering requirements, a greater depth of information is often needed than can be obtained through a questionnaire alone. For this reason, the development team believed that the combination of questionnaires and structured interviews would help them gain a better understanding of the needs of the future users of the Best Buddies Maryland web site and the constraints they face. During interviews, users were able explain their answers in greater detail and sometimes reveal some of the underlying reasons behind their answers. The interviewer is able to follow the user on interesting tangents that provide new and useful information. Additionally, when investigating the attitudes of users towards various styles of web sites and types of content, the interviewer is able to see the "body language" of the interviewee; this can be useful in determining the depth of the user's feelings about these issues.

Structured interviews have two main disadvantages: they are time consuming, and can be very costly if the user population is spread across a large area. The primary disadvantage of structured interviews in the case of the development of the Best Buddies Maryland web site was that they were time consuming. Only two weeks were available for conducting interviews and one week for the distillation and write-up of the information collected. Still, the development team intended to interview a cross-section of the users. All four employees of Best Buddies Maryland would be interviewed. Additionally, two volunteers from middle school, two from high school, two from college, and two people not currently involved with the Best Buddies program would be interviewed. All interviews were tape recorded (with the interviewee's permission) to ensure accuracy. All interviews were arranged well in advance at the user's convenience, and it was the goal of the development team to limit each interview to thirty minutes.

The information to be gathered during the structured interviews focused on users' attitudes about web sites and concrete content requirements (see Best Buddies Maryland Form C, Fig. 5.4, for interview questions). If the interviewers strayed from the format of the questions when unanticipated useful topics come up, they returned to the prewritten format for the final portion of the interview. The development team chose to limit the number of questions asked in the interview in order to allow time for rich, complete answers. Additionally, pains were taken to avoid loaded, leading, and biased questions.

As the development team intended to interview 12 users of the Best Buddies Maryland web site, one of these users was selected to test the interview questions in advance. As the test interview progressed, any unclear questions were identified and reformulated. Additionally, if the test subject provided insight into an interesting area not considered by the development team, questions were added to incorporate this new area into future interviews. Through the testing and use of questionnaires and structured interviews, the development team collected the information that would lead to the development of a successful web site for Best Buddies Maryland.

Questions for Initial Meeting with Clients

1. Do you have any objections to us tape recording interviews to ensure accuracy? (Question 1 applies only to the people directly asked.)
2. Would it be possible for you to provide users in the upcoming months for information gathering and testing of the web site?
3. What does the Maryland chapter of Best Buddies do differently than the international organization?
4. Who will be the users of the Maryland chapter's web site?
5. Is there an organizational chart for your chapter that we could have?
6. What type of content, in general, would you like on your web site (e.g., calendars, contact information, organization history, or other content)?
7. Has the Maryland chapter ever had a web site?
8. Where would you like your web site to be hosted?

Figure 5.2
Best Buddies
Maryland Form A

Figure 5.3

Best Buddies
Maryland Form B

User Questionnaire

Instructions: We are currently developing a web site for Best Buddies Maryland. The information gathered through this questionnaire will aid the development team in choosing the best approach in creating the site. Please circle the most appropriate response for each question. If you are unsure of any questions, we would prefer you select the Don't Know response rather than guess. If you select Other as the answer for any of the questions, please provide a brief explanation. Thank you for helping with this questionnaire.

Personal Information

1. How old are you?

    10–13   14–17   18–24   25–34   35–44   45–65   65+

2. What is your highest level of education completed?

    Middle school   High school   Some college   Associates degree

    Bachelors degree   Masters degree   Doctorate

3. Gender

    Male   Female

4. Do you have a computer at home?

    Yes   No

5. Are you involved with any other volunteer work? (If yes, please list.)

    Yes   No   Other volunteer work _____

6. Are you a native speaker of English? (If no, please list your native language.)

    Yes   No   Native language _____

Computer Information

1. Which style of computer do you use for World Wide Web browsing?

    Desktop   Laptop

2. Which type of processor do you have?

    486   Pentium I   Pentium II   Pentium III   Don't know
    Other _____

3. What type of connection to the Internet do you use?

    Dial-Up Modem   Cable Modem   ISDN   T1/T3   DSL   Don't Know
    Other _____

4. If you use a dial-up modem, what speed is it?

    9.6 kbps   14.4 kbps   28.8 kbps   33.6 kbps   56 kbps   Don't know
    Other _____

5. What size is your monitor?

    Laptop   14"   15"   15" Flat screen   17"   19"   21"   Don't know
    Other _____

6. What is the resolution of your monitor?

    640 × 480   800 × 600   832 × 624   1024 × 768   1024 × 870
    1152 × 870   1280 × 1024   1600 × 1200   Don't know
    Other _____

7. How old is the computer you use for browsing the World Wide Web?

    <6 months   6 months   1 year   2 years   3 years   4 years   >4 years   Don't know

8. Which operating system is on the computer you use to browse the World Wide Web?

    DOS 6.2   Windows 3.1   Windows 95   Windows 98   Windows 2000
    Windows NT   OS7   OS8   Unix   Linux   Don't know
    Other _____

Figure 5.3

continued

9. Which Internet service provider do you use?

America Online   Compuserve   Erols   Mindspring   Earthlink
Don't know   Other _____

Web Preferences

1. Do you prefer websites to have frames?

   Yes   No   No opinion   What is a frame?

2. How much animation do you like to see on websites?

   None   A few pieces   A lot   No opinion

3. Please rank from 1 (frequently use for this purpose) to 5 (rarely use for this purpose) your use of the World Wide Web.

   ____ Entertainment   ____ Research   ____ Work-related communication

   ____ Communication with friends and family   ____ School work

4. How often do you use the World Wide Web?

   Several times a day   Daily   Weekly   Monthly
   Few times a year   Never

5. How useful do you think the World Wide Web is as an information tool?

   Not useful   Somewhat useful   Useful   Very useful

6. How long have you been browsing the World Wide Web?

   More than 5 years   5 years   4 years

   3 years   2 years   1 year   Less than 1 year

7. From where do you usually browse the World Wide Web?

   Home   Work   Public Library   School   Other _____

8. Which web browser do you use?

   Netscape Navigator 4   Netscape Navigator 3   Internet Explorer 4

   Internet Explorer 5   AOL   Lynx   Don't know   Other _____

9. Please place a check mark next to the search engines you use most frequently.

   ____ Yahoo   ____ Lycos   ____ Ask Jeeves   ____ Hotbot   ____ AltaVista

   ____ Google   ____ Northernlight   ____ Don't use one

   ____ Other _____

10. What content would you find most useful on Best Buddies' web site? (Please rate: 1 (not important) to 5 (very important). You may use the same number more than once.)

    ____ Ways to volunteer   ____ History of the organization

    ____ Links to related organizations   ____ Ways to donate money

    ____ Guest book   ____ Office location and contact information

    ____ Other _____

11. Do you regularly use the websites of organizations with which you are involved?

    Yes   No   If yes, which site(s) _____

12. If you regularly use the websites of organizations with which you are involved, do you find any of them to be particularly useful?

    Yes   No   If yes, how is it useful _____

13. Please provide any additional comments regarding your use of computers, the World Wide Web, or any other content you would like to see on Best Buddies' web site.

Thank you for taking the time to complete this questionnaire.

> **Structured Interview Questions**
>
> Instructions to interviewer: These questions form the outline to be followed during the interview. Many of the questions, however, may lead the interviewee to provide useful, unanticipated information. It is your role to not only keep the interview on track, but to also formulate follow-up questions when the interviewee takes useful digressions.
>
> 1. What is your general opinion of the World Wide Web?
> 2. How would you characterize your usage of the World Wide Web?
> 3. Are you comfortable using technology involving computers?
> 4. What are your favorite websites?
> 5. Have you ever made the decision to join an organization based on information the organization placed on a web site?
> 6. In what ways do you use information collected from the World Wide Web?
> 7. Do you prefer more graphics or more text on websites providing information about organizations?
> 8. What kinds of information would you like to have available from the Best Buddies Maryland web site?
> 9. Please rate each of the items you mentioned in number 8 as either a *want* or a *must*. A *want* is something you would like to have available and a *must* is something the web site absolutely needs to be useful to you.
> 10. Please rank the wants you listed in number 9 on a scale of 1 to 5, with 1 being not too important to you and 5 being very important to you.

Figure 5.4

Best Buddies
Maryland Form C

CASE STUDY #2

▲ Institute of Notre Dame

The web development team working on the Institute of Notre Dame (IND) web site had the responsibility of redesigning the currently existing web site. Since the web site was being redesigned, the team had the luxury of talking to current users of the web site to determine what they liked, what they did not like, or what they would like to improve.

After receiving e-mails from the client organizational contact at the Institute of Notre Dame, Fred Germano, the development team decided to use two techniques to gather the user requirements. First they would interview Fred to learn more about technical issues, and then they would ask users to fill out surveys to learn more about their content needs. Based on our access to users, the team decided to utilize a web-based survey to gather requirements from the current user base. Since the IND web site already existed, we could place a link to a web-based survey directly on the current IND site. In addition, Fred informed us that the target users for the IND web site should all have access to the web, and therefore, a web-based survey would be appropriate. However, even with all the planning that was done, the web site development team was ready for unexpected results.

Interview

The team's first goal when they meet with Fred was to find out more information about the current web site. The team already knew that the site needed redesigning, but Fred was asked to give more information about the current site, to provide some insight on the current problems, and give suggestions for the new web site. IND Form A (Fig. 5.6) lists the questions that the team planned to ask Fred in the first interview.

Survey

Mr. Germano's feedback was used to assist in developing a survey for current users of the web site. Each group member created some questions that might provide useful data for the requirements gathering. The team then met and reviewed the questions. Most of the questions were very similar, except for wording, and these questions were condensed and reworded for clarity.

The survey was designed to provide a quantitative measure of user requirements as well as solicit detailed information in several key areas. The survey balanced open-ended and closed-ended questions. With the exception of the final two questions, all the open-ended questions in the survey were designed to clarify earlier closed-ended questions. By analyzing the results of the closed-ended questions, the team could determine usage trends among IND's target audience. Also, by studying the open-ended questions, the team could determine which aspects of the site needed the most attention. The survey questions are shown in IND Form B (Fig. 5.7).

After developing this paper survey, the development team turned it into a web-based survey and placed it at <http://onestop.towson.edu/IND>. A screen shot of the web-based survey is visible in Fig. 5.5. The results would yield an understanding of users' preferences. Besides the online form, the team also provided a hard copy of the survey, so that if users did not have access to the web or were not comfortable using the web, the team could still learn about those future users' needs. It was hoped that many of the users, such as faculty members and current students, would fill out the web-based survey. Furthermore, the team decided to send a flier home to the parents asking them to fill out the survey, either via the web, or the attached hard copy. Although they did not expect many parents to complete the survey, the team hoped to provide parents with a useful web site as well.

The web-based survey form was created using HTML and JavaScript. The JavaScript is supported by Internet Explorer 3.0 and above and Netscape 3.0 and above. The look of the survey was tested within many browsers, including Lynx, and the survey looked the same. Although it was not as easy to fill out the survey using Lynx, users still could respond to the survey using it.

Once the user clicked on the Submit Survey button, the form was sent to an Active Server Pages document where the information was retrieved and stored within a Microsoft Access database. Since the information was stored within a database, the team could create reports and analyze the data more efficiently. For the users who filled out the hard-copy form of the survey, their results were entered into the online version

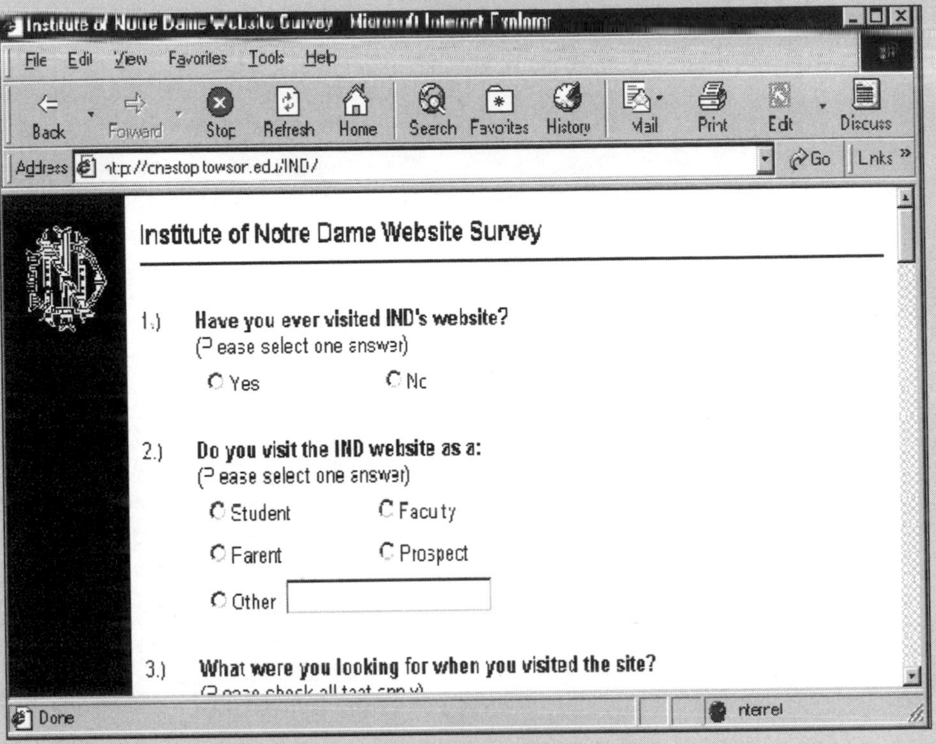

Figure 5.5

Institute of Notre
Dame web site survey

manually. This way all of the results were in one place and each group member could analyze the information.

Testing

Since the team had two forms of our survey, they tested both by providing three or four users with a paper copy of the survey and an additional three or four with the URL of the online survey. Pilot testers were asked to write their comments about the survey on the hard-copy version. All of the comments and/or concerns about the survey were taken into consideration. The team wanted to provide a survey that would meet the needs for collecting requirements, thus enabling them to design a web site meeting the needs of the users.

Questions for Interview with Fred Germano

1. Who do you plan to be the primary users of this site? Can we interview/survey some representative users from each of the user categories mentioned?

2. For each of the users, what kind of information would you like to provide?

3. For each of the user categories, on average, what is their level of experience in using computers?

4. Are there areas of the existing web site that you wish to expand upon? What information, such as the school's mission statement, history, and current events can we use in building content areas? What content do you feel is the most important to present to the different types of users?

5. Do you have any logs from your server that we can use to determine: what pages get the most activity and what pages get the least activity.

6. Who will be maintaining the site after it is released? What is their level of technical knowledge?

7. How often will the site be updated with new information?

8. What are IND's future plans for the web site?

Figure 5.6
IND Form A

Survey Questions

1. Have you ever visited IND's web site? (Please select one answer.)
   Yes   No

2. Do you visit the IND web site as a: (Please select one answer.)
   Student   Faculty   Parent   Prospect   Other

3. What were you looking for when you visited the site? (Please check all that apply.)
   __ General information about IND
   __ Information about upcoming events at IND
   __ Information about faculty
   __ Student honors list
   __ Application information
   __ Address and/or phone number of IND
   __ School hours and cancellations
   __ Information on extracurricular activities/clubs
   __ Class information (such as schedules)
   __ Links to other educational resources
   __ Other

4. Were you able to find what you were looking for? (Please select one answer.)
   Yes   No

5. How useful was the site? (Please select one answer.)
   __ Very useful: I will visit the site often.
   __ Somewhat useful: I will visit the site periodically.
   __ Neutral: I might come back.
   __ Not very useful: I probably won't come back.
   __ Not useful at all: I am not coming back.

Figure 5.7
IND Form B

6. Would you visit this web site again? (Please select one answer.)

Yes   No

If no, why not?

7. What would you like to see on IND's web site? (Please check all that apply.)

__ General information about IND

__ Information on upcoming events at IND

__ Information about faculty

__ Student honors list

__ Application information

__ Address and/or phone number of IND

__ School hours and cancellations

__ Information on extracurricular activities/clubs

__ Class information (such as schedules)

__ Links to other educational resources

__ Other

8. What is the one thing you like the *most* about the site? (Please select one answer.)

__ Color scheme

__ Navigation

__ General information about IND

__ Information about school events

__ Information about faculty

__ Application information

__ School schedule information

__ Information on extracurricular activities/clubs

__ Class information (such as schedules)

__ Links to other educational resources

__ Other

9. What is the one thing you like the *least* about the site? (Please select one answer.)

__ Color scheme

__ Navigation

__ General information about IND

__ Information about school events

__ Information about faculty

__ Application information

__ School schedule information

__ Information on extracurricular activities/clubs

__ Class information (such as schedules)

__ Links to other educational resources

__ Other

Figure 5.7
continued

10. Please list three of your favorite web sites (if you have any):

_____
_____
_____

11. Help us design a better web site. Please give us any comments or suggestions not covered by the above survey.

_____
_____
_____

Figure 5.7
continued

CASE STUDY #3

▲ Eastman Kodak Company

Introduction

In order to establish user-centered requirements for the kodak.com redesign, we needed to gather as much data as possible regarding users' needs and current behaviors. A number of different techniques were employed to obtain this data. Since the site had existed for over two years, Web server logs and search logs were available and useful in indirectly monitoring users' interests. Other data-gathering techniques, such as focus groups and usability tests, involved direct observation of test participants that fit in the targeted user population.

Kodak business goals also heavily influenced the design requirements for the kodak.com redesign, and so interviews with the Web teams of many business units and corporate groups within Kodak were conducted. In cases where a business unit served a particular hard-to-reach market segment—such as motion picture cinematographers or dentists—talking with business unit representatives was also an indirect way to determine user requirements, because the representatives were experienced in working with users in their particular targeted market.

Web Server Logs

Analyzing Web server logs helped determine what areas on kodak.com tended to attract the most traffic (hopefully corresponding to the areas of greatest user interest). Table 5.1 shows the average number of daily visits for *top-level pages*; Table 5.2 shows the average number of daily visits for *second-level pages* (those linked from top-level pages).

TABLE 5-1 Average Daily Accesses for Top-Level Pages, February 1996–January 1997

Page	Average Daily Accesses	Percentage
Digital Imaging	2879	25.19
Photography	2353	20.59
Search	1980	17.32
Product Info	1033	9.04
What's New	1019	8.92
What's Hot	828	7.25
Customer Support	712	6.23
About Kodak	397	3.47
Business Solutions	228	1.99
Total accesses at this level	11,428	100.00

TABLE 5-2 Average Daily Accesses for Second-Level Pages, November 1996–January 1997

Page	Linked From	Average Daily Accesses
KODAK Picture This postcards	Digital Imaging	13,144
Digital Cameras	Digital Imaging	1337
Guide to Better Pictures	Photography	987
Feedback/Guestbook	Customer Support	954
Alphabetical Product Listing	Search, Product Info	903
PHOTO CD	Digital Imaging	651
Kodak Professional	Photography, Business Solutions	575
Product Types	Product Info	452
Digital Products Dealers	Customer Support	403
Professional Motion Imaging	Photography, Business Solutions	370
(Digital) Product Info	Digital Imaging	346
Software Drivers	Customer Support	344
Technical Information	Product Info, Customer Support	301
Table of Contents	Search	251
Press Releases	What's New, About Kodak	237
Zoomable Spatial Layout	Search	234
Digital Learning Center	Digital Imaging	228
Product Families	Product Info	224
Desktop Scanners	Digital Imaging	204
FlashPix	Digital Imaging	182
Kodak Online Services	Customer Support	164
Advanced Photo System	Photography	163
Corporate Info	About Kodak	159
Photography FAQ	Photography	142
Dye Sub Printers	Digital Imaging	136

TABLE 5-2	continued	

Page	Linked From	Average Daily Accesses
FAQ	Customer Support	128
Call Kodak	Customer Support	128
Educational Solutions	Photography, Business Solutions	126
Capture, Manage, Store, Share	Product Info	122
Seminars/Events	Photography	121
Contact Kodak	About Kodak	111
Where to Buy	Customer Support	111
Business Units	About Kodak	94
Customer Chat	About Kodak	73
Business and Industry	Business Solutions	71
George Fisher, CEO	About Kodak	69
Graphical Overview	Search	68
Developer Relations	Product Info	62
Customer Equipment Services	Customer Support	62
Around the World	About Kodak	59
PHOTO CD Transfer Sites	Customer Support	55
Product Tradeshow Booth	Product Info	40
Service and Support	Business Solutions	35
Medical and Scientific	Business Solutions	32
Spatial Layout (Text)	Search	26
About This Server	About Kodak	25
Government Imaging Systems	Business Solutions	17
Image Magic	Photography	2

Search Logs

A search function was linked from the kodak.com home page and from the footer of every page in the entire site. Data on the most popular searches made by users was available in the form of logs. Table 5.3 lists the top 25 search requests in February–April, 1997, along with the total occurrences of each query. This was interesting and useful data because it showed that there needed to be easy access to the KODAK Picture This postcards feature and information on employment opportunities at Kodak. We knew that the KODAK Picture This postcards feature was the biggest traffic draw on kodak.com, but the fact that it was also the most popular search topic indicated that we needed to make it more easily accessible. We did not realize that employment was as popular a topic as it was, representing the third most-searched topic on kodak.com. In the new design, both areas were linked directly from the home page.

TABLE 5-3	Search Log Data for February–April 1997	
Top 25 Search Topics	Number of Queries	Percent of All Queries
KODAK Picture This postcards	17,247	6.77
DC50, DC120, etc.	5589	2.19
Employment	4934	1.94
Sample pictures/Digital Images	4238	1.66
PHOTO CD	2548	1.00
Scanner	1629	0.64
Advantix film, Advanced Photo System (APS)	1586	0.62
FlashPix	1250	0.49
Film	1196	0.47
Xtol	1062	0.42
Printers	1062	0.42
Digital camera	992	0.39
Software	907	0.36
Prices	851	0.33
Diconix	819	0.32
Image Magic	709	0.28
Greetings	694	0.27
Digital imaging	644	0.25
Picture Disc	572	0.22
Super 8	571	0.22
Driver	551	0.22
Download	550	0.22
Camera	550	0.22
Photo enhancer	531	0.21
Infra-red film	526	0.21
Above total	51,808	20.3
Total queries	254,933	

Interviews with Kodak Business Units

Eastman Kodak Company is a large corporation organized into business units that deliver products and services for specific markets. Examples of such business units include Kodak Professional, a unit that serves professional photographers and members of the printing and publishing industries, and Health Imaging, which markets medical imaging solutions to health care professionals, including radiologists, cardiologists, dentists, technicians, and hospital administrators. Each business unit has content developers and managers who handle the business unit's presence and content on kodak.com. Representatives from each business unit were interviewed to better understand:

1. The nature of their customers

2. The customer needs they wanted to meet and the value they wanted to deliver using the Web

3. The nature of their Web content

4. Any other objectives they had for the Web

The results of the interviews are presented in Chapter 6.

Focus Groups

Kodak enlisted the expertise of American Institutes for Research (http://www.air.org), a consulting firm specializing in behavioral and social science research, to plan and conduct these activities in different locations across the United States. Focus groups were conducted with two different groups within the target user population of the Kodak Web site: "consumers" and "dealers." Consumers were defined as Web users who were interested in photography—consuming at least four rolls of film annually but not working as a professional photographer. Dealers were defined as retailers of digital photographic equipment, interested in using the Kodak Web site to find information on products.

Focus group sessions were planned for three different U.S. cities: Lexington, Massachusetts, Dallas, Texas, and San Jose, California. Separate consumer and dealer focus groups were planned for each city, for a total of six sessions. Because the sessions were conducted by different moderators, very detailed moderator's scripts were necessary to ensure that the appropriate topics were covered. These moderator scripts are available in Figs. 5.8–5.11.

Usability Testing

Usability testing was performed on kodak.com with the current home page and top level in place, to determine usability issues that would need to be addressed in the redesign. With Kodak's guidance, AIR designed the test protocol and recruited 12 individuals to participate. The test was conducted in Waltham, Massachusetts, and the testing sessions were videotaped for future review. Participants were screened to fit the attributes of the "consumer" focus group participant, described in the previous section. The purposes of the usability testing were to: (1) test the usability of the Web site in realistic situations for which a customer would come to the Kodak Web site, and (2) discuss the features and aspects of the Web site with the customers. To represent the real browsing conditions of many kodak.com visitors, participants in the usability test had a 15-inch monitor and were connected to the Internet at 28.8 kbps. The usability test was planned to consist of a number of steps:

1. First, the participant filled out a participant agreement form, agreeing to take part in the usability test.

2. The participant then received an introduction on the purpose and process of the test (in Fig. 5.12).

3. The participant was asked to perform a number of information gathering tasks, such as "find a film that will work well in bright, sunny conditions" (the list of tasks is in Fig. 5.13).

4. The participant took part in a posttest interview, providing overall feedback about the Web site (in Fig. 5.14).

"Guest Book" Messages from Visitors

Several hundred messages per day are submitted through the kodak.com "Guest Book" (a form through which kodak.com users can send questions, requests, comments, and so on to the company). Typically, the vast majority of these entries are requests for product support, requests for additional information, comments about the company and/or its products, and less than two percent contain feedback about the Web site itself. However, these entries are the only regular means by which actual kodak.com users can provide direct feedback about the site. Therefore, we analyzed guest book comments from several months as part of our effort to understand user needs and desires.

We found that the majority of guest book feedback pertaining to the site itself was too generic to be useful (e.g., "Great site!"), and that most specific problems identified (e.g., broken links, misspellings, inaccuracies) tended not to be helpful in identifying usability problems. However, there were a small number of comments that inspired our thinking about opportunities to improve kodak.com. For example, a few comments brought up the issue that the essentially static appearance of the existing home page did not facilitate announcements of new product launches or the availability of popular applications (like the KODAK Picture This postcards feature); also, it gave no indication that new information was being added or that the site was being kept up-to-date. This helped motivate our desire to make the new home page more dynamic and flexible than the existing home page.

User Surveys

The results from a number of previously-performed user surveys conducted on kodak.com yielded valuable information about user characteristics and preferences. We gained insights into the reasons users visit (e.g., business or personal reasons), the frequency with which users visit, connection speeds, monitor settings, browsing habits, demographics, and so forth. These insights were extremely valuable during the development of user requirements for the new site structure.

Agenda of Topics for Consumer Focus Group

Introduction	5 minutes
Digital imaging associations	15 minutes
Worldwide Web usage	15 minutes
Kodak Web site	10 minutes
Web site features	15 minutes
Discussion of new product concepts	20 minutes
Most important features	5 minutes
Conclusion	5 minutes
Total time	90 minutes

Figure 5.8

Agenda of Topics for
Consumer Focus
Group

Introduction for Consumer Focus Groups

Thank you for taking the time to meet with us today.

We should start by explaining the purpose of our research effort and the role you will play.

We are working with a film manufacturing company that is gathering information about the types of services that photographers might want to have on the World Wide Web. As part of that goal, the company is holding focus groups around the country with consumers such as yourselves who are photographers and who already use the Web. The client will use this information to design and modify their Web site.

The client who is sponsoring this session wishes to remain anonymous. I work for an independent research company, so please feel free to say whatever is on your mind concerning photography and the Internet. I will not be offended. The client wants to know what is working well, and what is not.

During our 1.5-hour session, we are going to:

- ask you to talk about your thoughts concerning digital photography.
- ask you how you use the Internet.
- have you comment on two concept services that might be available on the Internet.

We are videotaping this session for future reference. Specifically, there are some members of the development team who cannot be here today who would like to see how things went.

As you can tell, this room is equipped with a one-way mirror. This makes it convenient for a few of our clients to watch, but not interfere with our discussion.

Keep in mind that there is no pressure to perform today. We want you to feel comfortable and enjoy yourself. If at any time you feel you want to withdraw from the study, you may do so. However, you would forfeit the honorarium.

This session will last about 1.5 hours. We encourage you to enjoy the food and drinks that are in the room while we conduct the discussion.

One more point. Before we get started, we would like you to read the statement that defines the terms of this session and requests confidentiality. If you are comfortable signing the form, please do so. When you have completed this form, please fill out this background questionnaire. Do you have any questions before we move on?

Figure 5.9

Introduction for
Consumer Focus
Groups

Selected Discussion-Starters for Consumer Focus Groups

- What aspects of the Web do you like?
- What aspects of the Web do you dislike?
- What makes the Web attractive to use? What makes it cool?
- For what types of things do you use the Web?
- How many of you buy products and services through the Internet or Web?
- How do you pay for them?
- Would you be willing to pay less or more for products you buy on the Web?
- Do you have any concerns about security on the Web for credit cards or financial accounts?

Let's return to the things you do on the Web.

- Do you use the Web or Internet to communicate with friends? With family?
- If your pictures could somehow get onto the Web, how interested would you be in sending pictures to your friends? To your family?
- What would make using the Web fun for sending pictures to people?
- What would make using the Web difficult for sending pictures to people?
- Do you have any concerns about other people seeing your pictures on the Web?
- Once your pictures are digitized, you have all sorts of options with your pictures.
- What kinds of things would you do with your digital images?
- Would you want to use digital manipulation on your images?
- Would you want to print out your images on other types of materials besides paper? Which materials?
- What would be the biggest problem with digital images?

Figure 5.10

Selected Discussion-Starters for Consumer Focus Groups

Selected Discussion-Starters for Dealer Focus Groups

We are going to start our discussion on the topic of how you send and receive information from Kodak. As we do so, let's keep the focus on your individual needs and feelings. We would like you to talk about how you currently receive information, and the types of information you need from Kodak.

Let's start by talking about the types of information you currently receive from Kodak.

- What are some of the things you receive in the mail from Kodak? Does anybody receive new product announcements, product updates, product usage tips, and invoices?
- Do you receive phone calls from Kodak?
- Does anyone from Kodak send you faxes? What types of information do they send?
- How many of you receive electronic notes or e-mail from Kodak? What types of information does the e-mail contain?

Let's continue by talking about the types of information you currently send to Kodak.

- What are some of the things you send in the mail to Kodak? Do you send payments, problem reports, contracts, purchase decisions?
- When do you call Kodak? What types of information are you looking from when you call Kodak?
- Do you send faxes to Kodak? What types of information do you fax?
- How many of you send e-mail to Kodak? What types of information do you send in your e-mail?
- Who's having problems with communicating with Kodak?
- What would improve your communication with Kodak?

In today's discussion, we have discussed mail, phone, fax, and e-mail. E-mail is carried on the Internet. However, we have not discussed a relatively new method of information delivery, the World Wide Web. The Web is the section of the Internet that contains Web sites or home pages for companies, groups, or individuals. I would now like to discuss further the Internet and the Web.

First, let's talk about the Internet.

- Does your dealership currently have Internet access?
- What would motivate you to get Internet access?
- What role could Kodak play in your decision to get Internet access?

Next, let's talk about the World Wide Web. Kodak currently has a Web site and it contains some information about the company.

- What types of information do you think would be located on Kodak's Web site? What information would you like to find on it?
- How many have used the Kodak Web site?
- What types of things did you do on the Kodak Web site?
- What were your impressions of the Web site? How would you describe it?
- How easy or difficult was it to find information on the Web site?
- How pleasing or not pleasing were the colors and graphics on Kodak's Web site?
- How would you improve the Web site?
- Concerning information delivery, how do you think the Web site would compare to mail, phone, fax, and e-mail?

Figure 5.11

Selected Discussion-Starters for Dealer Focus Groups

Usability Test Materials

Below are excerpts from the materials used in a usability test of kodak.com. The materials were developed and used by the American Institutes for Research (http://www.air.org) with guidance from Kodak.

Introduction

Thank you for coming today. I work for the American Institutes for Research, a not-for-profit consulting group that is hired by outside companies to conduct research about the usability of products, software, and services. Currently, we've been asked by Kodak to evaluate their Web site.

I will guide you through the evaluation and interview you about your impression of the Web site. The session will be videotaped, and there may be someone observing us. Remember, we are not evaluating you in any way: We are interested in evaluating the content and information in this Web site. The information that you give us will be used to improve the Web site.

I will give you several tasks to complete using the Web site. The tasks will be printed on cards in front of you. I'll ask you to read each task aloud and then try to complete the task.

As you complete each task, I will ask you to think aloud as you try to complete it. This will let me keep up with you.

Throughout the session, I will encourage you to freely express your opinions, to comment on what information is clear or unclear to you, and in particular, what you find confusing or difficult to understand.

Figure 5.12
Introduction

Task 1—Top-level Exploration, Talk Aloud Warm-up

Take a few minutes to explore this page. As you do so, please comment on what you think each of the links mean, and the sorts of things that you would expect to see if you were to click on each of the links. Feel free to comment whenever you come across aspects and features of the Web site that you like, you don't like, you find confusing, or you find helpful.

Task 2—Product Information (search without knowing product name beforehand)

Try to find a film that will work well in bright, sunny conditions.

At first encounter with product information page:
Please talk through what you think the different links on this page mean.

Return to the top page of the Web site, where you started out.
_____ Backup   _____ "Go" menu   _____ Footer   Other: _____

Task 3—Product Information (search for a particular product name)

Try to find out a page of information on the Kodak Cameo Auto Focus Camera.

Return to the top page of the Web site, where you started out.
_____ Backup   _____ "Go" menu   _____ Footer   Other: _____

Figure 5.13
Participant Tasks

Figure 5.13

continued

Task 4—Digital Photography (Digital Learning Center)

You have just heard about digital cameras and would like to learn more about what they can be used to do. You wonder if the Kodak Web site contains any online tutorials about digital photography technology and how it is used. Try to find this information.

Return to the top page of the Web site, where you started out.

_____ Backup _____ "Go" menu _____ Footer Other: _____

Task 5—Customer Support (Dealer Locator)

Try to find a dealer in Cambridge who sells the DCS 420, a professional quality digital camera.

Return to the top page of the Web site, where you started out.

_____ Backup _____ "Go" menu _____ Footer Other: _____

Task 6—Digital Photography (sample digital image)

Pictures taken by digital cameras can be viewed on the Web. Try to find sample pictures taken by the DC40 camera so that you can see the quality of the picture.

Return to the top page of the Web site, where you started out.

_____ Backup _____ "Go" menu _____ Footer Other: _____

Task 7—Customer Support (Frequently Asked Questions)

Try to find out whether walking through the X-ray machine at the airport will affect the film in your camera.

Return to the top page of the Web site, where you started out.

_____ Backup _____ "Go" menu _____ Footer Other: _____

Task 8—Customer Support (Guest book)

Imagine that you have searched the Web site for an answer to a question about a Kodak product that you own, and you are unable to find an answer to your question. What would you do at this point?

    If participants did not answer that they would e-mail Kodak:

- You have heard that there is a way on the Web site to e-mail questions to Kodak. Try to find it.
- How long do you expect it will take before you get an answer?
- What does the term "Guest book" mean to you? Can you suggest a better name for this function?

    Go back to the Customer Service page.

- Is this what you expected under Customer Service?

Return to the top page of the Web site, where you started out.

_____ Backup _____ "Go" menu _____ Footer Other: _____

Task 9—Product Information (compare search possibilities)

Let's return to the Product Information page. Six of the links on the page can be used to search for information on products, and we are interested in determining how well each of the search strategies work. I am going to give you a couple of things to search for, and I will ask you to use a particular link on the page to do the search.

    Try to find a page of information on the DC50 Digital Zoom Camera by clicking on the _____ link.

    Now try it from the _____ link.

Figure 5.13
continued

Which of the two search methods do you prefer? _____

Is there a different way of finding this information that you would prefer?

At the beginning of the session, I asked you to find an appropriate film to use in bright sun. Try to find this information from the _____ link.

Now try it from the _____ link.

Which of the two search methods do you prefer? _____

Is there a different way of finding this information that you would prefer?

In general, what do you think of having multiple ways of searching for products?

Return to the top page of the Web site, where you started out.

_____ Backup   _____ "Go" menu   _____ Footer   Other: _____

Task 10—Product Information (search, compare navigation aids)

I'd like to direct your attention to a particular page. Click on the Find function. What do you think this page is used for? What is clear or not clear?

Now, I'd like you to look at this section over here (point to *You can also search by:*) What do you think is meant by each of these links?

Try out each of the links.

Would this be helpful in finding what you need on the Web site? Which do you like best?

Post-test Interview
- What were the three things that you liked best about this site?
- What were the three things that you liked least about this site?
- If you could change one thing about this site, what would it be?
- If you could add one thing to this site, what would it be?
- Would you go back to this site?
- Would you recommend this site to others?

Figure 5.14
Posttest Interview

Conceptual Design
of the Web Site
Site Architecture
and Navigation

CHAPTER

6

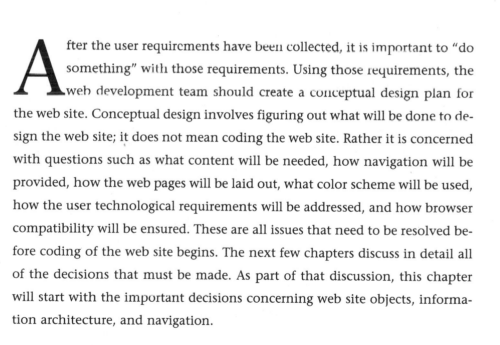

After the user requirements have been collected, it is important to "do something" with those requirements. Using those requirements, the web development team should create a conceptual design plan for the web site. Conceptual design involves figuring out what will be done to design the web site; it does not mean coding the web site. Rather it is concerned with questions such as what content will be needed, how navigation will be provided, how the web pages will be laid out, what color scheme will be used, how the user technological requirements will be addressed, and how browser compatibility will be ensured. These are all issues that need to be resolved before coding of the web site begins. The next few chapters discuss in detail all of the decisions that must be made. As part of that discussion, this chapter will start with the important decisions concerning web site objects, information architecture, and navigation.

▶ 6.1 CHARACTERISTICS OF WEB SITES

Web sites can be characterized by their degree of interactivity and by the content of their web site objects. These characteristics affect the conceptual design of the web site.

Static vs. Database-Driven

A majority of small-to-medium size web sites are static. That means that there are a specific number of HTML files with fixed content.[1] Fixed content is content that changes only when someone (such as the web developer) changes the data in the files.[1] In contrast, most larger web sites (including e-commerce sites) are database-driven. A database-driven site allows users to search for and request specific data, and most web pages are created "on-the-fly" by the database.[1] Additional functionality might also be designed into a web site using a database.

Interactivity

It is often important for a web site to be able to respond to user actions. A database provides one method for a web site to respond to user actions. There are a number of other options for adding interactivity to a web page. For instance, the web development team can add a "mouseover" using JavaScript.[2] A mouseover occurs when an object on the screen changes when the user places the mouse pointer over the object. Through use of JavaScript and other standards (such as cascading style sheets and the document object model), objects on the screen can change when the user rolls the mouse pointer over the object or clicks on the object.[2] For instance, when the user passes over a certain object, the background screen color can change, a message can pop up, or the font size can change. None of these actions are required for a successful web page, and these interactivity options, which can make a simple web page complex, should be added only when the user requirements support them, and when these interactivity options will actually improve the user experience.

Content—Determining Web Site Objects

To determine what content should be included on a web site, a good way to start is to go back to the requirements gathered, as well as to the web site mission as defined by the client, and think about what web site objects would be appropriate for the web site.[3] A web site object is a piece of content information that could be presented on a web site.[3] A web site object is not necessarily the same as a web page, because a web page could contain a number of different web site objects. However, since the web development team can define the granularity of a web site object, the distinction between a web page and a web site object is essentially meaningless.[3]

Prioritizing

In determining which web site objects should be included in the new web site, the data from the requirements gathering should be analyzed. Although it would be nice to include all web site objects requested by users, in most cases, this is not a realistic goal. If there were many different content resources requested by users (and suggested by the clients), then these requests should be prioritized. One way of prioritizing these web site objects is to count how often these objects were requested in the requirements gathering, and the most-often requested objects should be the ones to be included in the web site plan. If the requirements gathering asked targeted users whether they would be interested in certain content, a threshold percentage could be used. For instance, a web site object might be included on the web site only if 50% or more of targeted users indicated that they would be interested in the resources.

Based on the requirements gathering, possible web site objects could be defined into three categories: mandatory, desirable, and optional.[4] Mandatory objects are those that are necessary for a successful web site, desirable objects are those that would be helpful and should be added as soon as possible, and optional objects are those that might be useful to have, but will not affect the overall success of the web site.[4] Changes in time or money allocated for the web development project might mean that more (or fewer) of the desirable and optional web site objects will be included. If quantitative data is available, whether objects are perceived as mandatory, desirable, or optional, this data can be analyzed using decision-making models. In addition, there might be some web site objects requested by users that the clients are strictly against, and therefore, those objects cannot be included in the actual web site, at least at the present time. For instance, if users want chat rooms, content of a partisan nature, or information on competitors, the client might be strongly against including such content.

Listing the Web Pages

Assuming that the web site is not database-driven, once the content requests have been prioritized an important step is to make a list of all of the web pages that will be developed for the web site. For a site redesign, a list of the web pages on the current site should be made, and then that list should be modified. Making a list of all web pages that should be on the site can help to ensure that nothing will be left out, and will help to determine who will be developing the content. For each web page, the web development team needs to decide important issues such as:

1. The title of the web page
2. The purpose of the web page
3. The content that needs to be developed, and how that content will be developed
4. How often the data will need to be updated
5. Who will be responsible for updating the data

It might be helpful to develop a table that lists all of the web pages to be developed, as well as the pertinent information about each web page. An example of such a table appears in Table 6-1.

TABLE 6-1	Possible Web Structure for Towson Chapter of Omicron Delta Kappa (ODK) Web Page		
Title	Purpose	Content	Updated
History	Describe the history of the Towson ODK circle	from Towson ODK brochure	Once every few years
Induction	Present the most recent induction class into the Towson ODK circle	from induction program	Once a semester
Application	Provide an explanation of how one becomes a member of ODK	from national ODK	Infrequently
Meetings	Provide a list of meeting dates/ locations	from staff advisor	Once a month
Officers	List the current officers	from staff advisor	Once a year
Pictures	Show pictures of ODK events	from staff advisor	A few times a year

► 6.2 ORGANIZATIONAL STRUCTURE OF THE HOME PAGE

After it is determined how many and what web pages will be developed, the next question is how these different web pages will be organized into logical organizational units, or "sections," of the web site. When users access the home page of the web site, they are usually greeted with a number of different sections on the web site where content is available. Think about when you place a phone call to a company and get a voice mail menu, "If you want to place an order, press 1; if you want to talk to the customer service department, press 2; if you want to return an item, press 3; if you are interested in a job at our company, press 4." This is the same basic concept as the structure of the web site. The web site is saying, "If you are interested in upcoming events, click here; if you want to learn more about our organization's history, click here; if you want to learn more about our officers, click here." If card sorting was done during the requirements gathering phase (see the previous chapter), then the card sorting should strongly influence how the web site is logically organized. The home page can be organized in three different ways: topical, audience-splitting, and metaphor.

Topical Grouping

One way to organize the home page is based on similar topics. The home page can be split into topics such as "history," "leadership," "products," and other sections.[5] For a university, these topics could be academics, sports, libraries, and campus life.

Audience-Splitting

Another way to organize the home page is a technique called audience-specific or audience-splitting.[5,6] In audience-splitting, when there are numerous user groups that might be looking for different types of information, you set up sections for each user group. For instance, on many university web sites, there are separate sections for faculty/staff, students, alumni, and prospective students.

Metaphors

A third way to organize the home page of a web site is to use metaphors.[5] Metaphors relate the interface to objects and concepts in the user's everyday life, and they can sometimes assist the user in understanding the structure of a web site.[7] For instance, many e-commerce web sites use the metaphors of a "shopping cart" and a "check out." A baseball team could create a home page using the metaphor of a stadium, where users click on different graphical objects that represent content, such as a graphic of a seat to find out about purchasing tickets, a graphic of a dugout to learn more about the team players, a graphic of the concession stand to find out what food and memorabilia can be purchased at the ball park, or a graphic of a parking lot to find out how to get to the stadium; this metaphor could continue to be extended.

Maintenance

Whatever the organizational structure chosen, future maintenance should be a consideration. New areas of content might be added, some areas of content may be deleted, but content will change and certainly new web pages will be added. If the entire site structure is based on a limited metaphor, this may limit future growth of the site, or may hinder users from finding the information that they want. For example, where do you find information about the community service performed by baseball players if the entire web site is based on the baseball stadium metaphor?

▶ Sections of a Home Page can be Structured by:
1. Topic of the content
2. Audience-splitting
3. Metaphors (when appropriate)

▶ 6.3 INFORMATION ARCHITECTURE

A classic TV commercial asked, "How many licks does it take to get to the center of a Tootsie Roll Pop?" Mr. Owl found that it took three licks to get to the center of a Tootsie Roll Pop. When designing a web site, an important question to consider is, "How many clicks will it take for the user to get to the information that they want?" The number of clicks required of the user is influenced by the information architecture. *Information architecture* is the study of how web sites are structured, how users navigate through the web site, and how to plan for change and growth in the web site.[5] Although the hypertext that creates the foundation for the web theoretically allows the user to click from any page to any other page, web sites are generally set up in some type of organizational structure.[5] The best structure for web sites is the hierarchy, a top-down approach that is similar to a family tree or an organizational chart, which users can readily understand.[5] A hierarchical structure can be set up with a "top page" (your home page), "middlemen pages" (for content areas, or audiences), and content pages. It is important to plan ahead, and sketch out the paths that a user can take through a web site (more about this later).

Research on Menu Design

When the user is presented with a list of choices to click on a web page, this is in reality, a menu. There is a great deal of research on menus related to designing links and the information hierarchy on a web site. For instance, it is preferable to provide more choices on a single menu level, rather than offer numerous menus with fewer choices.[8] If you think of a menu structure as a tree, two aspects of the structure are the depth (the number of menus) and the breadth (the number of items on a menu).[8] Given a static number of menu choices, as you increase the number of menus, you decrease the number of menu items per menu. It is also important to keep in mind the human cognitive limits on information processing. A classic research article states that humans process information in chunks of 7 ± 2.[9] Both of these research findings need to be balanced to provide a successful experience for the user. For instance, a user should not be required to go through 50 menus, but if he or she is presented with a list of 200 choices, that individual will still be overwhelmed. These 200 choices need to be organized, or chunked, so that the user is not overwhelmed.

Two web sites, one that has chunked their choices, one that has not, show how chunking can be effective. The Firstgov web site (Fig. 6.1) has many different links on their web page, but they are "chunked" into major titles to make it easier to find what you want. The web site for the University of North Carolina–Charlotte (Fig. 6.2) offers too many links that are not organized in a coherent manner. There are links to the left of the picture, on top of the picture, below the picture, and to the right of the picture.

The Goal: Minimizing the Number of Clicks

How can the research work on menu design be applied to designing web sites? The fewer menu choices (hypertext links) per web page, the more web pages that a user will need to go through, and the more "clicks" that the user will have to make. Research findings indicate that the user may give up if they are required to go through more than four or five clicks to get to the desired information.[5] Therefore, all of these factors need to be balanced. A broad, shallow hierarchy structure is superior to a narrow, deep hierarchy structure for users on the web, since it will require fewer clicks by the user. Figure 6.3 shows an example of the two hierarchy structures.

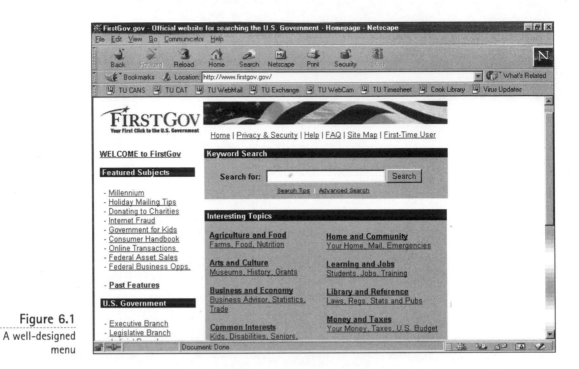

Figure 6.1
A well-designed menu

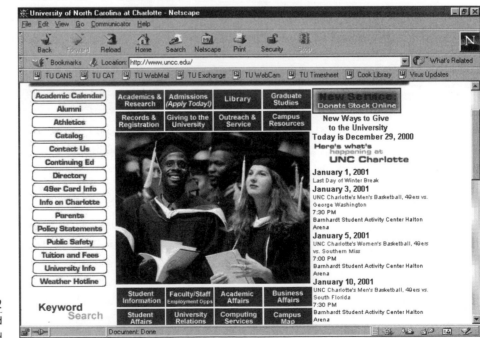

Figure 6.2
A poorly designed menu

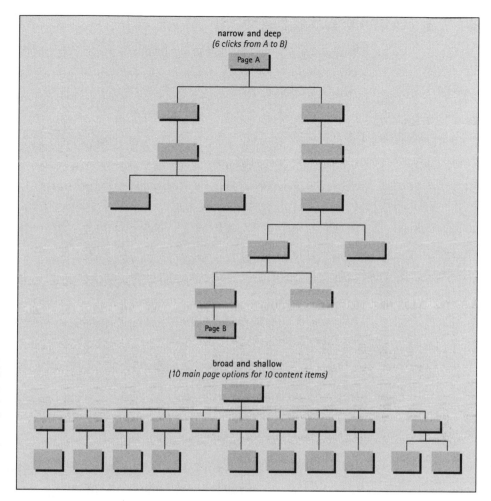

Figure 6.3

A broad, shallow hierarchy versus a deep, narrow hierarchy (Reprinted from *Information Architecture for the WWW*, by L. Rosenfeld and P. Morville).

Client Feedback

At this point, it might be useful to take the list of web pages and the organizational structure of the web site, and consult with the client contact. This can be a simple document sent to the client for approval.[10] If the client signs off on the conceptual design of the web site, a subsequent misunderstanding between the client and the web development team can possibly be avoided. Another possibility is that the content that is requested by users cannot be included (either because it is impossible or because the client is not in favor of it). By having the client approve the high-level conceptual design of the web site, many future problems can be avoided.

▶ 6.4 NAVIGATION

Navigation is one of the most important conceptual design considerations for a web site because it allows the users to know where they currently are in the web site, where they have been, and how to get where they want to go.[6,11,12] Navigation must be planned before any coding is done, because it must remain the same throughout a web site. Navigation should help indicate what is available on the web site, and what links lie outside of the web site, somewhere on that great big World Wide Web. Instructing users on where they have been is a feature already built into the browser. Users can check their recent history of web page visits using their browser, and textual links change color after users have clicked on them, appearing as "visited" links. However, web site developers still need to address the user questions of "where am I now, and where can I go?" There are many different considerations in designing navigation. For instance, where on the web page will the navigation go? What types of navigation choices will the user have? How will the navigation be coded? The next sections will address these questions.

▶ Navigation Should Let Users Know:
1. Where they have been
2. Where they are
3. Where they are going

Navigation Based on Web Site Topical Sections

The most common type of navigation on the web is navigation based on the top-level sections of the web site. For instance, for a community organization, the main sections of the web site might be history, mission, current officers, meetings, events, and so on. These would be the main topical areas for a web site. For a smaller web site, these might be the only content pages that exist, and the total web site would include, perhaps, 10–15 web pages. See the web site of the Maryland Science Center (Fig. 6.4) for an example of such a site.

For a larger web site, these main content areas would each provide information and links to web pages in that topical area. For instance, top-level content areas on a university web site could include academics, campus life, athletics, and libraries. When either of these links is clicked, the user would then receive a list of the 10–15 pages that relate to student services at that university. See the web site from Mary Washington College (Fig. 6.5), which provides an example of topical navigation.

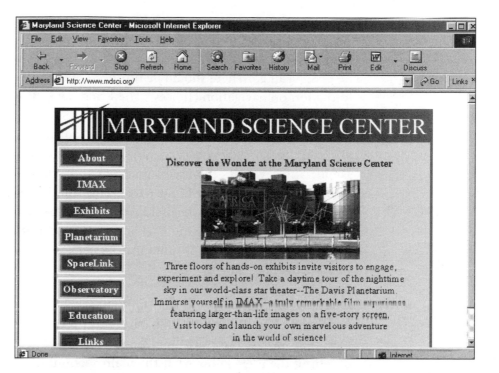

Figure 6.1

An example of
topical navigation on
a small web site

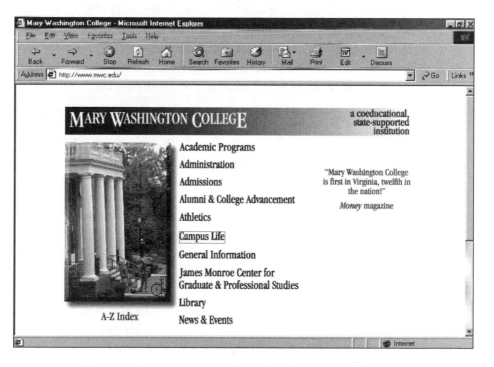

Figure 6.5

An example of
topical navigation on
a large web site

Regardless of the purpose of the web site or the number of web pages involved, some type of navigation *must* remain present throughout all pages on the web site. The user needs navigation choices in order to know where he or she can go. There should be no "dead-end" pages that provide no information on navigation choices.[6] The worst navigation is no navigation; a dead-end page provides no help on what to do or where to go for more information.[6] What if the user wants to find out more general information about the organization by accessing other sections of the web site? The skeptic will say that "the user only needs to click the Back button on the browser to get back to the home page." This solution does not always work, because it is possible that the user linked to the dead-end page from another web site, so that clicking the Back button would not take the user to the home page of the current site, but instead back to the web site that initiated the link to the dead-end page.

Navigation Based on Path Analysis

Another technique for providing navigation is to provide the user with the path that was used to reach the current page that they are viewing. Instead of letting the users know what the main sections of the web site are, path analysis navigation informs of the users of how they got to the web specific web page on a web site. Jakob Nielsen has called this approach to navigation as "breadcrumb navigation," because users are leaving breadcrumbs on their path to reaching a certain page.[12] For instance, a path analysis on a university web site might be the following:

www.towson.edu → campus life → student activities → Leadership Program

This path analysis shows the user the path taken to get to the web page for the Towson University Leadership Program. The leftmost web page mentioned is the broadest (the Towson University home page), and as the user moves to the right, each arrow represents one level lower in the web site hierarchy. Moving from left to right in the path analysis, the user moves from the home page (broad) to the current web page (specific) for the Leadership Program. In addition, each of the web pages mentioned in the navigation (www.towson.edu, campus life, student activities) should be a hypertext link, so that the user can click on any of the topics to get back to that web page. In addition, if a user comes to the Leadership Program web page from an outside web site without having read any of the other Towson University web pages, this path analysis would provide navigation guidance on how to access information on student activities, campus life, and Towson University as a whole. Figure 6.6 is an example of path analysis provided by Yahoo! that shows the hierarchical path taken to reach the current web page. In addition, Yahoo! also provides the path as a part of the web page title (see the path in the title bar). Yahoo! has also set up their directory structure so that the user could possibly be able to tell the path taken from the URL of the web page. Notice how the path analysis is displayed not only on the web page, but also on the title bar and URL. Since most web sites do not do this effectively, the URL cannot always be trusted as a source for path information.

Hierarchical Organization

To effectively use path analysis, the web site must be organized in a hierarchical manner, with a specific path to reach a certain web page. For instance, if the user could take 10 different paths to reach a certain web page, then it would be hard to provide a "trail" of how the user reached the web page. If the user could reach the leadership program web page under campus life, academics, libraries, faculty and staff, and so on, what path would be presented on the web page? It could be confusing, since the user would read the path and say, "but that's not how I got here!" Then again, a web page should not be able to fit under every topical content area on a web site, because if the content areas do not allow the user to narrow down their list of choices, how useful are the content areas?

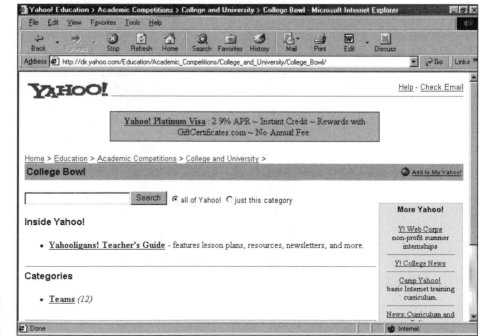

Figure 6.6

An example of path analysis

Search Engines

Many web sites offer search engines to help users find what they are looking for. There is no conflict between having a hierarchically structured web site and including a search engine. If users can find the web page that they are looking for by searching through the hierarchy of choices, that is great. But if they utilize the search engine to help them find the web page that they are looking for, the path analysis information is still useful, because it shows users how they could have found the web page in the hierarchy, and it provides context information for them on similar web pages that are available on the web site.

Mixing Navigational Schemes

It is important to note that navigation schemes based on topical sections and path analysis are not mutually exclusive. A web site can offer two navigation schemes: one displaying the main topical areas of the web site, and another offering a path analysis. In Fig. 6.7, the cnet.com web site provides the user with navigation information in two sections. In the black bar at the top of the screen, the user is provided with a list of content areas on the web site such as news, hardware, downloads, and games. In the bar below the "cnet news.com" graphic, users are provided with a path analysis of how they reached that web page (CNET→News→E-Business).

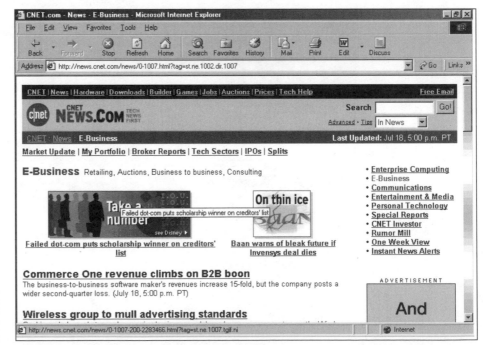

Figure 6.7

A web site that offers two navigation schemes

Another possibility for providing both topical area navigation and path analysis navigation is to provide navigation links that expand and collapse. The web site for L.L. Bean (Fig. 6.8) provides this type of navigation. At first, the user is presented with a list of the main sections of the web site (men's, women's, kids, and so forth). After the user clicks for more information on men's clothing, and then clicks for men's shirts, the navigation menu on the left expands to provide path information on how the user got to that point (see Fig. 6.9). So, there are a number of different ways that both topical navigation and path navigation can be presented at the same time.

Technological Requirements for Navigation

Navigation should be provided through text links. Navigation should not be provided through either graphics, buttons, JavaScript, and/or Java applets. Since navigation is a basic requirement for a successful user experience, navigation should be provided for the lowest common capability. Users might be browsing the web using an older browser that cannot handle advanced technology, or the user might be browsing with graphics turned off, JavaScript turned off, or Java Applets turned off. In an extreme scenario, a user might be using a text-based browser, such as Lynx. Use of graphics for

Figure 6.8

Navigation links that expand and collapse

Figure 6.9
An expanded
navigation menu
with path
information

navigation is not ideal; however, if graphics (such as icons, buttons, or text bars) are used for navigation, then the <alt> tags must be included to specify alternate text for those using text-based browsers, or for those with graphics turned off. This alternate text (e.g., <img src="washington.gif" alt="Washington, DC">) will appear if the graphics do not. If all navigation is provided using graphics or advanced coding, and no alternative text is provided, the user is out of luck. See Figs. 6.10 and 6.11 for the Jewish Community Center of Baltimore web site, one using Internet Explorer and the other using Lynx. You will notice that nothing appears on the Lynx-based interface. The web site for Yahoo! is a different story. It appears normally in Internet Explorer (see Fig. 6.12). Navigation also is functional using Lynx (Fig. 6.13). The navigation appears in text, and the user is able to navigate the web site using Lynx. In general, the simpler the navigation, the more accessible it is to people. This is especially true of user populations with special needs, some of whom use Lynx and speech synthesizers. (Accessibility is discussed in Chapter 8 in more detail.) The technical approaches for setting up navigation are discussed in Chapter 9.

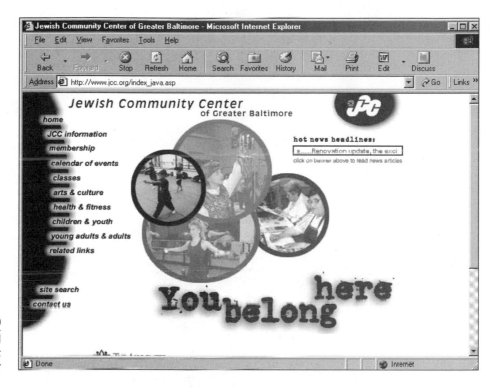

Figure 6.10

A web site viewed
with Internet
Explorer

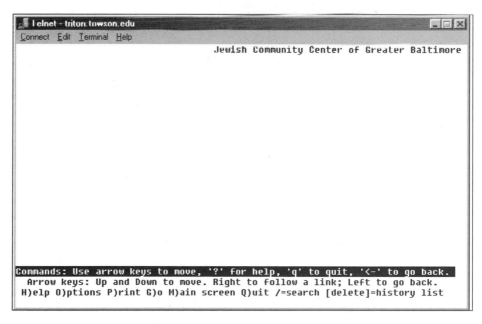

Figure 6.11

A web site viewed
with Lynx

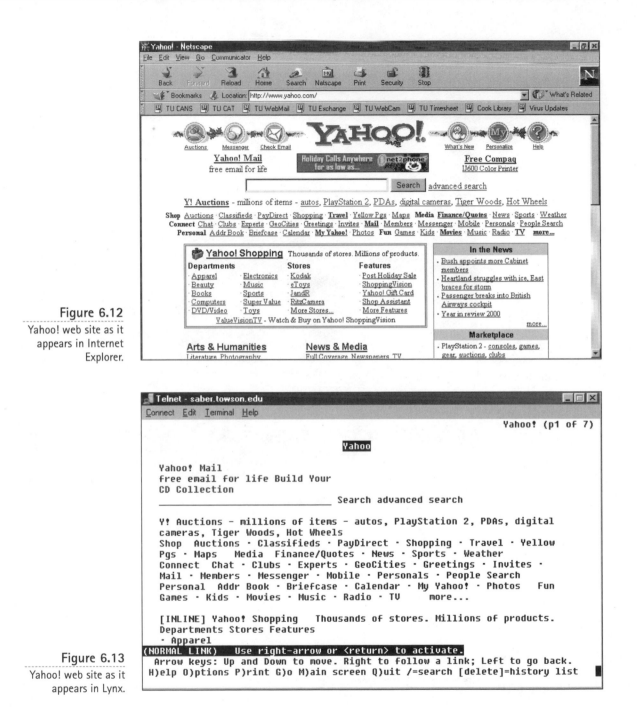

Figure 6.12

Yahoo! web site as it appears in Internet Explorer.

Figure 6.13

Yahoo! web site as it appears in Lynx.

Location of Navigation

Navigation is important to the user and needs to be ever present. The web site developer has the challenge of not knowing how much screen space is available—users may have different monitor sizes, different screen resolutions, and users may resize the browser window to any size that they would like.[2] Navigation needs to be easily visible, regardless of the size of the monitor being used or how the browser window is sized. This means that navigation needs to be provided on either the top of the web page, the left side of the web page, or with some combination of these two[1] because the leftmost side of the web page, as well as the topmost part of the web page, will always be visible to users.

If navigation is placed on the right side of the web page or the bottom of the web page, it is possible that the user might never see the navigation, and could then be confused as to how to navigate through the web site.[1]

For instance, in Fig. 6.14, the navigation for the main sections of the Virginia Tech web site (Academics, Administration, etc.) is provided towards the bottom of the web page. The user must scroll halfway down the page to see the navigation for academics, administration, libraries, and such. In Fig. 6.15, when the user views the top of the web page, navigation is not obvi-

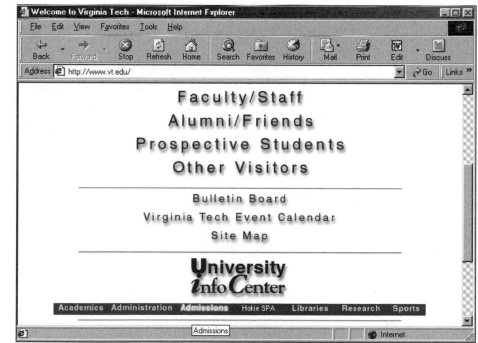

Figure 6.14

Navigation located in the middle of the page

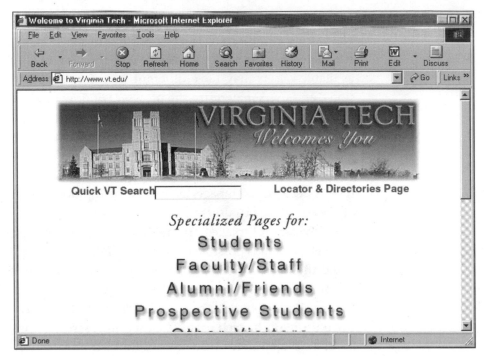

Figure 6.15
Navigation is hard to find

ous or easy to find. Olive Garden restaurants might provide wonderful food, and might be easy to find, but the navigation on their web page is difficult to find. It is located all the way at the bottom of the screen (Fig. 6.16), and it is doubtful that many users even see the navigation. In Fig. 6.17, when the user accesses the page, he or she has no idea where the navigation is located. On the Saturn automobile web site, the site navigation is provided on the right side of the screen (Fig. 6.18). This is fine if you have a large browser window open, but when the browser window gets smaller, the navigation disappears (Fig. 6.19).

Providing Current Location Information

When you stop at a rest stop on a busy highway, or when you check out the map of stores in a shopping mall, you will probably look for the phrase "You are here" on a map. Since in reality, navigation provides a map of a web site, navigation schemes need to provide some way of telling the user that "You are here."[13] Users need to know where they are in the overall structure of a web site. This is especially true if the user does not access the web site starting from the home page, but rather, links from another web site and enters the web site one or two levels down in the web site hierarchy.[13]

Figure 6.16
Navigation is located
at the bottom of the
web page

Figure 6.17
Navigation is hard to
find

Figure 6.18
Navigation located
on the right side of
the screen

Figure 6.19
Navigation disappears
on a smaller browser
window

Just saying "Well, when the user clicks on the link, it changes colors" is not enough. Usually, links change colors once users have clicked on them, to show that the users have already taken that link.[2] However, this is not sufficient to show current location. Once the user has followed all navigation links on a web site, the links will all be the same color. And, depending on how users have set up their browser preferences, those links might be displayed in the same color for a long time. With all links displayed as "visited," the user knows only where he or she has been in the recent past, but has no information on the current location.

Users need to be provided with information on where they currently are in the overall structure of the web site.[12] This can be done in a number of different ways. If the navigation links are textual, then when the user is viewing a certain page, the link to that page should be deactivated. This serves two purposes: The user knows the current location, and is not able to repeatedly click on the link again, which could cause confusion. An example of deactivation can be seen in the homepage for the ACM CHI (Human Factors in Computing) Conference 2001 (Fig. 6.20). When the user is on the home page, the navigational link to the home page is deactivated, and appears as plain text. Alternatively, a small symbol or graphic (such as an

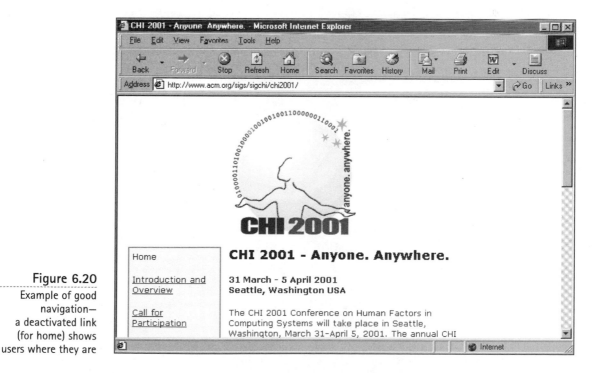

Figure 6.20

Example of good navigation— a deactivated link (for home) shows users where they are

arrow or a smiley face) could be placed next to the link, to symbolize to the user that "You are here!" If the navigation is provided using something like graphical buttons, then the graphical button providing a link to the current page should be darker, lighter, differently sized, differently colored, or provide some hint to the user of current location. For an example of this, look at the web site for the Department of Computer Science and Information Systems at the American University web site (Fig. 6.21). The navigation buttons change color when the user is viewing that specific page.

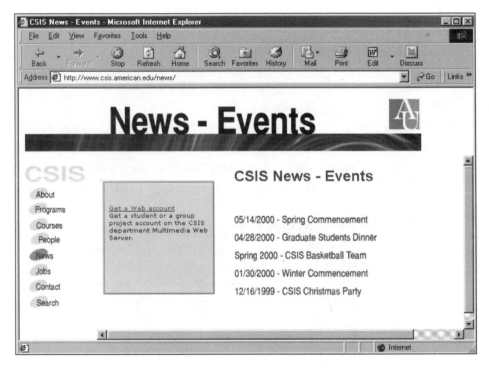

Figure 6.21

Example of good navigation— different color (for news) shows users where they are

SUMMARY

When user requirements are collected, they serve as a rich base of information. This information should be used to create the conceptual requirements for the web site. The web development team has to consider which web site objects should be included. Once the web site objects are defined, then the team must define the information architecture for the web site and plan for site navigation. A number of different approaches can be used for navigation, such as topical navigation or path navigation, and the navigation itself can be coded in a number of different ways.

Deliverables

At this point, you should have:

1. Fully analyzed the data collecting in the requirements gathering
2. Decided what content will be available and how that content will be distributed across web pages
3. Determined how much content already exists and how much will need to be developed
4. Decided upon the information hierarchical structure of the web site
5. Decided upon a navigation structure for the page layout

Discussion Questions

1. What is a web site object?
2. How do topical navigation and breadcrumb navigation differ?
3. What is audience-splitting, and why might it be useful?
4. How can a metaphor be used to organize the sections of the home page, and what might the drawbacks be?
5. What is information architecture, and why might a hierarchical structure be used in the development of a web site?
6. Why should site navigation not require the use of Java applets or JavaScript?
7. What is chunking, and how does the concept relate to web site design?
8. If the navigation is located at the bottom of the web page, describe a situation where the user may never see the navigation.
9. How does the browser provide navigation information on where the user has been?

REFERENCES

1. Powell, T., Jones, D., & Cutts, D. (1998). *Web Site Engineering: Beyond Web Page Design.* Upper Saddle River, NJ: Prentice Hall.
2. Niederst, J. (1999). *Web Design in a Nutshell.* Sebastopol, CA: O'Reilly and Associates.
3. Fuccella, J. (1997). *Using user centered design methods to create and design usable web sites.* Proceedings of the 1997 ACM Conference on Systems Documentation, 69–77.
4. Whitten, I., & Bentley, L. (1997). *Systems Analysis and Design Methods.* Boston: Irwin McGraw-Hill.
5. Rosenfeld, L., & Morville, P. (1998). *Information Architecture for the World Wide Web.* Sebastopol, CA: O'Reilly and Associates.
6. Lynch, P., & Horton, S. (1999). *Web Style Guide: Basic Design Principles for Creating Web Sites.* New Haven: Yale University Press.
7. Lazar, J., & Norcio, A. (2001, In press). User Considerations in E-commerce Transactions. In Q. Chen (Ed.), *Human-Computer Interaction: Issues and Challenges.* Hershey, PA: Idea Group Publishing, 185–195.
8. Shneiderman, B. (1998). *Designing the User Interface: Strategies for Effective Human-Computer Interaction* (3rd ed.). Reading, MA: Addison-Wesley.

9. Miller, G. (1956). The magical number seven, plus or minus two: Some limits on our capacity for processing information. *Psychological Review, 63*(2), 81–96.
10. Burdman, J. (1999). *Collaborative Web Development.* Reading, MA: Addison-Wesley.
11. Fleming, J. (1998). *Web Navigation: Designing the User Experience.* Sebastopol, CA: O'Reilly and Associates.
12. Nielsen, J. (2000). *Designing Web Usability: The Practice of Simplicity.* Indianapolis: New Riders Publishing.
13. Navarro, A., & Khan, T. (1998). *Effective Web Design.* San Francisco: Sybex.

CASE STUDY #1

▲ Best Buddies Maryland

The user requirements for the Best Buddies Maryland web site were gathered through a questionnaire, structured and unstructured interviews, review of organizational documents, and observation of the organization.

Interviews and Questionnaires

The initial interview took place with the staff of Best Buddies Maryland in downtown Baltimore. During the first client meeting, the development team collected documents relating to the history of Best Buddies, their mission, the schools participating in the Best Buddies program, and the group's organizational chart. The client also requested that the following general content be included in the web site: information for those who wish to donate time and money, information about upcoming Best Buddies of Maryland events, and contact information and links to the international organization and local affiliated schools.

The web development team attended the Best Buddies Maryland Friendship Games at the University of Maryland College Park. The event consisted of several group and individual games, a lunch, a concert, and a visit from the Baltimore Oriole's mascot. Members of the organization from Maryland, Virginia, and the District of Columbia participated in the event. Attending the Friendship Games gave the team an opportunity to observe, first hand, a Best Buddies event. The team also took advantage of this event to distribute surveys, take pictures, and perform a structured interview with the Program Director of Best Buddies International.

A week after attending the Friendship Games, the development team conducted structured interviews with the director, the two program managers, and a staff member for Best Buddies Maryland at their headquarters in Baltimore. In addition, the web development team interviewed two young adults with mental retardation who have been involved with the Best Buddies chapter at Towson University. The format of the interviews was one-on-one, with each of the interviews being taped to ensure accuracy.

In addition to the interviews, a questionnaire was developed to assist in collecting the user requirements (see previous chapter). After pilot testing the questionnaire with three users, the development team distributed them to potential users of the Best Buddies Maryland web site. These surveys were distributed via a variety of methods. Several were handed out at the Friendship Games; a dozen were handed out at the ARC (formerly known as the Association for Retarded Citizens) of Carroll County, a charitable organization that assists retarded citizens in Westminster, Maryland; several were distributed via e-mail; and one was sent via facsimile machine. A total of 45 completed questionnaires were returned to the development team.

Interview Results

To the five questions in the structured interviews, the seven interviewees provided very similar answers. The interviewees each had a positive general opinion of the World Wide Web. They characterized their usage of the web as "frequent." They were all very comfortable using technology involving computers. All listed informational sites (e.g., mapquest.com and msn.com) as their favorite sites. Although they had not made the decision to join an organization solely based on its web site, they had used organizations' web sites to help in making the decision. The other two interviewees restricted their answers to a general acknowledgment of usage of the World Wide Web and a few suggestions relating to content. The results of the interview questions relating specifically to content were used to determine whether specific content was considered by users to be a "must" or a "want." These results are described more fully in the next section.

Descriptions of Possible Resources

Link to International Organization

This requirement calls for a hyperlink to the Best Buddies International web site (www.bestbuddies.org). In addition to the link, a brief explanation of the history and mission of the international organization would be included. Score: Must

Program Information

This requirement calls for the web site to include a page detailing the various programs undertaken by Best Buddies Maryland. Score: Must

Donation Information

This requirement calls for the web site to include a page detailing the procedure for donating time or money to Best Buddies Maryland. Score: Must

Affiliated Schools Information

This requirement calls for the web site to include a page listing the schools affiliated with Best Buddies Maryland, including contact information and year affiliated. Score: Must

Contact Information

This requirement calls for the web site to include telephone numbers, fax numbers, e-mail addresses, and the mailing address for Best Buddies Maryland. Score: Must

History of the Organization

This requirement calls for the web site to include a brief summary of the history of Best Buddies Maryland. Score: Must

Guest Book

This requirement calls for the web site to include a page where visitors can leave a message and see messages left by other visitors. Score: Must

Calendar of Events

This requirement calls for the web site to include a schedule of upcoming Best Buddies Maryland events. Interested parties could find out where and when an event was being held and what type of event it was. Score: Must

Pictures of Events

This requirement calls for the web site to include photographs and text descriptions of previous Best Buddies events. Score: Want

Media Coverage

This requirement calls for the web site to include a page for posting articles that have appeared in the print media about Best Buddies Maryland. Score: Want

Links to Related Organizations

This requirement calls for the web site to include a page of links to organizations performing work similar to that performed by Best Buddies. The users offered the Special Olympics and the various ARC organizations around the state as examples of related organizations. Score: Want

Matches of the Month

This requirement calls for the web site to include a page featuring a success story of the month. A photo of the two Buddies and a text description of who they are and what activities they enjoy would be included. Score: Want

Other Things Learned

History of the International Organization

Best Buddies Maryland, a state branch of an international organization, is dedicated to improving the lives of people with mental retardation by creating opportunities for one-to-one friendships and integrated employment. Anthony Kennedy Shriver founded the international organization in 1989 with a single chapter on one college campus. The organization has now grown to 400 chapters located on middle school, high school, and college campuses in the United States, Canada, and Greece. More than 80,000 individuals have volunteered in the past ten years and the organization hopes in the next decade to bring Best Buddies to every corner of the United States. Best Buddies' mission is to successfully integrate people with disabilities into schools, workplaces, and communities, ultimately making Best Buddies' services unnecessary. Until then, Best Buddies' vision is to educate high school and college students, corporate and community citizens, and employers about the needs and abilities of people with mental retardation.

The Maryland Chapter

Around the world, Best Buddies International has currently enriched the lives of people with mental retardation with the help of 261 colleges, 139 high schools, and 3 middle schools. Maryland's branch of Best Buddies participates with the help of 25 colleges, 24 high schools, and 3 middle schools. Maryland has made the second greatest commitment to helping to enrich the lives of people with mental retardation, right behind Florida. The Maryland chapter employs a staff of four at offices in Baltimore and Silver Spring.

The User Population

Members, employees, and potential members of the local Maryland chapter of Best Buddies International are going to be the development team's major focus when building the web site. The development team has collected a variety of information from this user set. Because the user set included people from all walks of life and levels of education, care was taken to word questions used in the questionnaire and structured interviews to be as clear as possible. Additionally, in the questionnaire the options of "Don't know" and "Other" were offered as answers to most questions to keep technically unsophisticated users from guessing.

Survey Results

Personal Information

From the personal information section of the questionnaire, the development team learned that the largest percentage age group that will be using the web site consists of people between the ages of 18 to 24. This indicates to the development team that the prime group of people that will be accessing the web site grew up with computers in their lives.

In addition to considering the user's age, the team learned that user's level of education must also be considered. Users represented all educational levels. (It is likely that a college group's Best Buddies advisor will have a Ph.D., even though no one with a doctorate responded to the questionnaire.) Since there was such a wide range of education, the development team would have to concentrate its entire wording of text towards all levels of education in order for all of the users to be able to fully appreciate the web site.

Eighty-seven percent of the users have a computer at home. Users will likely be in the comfort of their own home and will not likely feel rushed as they look through the site. English is the native language of the majority of users of the Best Buddies Maryland web site; the other nine percent of users' native language is Chinese; therefore, the development team would consider certain international issues such as potentially offensive colors and language when developing the content of the web site.

Computer Information

The second category of information collected in the questionnaire included computer hardware and software considerations. Not only was information about specific types of hardware and software collected, but also information relating to the level of technical knowledge enjoyed by the users. The development team learned that 80% of the user population utilizes desktop computers for browsing the World Wide Web. The majority of users are not certain as to which type of processor they have in their computers. However, the development team deduced that the majority of these users have processors that are faster than 486s and the original Pentiums because over 67 percent of users purchased their computers within the last two years.

Generally, the development team deduced that download time would be a big issue because the majority of users access the Internet with dial-up modems, and the majority of those users aren't sure of what their dial-up modem speeds are. Only 10% of respondents said they used a cable modem, and 2% said they used an ISDN line. Therefore, care would be taken to not overburden these slow connections with large graphical files. Another interesting piece of information was that 59% of the users browse the web with America Online's browser, which has been proven to be a slower avenue to browsing web sites throughout the Internet.

Lastly, the data gathered in the computer information section of the questionnaire played a role in how the development team made decisions regarding the actual layout of the web site. It is very important to understand users' screen size as well as their resolution size so that the design can keep the web pages within useful limits for most users. However, the development team learned that there is a wide diversity of screen sizes being used by the user population. Of the users who knew their monitor's resolution, most of them reported it to be 800 × 600, which gave the development team little reason to create a web site with any wide graphics or pictures. Unfortunately, most of the users surveyed knew neither the size nor the resolution of their monitor. Therefore, the development team needed to assume that the users had smaller monitors with low resolution so that the web site would be viewable on every monitor, regardless of size or resolution.

Users' Web Resource Needs

The very first question in the Web Preferences section was whether or not users preferred to have web sites with frames. Frames can be very useful in keeping navigation consistent between different pages on a web site. However, over half of the users surveyed did not know what a frame was. This information speaks to the users' lack of familiarity with web technologies and terminology. As the web site of Best Buddies International contains frames, the development team may choose to use them to provide some consistency between the two web sites.

The users' responses to the question regarding how much animation users would like to see on the web site seemed to be mixed. The results were as follows: none 9%, a few pieces 35%, a lot 23%, and no opinion 33%. Taken with the information over download times on dial-up modems, this result led the team to decide to either eliminate animation from the plan for the site, or limit it as much as possible. The last thing the development team wanted was to design a web site that is at best annoying and at worst overwhelming.

Communication with friends and family ranked highest among the users' purposes for using the World Wide Web, followed by schoolwork, entertainment, research, and, lastly, work-related communication. If the users had used the web to conduct high-level research on the web, a plainer, more direct approach to presenting all information would be taken with the Best Buddies site. The users, however, reported a more casual use of the web, so it might be possible to consider providing information in more interesting, visually appealing ways. Additionally, most of the users surfed the World Wide Web on a daily basis and 90% of users feel that the World Wide Web is useful as an information tool.

The number of years of World Wide Web browsing experience was reported as being from 4 years to less than 1 year. This further illustrates the diversity of the user population. The experience level ranged from expert World Wide Web surfers to novice. Consistency of navigation, use of "plain English," and making certain the site is viewable without extra technology (e.g., plug-ins) is very important when designing for novice users. Therefore the development team would avoid building in any complicated functions or confusing navigation. The goal of the site was to bring people to the organization, not drive them away in frustration.

Because most of users surveyed use either Netscape Navigator, Internet Explorer, or AOL, the Best Buddies web site would need to perform equally well when viewed by each of these browsers as a minimum requirement. For the purpose of marketing the site later in the implementation phase, the development team queried the users' search engine preferences. According to the results of the survey, Yahoo! was the most used search engine, followed by Alta Vista, Lycos, Ask Jeeves, Google, Hotbot, and Northernlight. This was a question where users showed a little more sophistication, adding Infoseek in the eighth position as an "Other" option.

Finally, the development team asked the users what they would like to see on the Best Buddies Maryland site in terms of content. In the questionnaire, users ranked "ways to volunteer" as the most important, followed by "office location" and "contact information," "ways to donate money," "history of the organization," and "Guest Book."

This information came from closed-end questions, so space was provided at the end of the questionnaire for writing in content users would like to see. Unfortunately, only six users added comments in this area. There was, however, some agreement among them. Four people wrote that they would like to see success stories (called Match of the Month by some users, a moniker adopted by the development team) highlighting a different Buddy pair each month. Four wrote that the web site should contain pictures from previous events. One person wrote that a calendar of upcoming Best Buddies events was vital and another mentioned a Guest Book as being useful.

Web Resources to be Designed

Through questionnaires and structured interviews, the development team investigated the purpose, scope, and user issues involved in developing a web site for Best Buddies Maryland. The Best Buddies Maryland web site was planned to fulfill several purposes. First, it will provide information to those who would like to join the organization. Second, it will act as a conduit for donations. Third, it will provide information about upcoming events to those presently involved in the organization. Fourth, it will provide a means for former members of the organization to stay in touch with other members and to stay abreast of activities taking place within the organization. Finally, the web site will provide a way for Best Buddies Maryland to celebrate their successes by prominently featuring successful Buddy match-ups.

The users of the future Best Buddies Maryland web site identified 13 possible web site object requirements. One of them, a page with stories appearing in the media, was recommended by only one user and that user considered it to be relatively unimportant, so the development team chose to develop the following list of 12 resources.

International Site Link

The purpose of this resource is to allow users to visit the international site of Best Buddies. The Best Buddies Maryland web site will offer a direct link to the international site where users can obtain information about other activities such as E-Buddies, an alternative volunteer opportunity (not offered by the Maryland chapter) for people who have access to the Internet. While a link to the international site was mentioned by only two of the interviewees, both ranked it as a must and the development team would have likely included it had none of the users mentioned it. Additionally, the page with the link to Best Buddies International will contain a brief sketch of the international organization so casual viewers need not leave Best Buddies Maryland to learn more about their parent organization.

History of the Organization

The purpose of this resource is to offer background information about the organization to prospective and current volunteers. This resource will educate visitors about the purpose of Best Buddies and the organization's goals. From the results of the requirements gathering, the development team found this resource to be a must among volunteers and nonvolunteers.

Donation Information

The purpose of this resource is to offer visitors to the web site information on how to donate money to the organization. This resource will offer contact information such as e-mail and address information. If the user wishes to e-mail the organization for more information, all he or she will need to do is click on the link that says e-mail and an additional window will open for him or her to send his or her request. From the results gathered, the development team found this to be a must for the client. This information is crucial to the survival of Best Buddies Maryland because they are a nonprofit organization.

Guest Book

The purpose of this resource is to enable visitors to leave questions, contact information, and comments posted for others to see. The Guest Book will enable members who are not actively involved with the organization to contact old friends. This will also offer a means for asking questions about the organization or about anything of interest and have someone post the answer for everyone to see. From the results gathered, the development team found this to be a must among the clients and the volunteers of Best Buddies.

Calendar of Events

The purpose of this resource is to inform visitors about any upcoming events. The Calendar will enable people to make plans to attend the events that interest them. From the results gathered, the development team found this to be a must among the clients and volunteers of Best Buddies.

Previous Events

The purpose of this resource is to offer information and photographs on past events. This will offer visitors a look at how much fun they could have at Best Buddies outings, perhaps encouraging nonmembers to join the organization. This was considered to be a strong want.

Related Organizations

The purpose of this resource is to offer links to organizations similar to Best Buddies, such as Special Olympics. This was considered to be a must.

Forms for Volunteering

The purpose of this resource is to offer visitors a printable application to become a volunteer at Best Buddies. This application will standardize the information collected from volunteers. This resource was considered a must among the individuals who participated in the requirements gathering.

Affiliated Schools

The purpose of this resource is to offer visitors a list of affiliated schools, including the contact information and the year they joined Best Buddies. This resource could assist visitors in finding out if their school is involved with Best Buddies, and if not, then help them to take appropriate steps to form a Best Buddies group on campus. This was considered a must among users.

Match of the Month Success Story

The purpose of this resource is to recognize a Buddy and a volunteer for their work during the month. This will encourage members to work hard in order to achieve this honor. Additionally, it will highlight for those not involved with the organization the good work done by Best Buddies. From the information gathered, this was rated a strong want, but not a must.

Contact Information

The purpose of this resource is to provide a way for visitors to the web site to contact or send information to Best Buddies. This resource will include e-mail addresses, phone numbers, fax numbers, and the organization's street address. Users rated this resource as a must.

Program Information

The purpose of this resource is to provide detailed information about the various programs undertaken by Best Buddies Maryland. Users rated this resource as a must.

User Issues

As was discussed earlier, the user population of the proposed Best Buddies Maryland web site is diverse in terms of age, education, and web-browsing experience. For this reason, the development team needed to be very careful not to design a site that would be useful only to very sophisticated users. This caution applies to both the level of language used on the site and the use of advanced technology. Additionally, the relatively slow Internet connections used by the future viewers of the web site made heavy usage of animation or graphics impractical. The purpose of the web site is to inform visitors rather than entertain them.

The web resources selected for development lead to other issues. The privacy concerns of those involved with the organization must be respected. No information about anyone involved with the group will be placed on the site unless the person in question explicitly agrees to it. This agreement applies to the placing of contact names for affiliated schools and related organizations as well as to information about Best Buddy Matches of the Month. Additionally, the site's Guest Book will have to be monitored for vulgar or rude remarks entered into it.

CASE STUDY #2

▲ Institute of Notre Dame

Interview and Questionnaires

The web development team began the requirements gathering by conducting a fact-finding interview with Fred Germano, computer coordinator at the Institute of Notre Dame. During this interview the team obtained some of the pertinent information needed for the redesign the school's web site. Mr. Germano gave some general information about the school and its development, as well as some in-depth facts about the existing web page and IND's expectations for the future. Mr. Germano expressed to the team that IND was in need of a new look for their existing web site. They were interested in a site that resembled that of the Archdiocese of Baltimore, Maryland. The redesign should not consist of any frames or flashing graphics. Mr. Germano also reminded the team that the web site will have a number of different user groups, including faculty, parents, and the student body, who are all females ages 14 to 18.

Listed below are a series of interview questions that were presented to Mr. Germano along with a summary of his responses.

Who do you plan to be the primary users of this site?
Students, faculty, parents, and prospective students

For each of the users, what kind of information would you like to provide?
For students: Departmental Links, School Calendar, and Athletic
    Calendar. A Homework page would provide the daily homework
    issued by each instructor. This page would also provide the ca-
    pability to do various assignments online.
For faculty: A calendar of faculty meetings, bulletins, and a se-
    cured page where instructors can post students' grades.
For parents: A schedule of events, Departmental listings, teachers'
    e-mail addresses, newsletters, and tuition information.
For prospective students: General information about the school,
    school curriculum, clubs, and athletic groups.

What is the level of computer experience for each of the user categories?
According to Mr. Germano, the students have the highest level of computer experience. IND incorporates lab time in the student curriculum. The younger teachers have a mod-

erate amount of experience and the older faculty members have the least amount of experience. The parents have a fair amount of experience because 90% of them have computers in their homes or at work.

Are there areas of the existing web site that you wish to expand upon?
IND is interested in incorporating the school's mascot into the page design. The new mascot is "Winnie the Penguin." The former mascot was a Native American girl.

Do you have any logs that document the pages that are most frequently viewed?
IND has a tracking system, but Mr. Germano had not evaluated these logs. The web development team was allowed to view the logs and take copies for further evaluation.

Who will be maintaining the site after it is released? What is the level of technical knowledge?
Fred Germano will be the person in charge of maintaining the web site. He has performed all the maintenance on the site thus far.

How often will the site be updated with new information?
Once the site is redesigned, Mr. Germano will update it daily with new information.

What are IND's future plans for the web site?
IND is interested in developing an online bookstore. Mr. Germano did not go into detail about the items that will be sold or the method of payment. IND would also like to add the capability of downloading the school's newsletter and bulletins. IND would like the ability to take applications over the Net while maintaining the individual's privacy. Within the next year or so, Mr. Germano will be teaching a selected group of students how to maintain and update the web site, and the students will be managing the IND web site.

Analysis of Survey Responses

All the responses that were collected were from the online survey. Fred Germano provided a link to this survey from IND's home page. Thus, we were able to obtain responses from actual users of the site. In addition, he arranged for IND's students to fill out the online survey during a class period. Even with this arrangement, the actual response rate from students was lower than expected. However, since the student body and faculty were solicited to respond to the survey, there is a much higher proportion of responses from them than from any other category of user. This fact was taken into account during the analysis of the data. A total of 54 survey responses were received.

Since all the responses were from the online survey, it was expected that almost all the respondents would have visited the site in the past. This was borne out by the results of the survey, with over 80% stating they had previously visited the site. Had the web development team been able to distribute a paper survey and had time to receive and analyze the results, this question might have provided more information about what proportion of IND's target audience actually has used the site.

Since attracting new students is an important mission for the site, the needs of potential students have to be considered in designing the web site, even though they were not a part of this information gathering process. Similarly, the low response rate from parents was expected from an online survey, but parents' needs still must be considered. Several alumnae did respond to the survey. This was a category of user that was not included in the survey. The existence of this new category means that the team should evaluate the needs and interests of IND's alumnae and develop suitable content for them as well as parents, students, faculty, and prospects.

An important set of questions on the survey asked what the respondents were looking for on IND's site and what they would like to see on the site. From these questions and related comments to other questions, we identified five key areas of development.

Schedules of Events

First, most people responded that they were interested in information on upcoming events at the school. There appeared to be a demand, especially among the students, for information about class schedules and extracurricular events. Among the open-ended responses to this question were requests for more information on sporting events, a student activities calendar, and schedules of tests and homework assignments. One comment requested a calendar for the entire year instead of just the current month. The number of these responses indicated that one of the main focuses of IND's site should be in providing detailed calendars of activities occurring at the school, including class-related and extracurricular activities as well as the school's hours of operation and information about weather-related closings. This information would be useful when organizing the content areas of the site; each section should make related schedules easy to locate. Additionally, the team might want to evaluate the creation of an overall schedule of events that ties together information from different schedules on the web site (along with links deeper into the site to more detailed information about events on this schedule).

Currency of Content

The creation of more schedule-related content was related to a second concern about the web site: the timeliness of the content. Several respondents to the survey were critical about the lack of up-to-date information on the web site. If more content areas are developed to provide information about upcoming events at IND, this information must be kept current. At the moment, Fred Germano is the sole person responsible for updating information on the web site, but future plans for the web site include allowing the faculty to update some information themselves as well as having the students make supervised changes to the content of the site. These steps will help keep the site's content current. Realizing that several people with differing experience levels will eventually become involved in maintaining this site, the web development team planned to design the site in such a way that it would be easy to make revisions to content while still maintaining a consistent page layout across the site.

Faculty Information

A third area of interest revealed by the survey is the expansion of faculty information. Responses to the survey indicate that faculty-related information is a popular request, but that the current web site does not fulfill the needs of its users. The current site contains a basic directory of faculty. This can be expanded to not only provide basic contact information (department, telephone number, and e-mail address), but also a brief biography of each faculty member, links to classes currently being taught, and other information that might help make this section of the web site seem friendlier. (Similarly, another section could be used to spotlight students who are involved in activities at the school.)

Pictures of the School

Fourth, several responses indicate an interest in more pictures of the school on the web site. This would include pictures of the school exterior and interior. The interior of the Institute of Notre Dame has a very grand feel due to its architecture and design; the proper use of pictures on the site along with more detailed information about the school would not only be interesting, but might also influence people who are considering enrollment at IND. The use of pictures on the site might also extend to the addition of pictures of faculty, students, and alumnae.

Content and Links of Interest to Students

Finally, a couple of student responses indicate that we need to consider not only what would be useful to the students, but also what would be interesting to them. In this case, we are dealing with an audience, in part, consisting of teen-aged girls. This audience will influence choices in both content and design. The current site offers little to draw them back. The survey responses provided the development team with the names of several sites that the students considered to be interesting. Additionally, since Fred Germano planned to have the students participate in updating the site, the site might include an area in which the students could develop pages of interest to them. This might take the form of student home pages, or an online school paper.

Analysis of the Current Web Site

The web site development team also tried to discover how useful the target population felt the current site to be. Thus the team analyzed the responses to this question by type of user and then compared those answers to what the users said they wanted. From both of these analyses, the team found that most users were either neutral about how useful the site was or found it to be only somewhat useful. The most positive responses in the "Neutral" and "Somewhat Useful" categories were for people looking for information about upcoming events, general, or other school information. Educational resource links and links to application information were fairly balanced across the "Neutral," "Somewhat Useful," and "Very Useful" categories, but these two responses also ranked lowest among the types of information requested. The heavy concentration of "Neutral" and "Somewhat Useful" responses seems to indicate that the current web site is providing the basic types of information desired by visitors, but falls short in developing that content. This indicated that the team could improve the site by building on the current content and organization instead of redesigning it from the ground up.

Another aspect of the current site's usability involves whether visitors are able to find the content on the site that they are interested in. Of all the responses to the survey, over one-third of them claimed to have problems finding the information they were looking for. This indicates two things: the need for more thorough and current content, and the need to improve navigation within the site. As stated earlier, the team has identified several areas in which they planned to expand upon the content currently provided. The web development team planned to make the navigation as clear and flexible as possible.

Two questions on the survey related to both the current content of the site and the usability of the site. These questions asked the respondents to identify the one thing they liked the most about the site and the one thing they liked the least about the site. It should be noted that there was a problem with the survey design that caused some of the responses to the question "What one thing do you like the least?" to be lost when the completed survey was written to the database. This error was discovered and corrected fairly early, but not until 29 people had already submitted their survey. Most of these responses were from faculty. Thus the number of valid responses to this question was relatively low and difficult to analyze for any user category other than students. Among students, event information received more than twice as many responses as any other choice as being the most liked part of the site. The remaining choices all scored very low. Surprisingly, navigation scored the highest among faculty. This contradicted the results from other questions in this survey and the team's own evaluation of the site that indicated that the navigation needed improvement. This response might indicate a misunderstanding of the question, or it might also mean that the navigational elements for the sections of the site that faculty visit are better developed than those on the rest of the site. In contrast, navigation was the least-liked site element for students. Neither parents nor alumnae had enough responses to be significant.

The final question on the survey was a free-form request for comments. This was a useful addition to the survey since it allowed the respondents the chance to give opinions outside the scope of the closed questions. Responses in the comments confirmed what was observed from the responses to the other questions, especially that more detailed content is needed about current events, clubs and athletics, class information, and faculty information.

To summarize, the web team's analysis of the online survey revealed the following:
- Five audiences must be addressed: students, faculty, parents, alumnae, and prospective members of the school.
- Content development will be a major part of the site redesign efforts.

- The most important content to develop in order to satisfy the site's users are:
  - Calendars of current and upcoming events including meetings, sporting events, and extracurricular activities
  - Class information—especially schedules of homework and tests
  - Expanded faculty information
  - Pictures of the school
  - Content targeted toward the interests of teen-aged girls in order to keep students visiting the site
- Timely information is vital. The site must be designed in such a way that it is easy for both faculty and students to update.
- Navigation needs to be improved in order to make it easier for visitors to find desired information.

Web Design Decisions

Based on the information gathering, the web development team was able to determine content needs. They decided to use existing content and incorporate it with new content based on the results of information gathering. In order to make web site maintenance easier, content will be displayed using a template. Fred Germano, who currently manages the site, would eventually like to have the students and faculty take over the daily management. The team believed that the use of templates would make this transition easier.

The team planned to provide a description of IND's Alumnae Association, information on how to become a member, a schedule of alumni events, and a variety of other kinds of information of interest to alumnae. The team asked Fred Germano to e-mail documents that would form the basis for a lot of the content.

After the meeting with Mr. Germano, the team began a new design for the web site. The team asked Mr. Germano what browsers most of the users used, and, answering for only the students, he said that they used Internet Explorer. The team copied the web server's logs and analyzed them using Microsoft Site Server. The results of the logs also showed that most of the users logging into IND's web site were using Internet Explorer 4.0 or greater. This was consistent with the fact that the computer labs at IND were running Internet Explorer. However, there were some users using other browsers, such as Netscape. Taking this into account, the team decided to create a site that would have a similar look in all browsers, including the text-only browser, Lynx. They decided to implement the main navigation across the top of the screen. Within each section of the web site (Students, Faculty, etc.), the team decided to also implement navigation along the left side of a screen that is section-oriented. For example, under the Alumni section, they would include links to reunion schedules. Fred Germano mentioned that he did not want to use frames or any new technology, since he would like the students to be able to create web pages. He wanted it as simple as possible without losing any design qualities.

Frames have a lot of pitfalls if implemented incorrectly. These pitfalls include not being able to bookmark a web page easily, not being able to change the title of a web page easily, and the fact that if someone enters a site indirectly through a search engine, the user may not even get the navigation bar whatsoever. Therefore, the web development team decided against using frames, and instead chose to use tables for the best user experience.

The requirements gathering helped in determining how the IND web site could be improved. It was confirmed that current navigation was a problem. Therefore, the group decided to implement table-based navigation, which would help users find what they are looking for on the web site. Web design decisions were thus made based on an extensive examination of site architecture and the navigation requirements of the IND web site.

CASE STUDY #3

▲ Eastman Kodak Company

Introduction
As described in the previous chapter, many different information-gathering techniques were used to collect data about users' needs and desires and Kodak's business objectives. The next steps for us were to synthesize requirements, develop design requirements based on the data and begin the actual design process itself.

Business Unit Interviews
This exercise helped us to better understand some of the specific markets and audiences Kodak was trying to reach and some of the specific goals Kodak was trying to achieve through the Web. The following overall design requirements for the new kodak.com top level resulted from the interviews with business units.

- Present information in a user-centric way, without regard for corporate business unit boundaries.

- Provide information on applications of products as well as the products themselves.

- Provide a more intuitive and direct path to Kodak's various markets. ("Business Solutions" is not an adequate catch-all.)

- Broaden the choices at each level so that the site is "shallower" (i.e., not requiring so many clicks to get to information).

- Provide areas for announcements, highlights, education, and enticement directly on the home page.

- Provide branding and visual design guidelines that support the diversity of Kodak—its various businesses and markets, its worldwide presence.

Consumer Focus Groups

The consumer sessions focused on participants' expectations and understanding of digital imaging terminology and technology, impressions of the digital imaging marketplace, and expectations and preferences for Kodak's offerings on the Web. Twenty-two consumers participated in the three consumer focus groups. Several interesting observations surfaced.

Many focus group participants were confused by terminology related to digital imaging and pictures. Some participants were not aware that Kodak made digital imaging products at all. In terms of general Web usability preferences, participants indicated that they disliked Web sites that took a long time to load, and that flashing pictures were annoying. Participants also sometimes found it hard to find the information that they were looking for. Regarding the Kodak Web site specifically, participants were excited at the possibility of sharing pictures with family and friends over the Web. Interestingly enough, none of the focus group participants had ever visited the Kodak Web site. However, the focus group participants indicated that they would be interested in visiting the Kodak Web site if it offered information on products and instructions on how to use those products, and also photography advice (on how to take good pictures, what type of film to use, and so forth). Finally, participants were enthusiastic about the idea of Kodak delivering customer support for products directly through the Web site.

Dealer Focus Groups

The dealer sessions focused on the dealers' relationships to Kodak and how they could be improved because of Kodak's online presence. Dealers were asked to comment on their current communication with Kodak, and indicate what Kodak could do over the Web to make that interaction more effective.

Twenty-seven digital equipment dealers took part in the dealer focus groups. The dealers who took part tended to focus on what resources Kodak made available on the Web. Some participants felt that the information sent out by Kodak through traditional means was geared towards larger consumer dealerships, not smaller organizations, or those who needed more information that is technical. Approximately half of the focus group participants had visited Kodak's Web site, and many of them felt that the Kodak Web site was geared towards consumers, but should provide adequate information for the dealers. Such information could relate to new products, product availability, product specification sheets, and technical questions. The main advantage given for having this information available on the Web site was 24-hour-per-day availability. The participants commented that some information (such as dealer pricing information) should not be available to all (including customers) on the Web site. Overall, focus group participants did not like the design of the current kodak.com home page. For instance, the difference between "What's Hot" and "What's New" was not clear. Many of the categories were seen as confusing by the dealers, who requested easier paths for finding the information that they wanted.

Usability Tests

The usability administrator sat with the participant during the usability test. Participants had some problems finding information about specific products, but they experienced even more difficulty when they looked for any information without specific product names (such as advice for taking photographs). Users were given tasks to perform that would lead them to all of the links on the home page. The search engine for the Web site was perceived as being hard-to-use. When doing searches, users commented that many of the Web pages were too cramped with text, and therefore were hard to read. The frequently asked questions page was perceived to be useful, but users in some cases weren't sure what "FAQ" meant, and therefore, advised that the name "Frequently Asked Questions" should be spelled out. In addition, users had trouble finding the location to e-mail questions and comments to Kodak.

During the interviews that took place after the usability test, participants commented that the kodak.com Web site seemed too cluttered. Users indicated that many of the resources that they wanted were already available on the Web site, but users were hindered by the confusing terminology. Users also indicated that the search engine should be improved. Overall, users liked the resources offered at the kodak.com Web site and would be interested in returning to the Web site if it was made easier to use. All of this data was valuable in developing design requirements for the redesign.

Synthesizing Requirements

Based on our understanding of user needs and behavior, we defined a set of user requirements that guided the design of a new top-level site structure. Some of the specifics of these requirements are described below:

Information Segments

As described in Chapter 3, kodak.com visitors fall into a few broad segments based on information interest. We identified at least five major segments of information in which visitors could potentially be interested: (1) consumer photography and imaging, (2) business and professional applications of imaging, (3) Kodak as a company, (4) working with Kodak to deliver products and/or services, and (5) nothing in particular. All of these information segments needed to be accommodated by the new top-level site structure, and eventually formed the basis for the information "chunks" we developed for the home page.

Products versus Solutions

Some visitors come to kodak.com seeking information about a specific product; others come with a need or problem in mind but without knowing the product or service that can best meet that need. Both needed to be accommodated by the new top-level site structure.

Technological Requirements

Based on surveys, guest book comments, feedback from focus groups, and existing literature on Web site usability, we made fast download times, pages viewable on monitors of varying resolutions, support for textual navigation, and other such qualities requirements for our new top-level site structure. These requirements included:

1. Total file size for the home page, including graphics, should be kept to a minimum (ideally, around 45K).
2. The main navigation and graphics should be viewable without scrolling on a low-resolution monitor. The width of the page should not exceed 472 pixels; no horizontal scrolling or window expansion should be necessary. The vertical constraint may be relaxed with proper design that gives clear visual indication of additional material and entices user to go there.
3. No frames.
4. No gratuitous, incessantly looping animations, or blinking text.
5. The page should be completely navigable with image loading turned off (for text browser users).

Conceptual Design

We had gathered a tremendous amount of knowledge—user needs and characteristics, content requirements, and marketing requirements. The next step was to use that knowledge and requirements to architect the design of the home page and top level of kodak.com.

As is usually the case with design, there was no systematic process we could follow to take us automatically from requirements to design. We had to rely on creative problem-solving to generate a first prototype, which we could then improve upon using usability testing to drive design iterations. We assembled a multifunctional team consisting of visual designers, a project manager, a Web editor, a Web developer from one of Kodak's business units, a manager with a background in user experience, and usability experts to examine the requirements and brainstorm possible designs for a new top level for kodak.com.

Our primary focus was the design of the home page. Once we settled on the design of the home page, we identified the need to create new top-level "hub pages" to pull together links to related pieces of content throughout kodak.com. For example, one "hub page," "Digital Cameras and Technology," was developed to include links to Kodak's various digital products, including digital cameras, inkjet products, and CD products. We spent less time on the design of these hub pages relative to the time we spent on the home page. We did not usability test the hub pages. The remainder of the links from the home page pointed to existing "sitelets" (subsites) within kodak.com which, for the most part, we did not alter.

We had several multihour working sessions. Based on the user interface requirements we had defined, we knew that in order to make navigation more efficient, the new home page would need to contain more links than the previous one. We also knew what content those links had to account for. Our challenge during the design process, then, was to:

1. Establish the exact wording for the links, understanding that both the descriptiveness of the links themselves and their context among neighboring links on the home page would impact usability.

2. Divide the links into groups to help the user evaluate them more quickly and easily. In going from roughly 10 to roughly 30 links, we knew we didn't want to simply add 20 more gray buttons to our current home page.

3. Design the look of the home page, incorporating imagery into a primarily textual home page to achieve a compelling look befitting the "World Leader in Imaging."

To achieve the first two tasks, we wrote the tentative names of the various sections of the site on sticky notes, and spent many of our working sessions moving these notes around on large pieces of posterboard. We discussed the sections of the site, their relative importance to users and to the company, and how they could be grouped and organized. For inspiration, we conducted a benchmark comparison of the Web sites of 10 corporations, making note of:

1. Theme, if any
2. Visual motif
3. Organization of major sections of the site with descriptions
4. Navigational model/tools
5. Common page elements
6. Number of choices from home page
7. How the following are handled on the home page:
   - The path to product information
   - International content
   - Online commerce, if any
   - Special relationships (e.g., with dealers and/or developers)
   - Feedback/guest book mechanism

Evaluating these sites helped us to identify design and interaction elements and words/labels that we found effective.

Information Architecture

When we created groups, we discussed the wording of the links so that the juxtaposed links would not create confusion. After several sessions, we arrived at groupings that we thought were reasonable (see Table 6.2 below):

TABLE 6-2	Groups within the Information Architecture for the Redesigned kodak.com Web Site

Group 1 Find Site Map Product Catalog Customer Support On-line Store	**Group 6** .further KODAK Picture This postcards Photo Chat
Group 2 What's New at www.kodak.com	**Group 7** All About Photography Guide to Better Pictures Digital Learning Center
Group 3 About Kodak Press Center Investor's Center Career Center	**Group 8** Advanced Photo System KODAK GOLD Films Digital Cameras and Technology
Group 4 For Dealers and Developers	**Group 9** KODAK Photonet online
Group 5 Professional Photography and Graphic Arts Motion Picture Imaging Business and Office Applications Health and Medical Imaging Aerial, Space, and Scientific Imaging Government and Law Enforcement Imaging Imaging in Education	**Group 10** Periodic Feature **Group 11** Kodak Around the World

Iterative Design with Usability Testing

We subjected our design to an *iterative design process*. That is, we conducted one usability test, fed the results of the test into the next iteration of the design, and tested again to further refine the design. The first usability test was paper-based.

Usability Testing, Round One

After developing a first draft of the links and groups we wanted for the new home page, we subjected it to paper-and-pencil usability testing. This was called "round one" of usability testing. Twenty participants were recruited for the study, which consisted of three stages.

In the first stage, each participant was presented with a simple listing, on paper, of the links we intended to have on the home page (see Table 6.2).

Links were presented in the major groupings ("chunks") we had agreed upon, but no other visual design was employed. Each participant was given the same set of 30 tasks (presented in random order). Tasks were designed to cover a broad range of content on kodak.com, including information most frequently sought by users. For each task, the participant was asked to identify the home page link most likely to lead to information that would support the completion of that task, and to give a rating from 1–3 of his/her level of confidence that the targeted information would be found using that link. This first stage was intended to examine how well our proposed home page links were differentiated; that is, for a given set of representative tasks, whether the user knew which link to choose to find a particular piece of information.

Table 6.3 shows the percentage of participants, for each task, who picked as their first choice the correct home page link that would lead to the completion of the task. This was the most useful stage of the test, as it provided a preview of what it would be like for a user to use the new home page.

TABLE 6-3	Phase I Usability Testing Results—Percentage of Participants that Identified the Correct Home Page Link on the First Try

Task	% Succeeding
1996 Annual Report	100%
How digital cameras work, digital technology in general	100%
Police department fingerprint work	100%
Help with a malfunctioning Kodak camera	95%
Multimedia postcards	90%
Products and services in other countries	90%
Finding a job at Kodak	90%
Professional photographer tips and tools for archiving portfolio	85%
Insurance solutions	85%
Difficulty connecting digital camera to computer	80%
Where to buy the DC120 digital camera	75%
Gift items that can be bought online	75%
Interactive application to share and discuss pictures online	75%
Vacation photography tips	70%
Learn about new consumer digital camera	70%
Training modules in German and Spanish	65%
Learn about consumer color scanner	50%
Whether extreme temperatures will affect single-use cameras	50%
Digital system for motion picture editing and special effects	45%
Communicating a positive comment to Kodak	35%
Learn more about PhotoCDs	30%
Online service to access, share, and store pictures	25%
Advanced Photo System cameras	20%
Sample pictures	5%
Discussion forums	5%
Interactive applications to experience pictures in new ways	5%
Photo club	0%
Holiday contests or events	0%
Putting images on mugs, T-shirts, calendars, etc.	0%
How to obtain Picture Postcard software	0%
(Number of participants = 20)	

In the second stage, we asked each participant to go through the entire list of links on the home page and describe what s/he would expect to find "behind" each link. This second stage was intended to examine the predictability of the links we intended to offer on the home page. Table 6.4 shows the percentage of participants making correct predictions for each link.

TABLE 6-4	Phase I Usability Testing Results—Percentage of Participants that Correctly Predicted the Content Behind Each Link			
Term	Correct	Partially correct	"Don't know"	Incorrect
Around the World	100%	0%	0%	0%
Career Center	100%	0%	0%	0%
Guide to Better Pictures	100%	0%	0%	0%
Product Catalog	100%	0%	0%	0%
Customer Support	100%	0%	0%	0%
What's New at www.kodak.com	100%	0%	0%	0%
About Kodak	95%	5%	0%	0%
Online Store	95%	5%	0%	0%
Digital Learning Center	90%	0%	10%	0%
Investor's Center	90%	5%	0%	5%
Health and Medical Imaging	85%	0%	15%	0%
Digital Cameras and Technology	80%	10%	10%	0%
Aerial, Space and Scientific Imaging	80%	5%	15%	0%
PhotoChat	80%	15%	0%	5%
Business and Office Applications	75%	15%	10%	0%
All About Photography	75%	10%	15%	0%
Professional Photography and Graphic Arts	75%	5%	20%	0%
Gold Films	75%	5%	15%	5%
Press Center	60%	10%	30%	0%
For Dealers and Developers	55%	25%	15%	5%
Imaging in Education	55%	5%	25%	15%
Find	50%	35%	15%	0%
Government and Law Enforcement Imaging	50%	15%	35%	0%
Motion Picture Imaging	50%	20%	15%	15%
Site Map	50%	20%	10%	20%
KODAK Picture This postcards	30%	30%	10%	30%
Advanced Photo System	30%	15%	15%	40%
.Further	0%	15%	65%	20%
Kodak Photonet online	0%	30%	15%	55%
(Number of participants = 20)				

We found this stage of testing to be helpful in that it identified unfamiliar or ambiguous terms, and terms for which the users' expectations differed from our intent. It also provided insight into possible misinterpretations of terms, and how pervasive these misinterpretations were likely to be. For example, we discovered that 80% of our test participants were unfamiliar with the term "Advanced Photo System," and did not realize that the term refers to an industry standard for general consumer photography. As another example, we constructed a link to "What's New at www.kodak.com" hoping that users would realize that it linked to recent updates to the Web site, not necessarily "what's new" with Kodak. However, we found that 75% of test participants did not make this distinction, and for the final design we dropped the words "at www.kodak.com" from this link.

In the third stage, we again went through the entire list of links on the home page with each participant and explained the content we intended to offer under that link. We asked the participant to give a rating on a seven-point scale of how well the link name we chose described the content we intended to offer "behind" it. In this stage, we were attempting to discover how accurate the participants found the names we devised. We discovered that this stage of the study was not particularly useful, since participants tended to give us high accuracy ratings for almost every link. We found that the fact that because a link name is accurate does not necessarily mean that it is predictable, or well differentiated from surrounding links, or otherwise useful to the user. As an illustration, a link marked "Information" may accurately describe what is found behind the link, but is not of much use to the user because it is not at all predictable or differentiable from other links. A specific example from our study is that we had a link marked "All About Photography" on our prototype home page. Five of the 30 tasks could be completed using this link, but for four of these five tasks, none of the 20 participants chose "All About Photography" as either their first or second choice links. Yet, when the participants were told the content that would be offered through "All About Photography" (tips for taking great pictures in various situations, suggestions on how to do more with pictures, information about photography clubs, seminars and events, information about Kodak photographic products, and more) all participants gave the name a high rating in terms of accuracy. The problem was that although the title "All About Photography" was accurate, it was not well differentiated from its surrounding links (many of which had to do with photography, as well). In addition, because of the great diversity of information to which it pointed, it was difficult for users to predict what lay behind the link. Because of this and other experiences, we concluded that this methodology was not useful for measuring the usability of the proposed site structure, or for identifying changes that would increase usability.

When the results of the first set of usability tests came back, we were ready to perform our first iteration on improving the proposed home page design. Based on the usability test recommendations, we cut down on the number of home page links—subsuming some in others—and recasting the focus of some of the proposed hub pages. Of the home page links that remained, we worked on renaming those that had caused confusion.

Conceptual Design of the Web Site
Page Layout

A web site might be a series of web pages, but the user only views a single web page at a time. Although a web page incorporating frames might actually consist of three or more HTML files, the user still perceives it as a single page. The issues involved in page design can make or break the user experience.

The web page is at the heart of the user experience. We need to consider what should go on a web page, and what factors can affect or have an impact on the user experience when viewing that web page. If months have been spent on collecting user requirements, but the user doesn't have the plug-in application needed to properly view the web page and cannot figure out how to download the required plug-in application, what is the point of the web page? All of the work to develop a web page might not really make a difference if the viewer cannot properly access the page. This chapter will discuss how to make a web page that is easy to use, and that will meet the needs of the user, delivering the information in a quick and easy manner. The chapter will also discuss the issues that can help or hurt the user experience when viewing a web page.

► 7.1 TECHNICAL CONSIDERATIONS

Download Speed

When requesting any web page, the user wants it to appear in a short amount of time. The human–computer interaction research is clear on this; users want a quick response to their request.[4] Not only are users likely to give up if the web page takes too long to download, but the download speed can also affect the perception of the quality and usefulness of the material on the web page.[5,6] Download speed is the number one concern of web users.

The time it takes for a web page to download is the product of a number of factors, including the user's connection speed to the Internet, the Internet service provider's capacity and speed, and the size of the web files being requested. Only one of these factors is really under the control of the web development team: the size of the files being requested. The user controls the connection speed to the Internet. (Depending on how little or how much the individual is willing to pay, he or she can get a 28.8 up to a T1 connection.) The client organization decides which Internet service provider to use, which may determine the server response speed. But it is the web development team who determines the size of the web files.

When users request a web page, they are requesting the HTML document that contains the majority of the content and presentation, as well as any graphics, Java Applets, Sound files, or other objects. As more of these objects are requested, the download time is increased. An HTML file that is 20K will not take long to download; however, the 2MB of graphics that come along with the HTML file take longer to download and that wait can frustrate the user. If the files take a substantial time to download, users may even perceive that they have made an error.[7,8]

The download time should be minimized by limiting the amount of data that is being downloaded. If plain textual content will do, there is no need to provide 15 graphics. The download file size should be minimized by limiting the use of graphics, sound, animation, and Java applets. These extras only hinder the user experience by increasing the time it takes for the files to download. Web developers should attempt to address the issue of download speed.[4] One guideline states that a web page, including all required download objects, should be between 10K and 50K.[9]

Plug-Ins

Plug-in applications, or helper applications, such as PDF (Portable Document Format), RealAudio, and Flash, can assist in presenting data in an appropriate and useful manner. However, these plug-in applications are helpful only if the user has them installed. If the user does not have the plug-in application, then requiring it can become a hindrance to the user's browsing experience. The conventional (and incorrect) wisdom is that "as long as the plug-in is available for free, we can provide a link to download the plug-in application." The unconventional, and correct, wisdom is that requiring users to download a plug-in application will take a few minutes. This has the same effect as increasing the file size so that it takes a few minutes to download. There is also the possibility that (1) the user will not want to download the plug-in application, (2) the user will not be able to figure out how to download the plug-in application, (3) the user will attempt to download the plug-in application and make an error, or (4) the user's local area network will not allow the user to download applications because of security reasons.

It is safe to require use of a plug-in application only when you know that almost all of your targeted users will have the plug-in application already installed. For instance, it is relatively safe to assume that all Computer Science and Information Systems researchers will have the Adobe Acrobat reader (for PDF files) installed, or will feel comfortable installing the reader. A number of web sites for conferences provide the call for papers as well as the papers themselves using the PDF format. Based on the information gathered on the user computing environment as a part of the requirements gathering, the web development team might know, for instance, that 90% of targeted users have RealAudio installed. It would then be safe to require the use of RealAudio on the web site.

Animation

Animation is appropriate only for a very limited number of web sites. Animation can be very distracting to users and generally is not appropriate on informational or e-commerce web sites. Research has shown that animation on web pages will decrease the performance of information retrieval.[14] Animation can be appropriate for web sites that will primarily used by children, because it helps to keep their attention. Also, animation is appropriate on web sites whose purpose is to entertain, because the animation (the entertainment) is the content itself. And animated graphics are not equivalent to video. Video is content that the user chooses to view as content. An animated picture is a picture that moves and changes shape or form, and unless users turn off all graphics, the user can not force the animation to stop moving.

Imagine reading a book where there were pictures, and the pictures began to move. It would be very distracting to read while there were moving pictures. Animation is no different. Animation distracts the user's attention from the current task.[4] Think about an animated graphic that is serving as a banner advertisement at the top of a web page. The whole purpose of the animated ad is to grab the user's attention. The movement is great if you are the company sponsoring the advertisement, but this is not so great if you are the content provider because the attention has been taken away from the content and from your message. Why would a web designer want to purposefully distract users from their original purpose in coming to the web site?

▶ 7.2 DESIGN CONSIDERATIONS

Cluttered Design

People think that it is better to add as many graphics, objects, and sounds to a web page as possible—"more is better." However, overloading the page is simply not good web page design. Based on what we know from human–computer interaction research about interface design and user reactions, we know that cluttering up your web page will actually decrease the usability of your web page. Think about going to an art museum. You don't see 50 paintings all closely displayed on one wall. Too many paintings presented together would be overwhelming to the museum visitor and would not enhance the viewing experience. When you are at an airport and looking for directions, you don't see clustered images for 25 locations such as restroom, gift shop, customs, and security. That's because providing 25 icons of airport amenities would be overwhelming to the airport visitor. Providing a cluttered screen of many graphics, all clamoring for attention, is just as much of a mistake. Human–computer interaction research has found that the related concepts of short-term memory and chunking give the physiological foundation to explain these phenomena. As humans take in data from their sensory environment, that data is processed in short-term memory.[1] But humans have limits on how much data can be held in short-term memory.[1] Specifically, humans can process 7 ± 2 chunks of data at a time.[1,2,3] A chunk can be a letter, a word, a concept, or a category. If 30 choices are presented to the user, this entire grouping can be overwhelming, but if these 30 choices are chunked into six categories of five choices each, they can be more easily processed by the user.

Organizing choices into categories can assist users in finding what they want. The goal of a web page should be to deliver information to users in a quick and easy manner, rather than to "make a statement."

Background Patterns

The background on a web page should be plain; it should not "jump out" at the user and scream for attention. In most cases, a clear color should be used, and a background graphical pattern should not be used at all. However, there are certain circumstances where a background pattern, if subtle, can be visually appealing. For example, a background could be set in a papyrus-type document graphic. This could look stylish and not distract the user's attention. However, an obviously repeating graphic should not be used to tile the background. If the client organization is interested in placing a seal or other identifying mark of the organization on the web page, such a graphic should be used only once. Repeatedly displaying the graphic does not improve user recognition of the web page; however, it will decrease the ability of the user to focus on the task and in many cases, it will hinder the user's ability to read the text. See Figs. 7.1 and 7.2 for good and bad examples of using background graphical patterns.

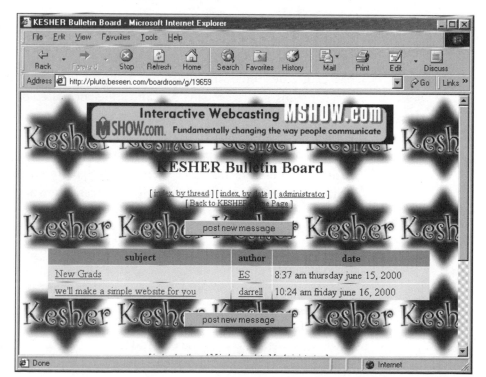

Figure 7.1

Bad use of a background graphical pattern

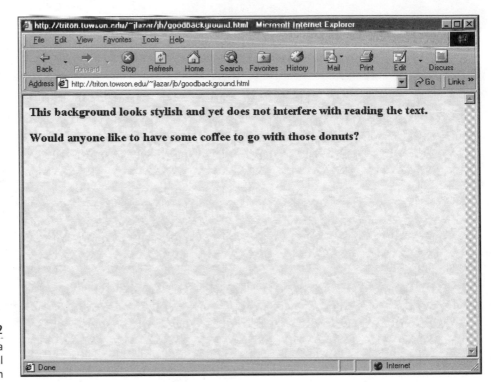

Figure 7.2

Good use of a background graphical pattern

Color

In the physical world, color has embedded meaning, usually culturally based. In the American culture, at a simplistic level, red means stop and green means go, red means hot and blue means cold, black means death and white means birth, and green represents money and greed.[16,17] These embedded meanings of color differ from culture to culture; for instance, the color white is symbolic not of birth, but of a funeral in Japan or India.[16,18] Although there are universal symbols that represent basic needs such as restaurants, lodging, and handicapped access, there are no universal meanings for color. Different cultures can interpret colors very differently.[16] If a web site is going to be used by an international audience, web designers should be sensitive to this fact, and should not overuse colors that could have a negative connotation for the targeted users. More information on designing for international user populations can be found by reading DelGaldo and Nielsen.[19]

On the web, the color of text also may have embedded meaning. Although there is no specific cultural meaning behind it, the early standards for text colors were that blue text indicated a hyperlink, and purple or red text indicated a hyperlink that had already been visited.[4] Because this has been a standard, users may expect that, when they see blue or purple text, they are looking at a link, even if the link is not underlined.[4] Therefore, blue text or purple text should not be used unless the text is a hyperlink, since the user may interpret blue or purple text that way.[15] In addition, since users are familiar with these web standards and what they mean, the web developer should not change these default link colors of blue for unvisited links and purple for visited links. For instance, if the web developer were to make all links, visited or unvisited, the color blue, this would decrease the amount of navigation information available to the users. They would not know whether they had visited the web page at the other end of the link.[20,21]

The color of text must have a planned contrast to the background color. Black text on black background will obviously not be perceptible, but combinations such as blue text on a black background or yellow text on a white background can also be difficult for users to discern. A good guideline is to use dark text (such as black) on a light background, or light text (such as white or yellow) on a dark background. Figure 7.3 shows an example of yel-

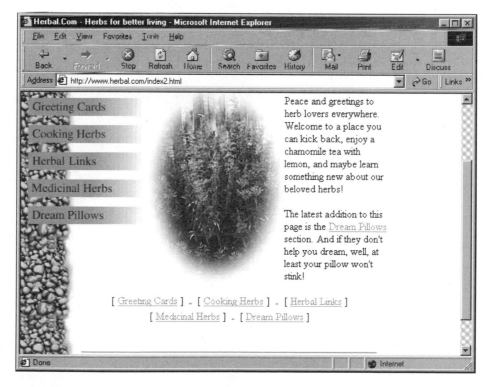

Figure 7.3

An example of yellow text on a white background

low text on a white background, which is very hard to read. Also, avoid using words in which each letter is a different color, because it is the equivalent of each letter jumping out, saying "look at me!" and this makes it very hard for the user to comprehend the entire word. A user's home page (shown in Fig. 7.4) provides an example of this faulty technique. The same rule applies to multicolored backgrounds; they "jump out" for the user's attention, and make it harder for the user to read the text. Regardless of what color combination is used, it is important to not use too many different colors. Human factors guidelines suggest using no more than four colors on a single display and seven colors on a set of displays, so as not to overwhelm the user.[3]

Figure 7.4
An example of a
multicolored word

Text

On the web, most content is provided in the form of text. There are a number of different qualities related to the presentation of the text. Text color was discussed in the previous section. The next paragraphs will discuss font size, font face, text spacing, and text length.

Font Size and Face

Font size is an interesting attribute. The web developer can set a font size, either using the headers, such as <h1>, the <font> tag, or style sheets. However, the user can overrule any of these, and make the font appear in the size that they prefer. Generally, font size remains the same throughout most of the text. Larger font sizes are used to emphasize certain sections, or for subheadings or titles. Different font sizes should not be used to show different topics. Instead, to show different sections, the web developer should use techniques such as titles, subheadings, bullets, horizontal rules, and extra white space. In addition to the font size, the web developer can also specify the font face (also known as the typestyle). Like the font size, the choice of font face can be overruled by the user. Furthermore, all browsers can handle different sizes of text. However, browsers cannot necessarily handle all different font faces. The available font faces depend on which font sets are installed into the computer.[22] The web developer should not specify one font only, but rather, should provide a list of fonts, in case one of the fonts specified is not available.[22] Fonts that are available on most browsers include Times New Roman and Arial, so it might be appropriate to specify one of those two fonts as the last alternative in the list of fonts. Finally, although it should be obvious, all text should not be in capital letters, which has the presentation effect of "screaming."[15]

Text Spacing

The text on a web page should not be one continuous blob of text. Instead, the text should be broken up into sections. This aspect of page layout comes from the area of graphics design. The text that appears on a web page should be easy to scan for the user.[4] Most users do not read all of the text on a web page. Instead, users tend to scan the content to find exactly what they are looking for.[4] Therefore, the text should be broken into sections, with titles for each section, and headings. When possible, there should be some type of overall layout scheme in the web page. Objects and text should not be inserted randomly on the page, with a picture on the left, with text centered, then a picture on the right, with the text left-justified. This type of layout will just frustrate the user. Instead, a grid structure should be chosen, such that the certain objects, content, titles, etc., always appear in the same location on the web page.[20] For example, if the graphics are always centered, the text is always left-justified, and the titles are always bolded and left-justified; this will provide some structure for the user. The user will expect to find certain information located in certain parts of the web page, and by providing an overall structure that is similar throughout web pages, the user will have a more positive and less frustrating experience with the web page.[20] Some of techniques for spacing text throughout a web page include bulleted lists (using the <UL> tag), line breaks (using the <br> or <p> tags), and horizontal rules (using the <HR> tag).

Text Length

A web page should not be too long. There is no standard definition for "too long," since it all depends on a number of factors, including screen size and browser window size. For example, the Yale Style Guide suggests approximately four screens full of information.[15] Common sense should be used in deciding on the length of a web page. A user should not usually need to scroll down through 35 screenfulls of information. Occasionally, a web page must be long due to the nature of the information. (For example, see http://thomas.loc.gov, the Thomas web site sponsored by the Library of Congress.) In that case, a relatively long page is acceptable as long as the user is aware that this is a long document, and provided that some type of navigation through the document (such as anchors to the major sections of the document) is available.

▶ 7.3 CONTENT CONSIDERATIONS

Content

Content is at the heart of the web page. Users are coming to a specific web page because of the content (in most cases, the information) that it contains.[10] Without content, the users have no reason to visit a web site.[10] The requirements gathering should have assisted in determining what types of content the users want (for more information, see Chapter 4). At this point, it should have already been determined what content will be included in the web site. The content should be provided by the client or developed by the client with the assistance of the web development team. In developing the content, the terminology and the writing style used in the content should be appropriate to the targeted user population. Writing for an audience of 10-year-olds should be very different from writing for an audience of surgeons.

Users should perceive that the quality of the content is high.[10,11] Content should be accurate, timely, grammatically correct, and appear to be trustworthy and believable.[11] Out-of-date content (unless posted for historical purposes and clearly stated as such) can affect the user's perception of quality content. Recent research has found that as users get acquainted with the structure and navigation of the web site, the usability becomes less of a consideration (because it becomes habitual for the user), and the importance of quality content increases.[12] Content is a factor in an emerging concept called *motivational quality*, which determines why users return to web sites.[13] If content appears to be out-of-date, biased, or incorrect, it tends to negatively color the user's perception of the quality of the web site, decreasing the chance that the user will return. Content should be continuously updated and improved, providing a meaningful reason for the user to return to the web site.

Identification

Let's compare various print media. When reading a typical book, people usually pick up the book and read it starting from the beginning.[15] It is rare for the reader to "jump into" the middle of the book.[15] All of the pages in the book are contained within the physical book covers, so if the reader is reading a page in the book, there are physical clues as to the overall layout of the book. The title page provides information on who the author or editor of the book is, and when the book was published. Compare the book with a newspaper. The newspaper has a new issue every day. Each article can be read individually; there is no need to read the articles in a certain order or pattern. Each newspaper article can be written by a different person. In a newspaper, each article clearly identifies who wrote it. The top and bottom of a newspaper page include information such as the name of the newspaper, the date published, the newspaper section (sports, metro, arts, etc.) and the page.

Context Information

In this example, a web page is similar to a newspaper. The user can jump from article to article, and there is no logical order necessary for comprehension. The user can jump from another web site directly into a web page deep within a web site. Because of these considerations, when viewing a web page, the user needs to have context information on who is speaking, and when the information was last updated.[15] Each page should include this information, and be able to stand alone. Users should be aware of how current the information is. If the information is out of date, users may have a low opinion of the quality of the web site. Furthermore, out of date information may not provide any useful content for the user.

Sponsor Information

It is also important to clearly identify who is sponsoring the web page. This can be as simple as a line at the bottom of the web page, or a copyright statement. On the web, the source of the information can sometimes be unclear. The source of the information is directly related to the quality of the information. Data coming from the Department of Education will usually be reliable, whereas data coming from a sixth grader who was doing a science project might have questionable validity. If the users don't know who is supplying the information, how will they be able to trust the information? The issue of trust is becoming increasingly important with e-commerce sites, but the trust issue is not limited to this type of site: Users want to interact with a web site that they can trust. They do not want to interact with a web site that provides untrue or questionable information, and if they discover questionable content, chances are good that the user will not return.

Contact Information

Users may have questions about the organization that are not answered by the web page. Therefore, contact information should be included at the end of every page. At minimum, an e-mail address should be provided. Ideally, the phone number, fax number, and mailing address of the organization should be provided somewhere on the web site.[15] If it is possible, this information should be offered at the bottom of every web page, for users to easily locate. If this is not possible, then there should be one web page on the web site that provides all of this contact information.

An example of a web page that does not follow any of these rules is Potlatch Paper (see Fig. 7.5). When you access the home page, it does not identify who sponsors the web page, what the web page is about, when the web page was last updated, or who to contact with questions. The same problems are true of the Napkin Design web site (see Fig. 7.6). On the other hand, the web site of the Decision Sciences Institute provides a header at the top and at the bottom of the web page and provides the date last updated, as well as an e-mail address to contact with any questions (see Fig. 7.7).

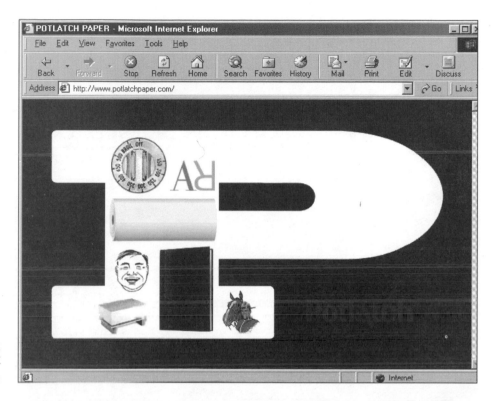

Figure 7.5
A web site with poor
contact information

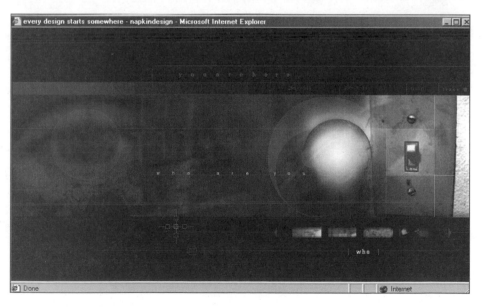

Figure 7.6
A web site with poor
contact information

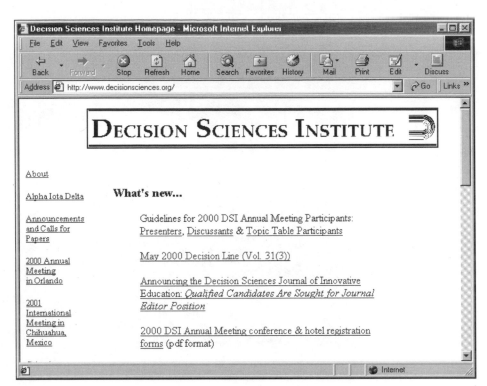

Figure 7.7
A web site with clear
sponsor information

Page Titles

Each web page should have a clear title. The title should tell what the user can expect from the content on that web page. There are actually two different titles on a web page: one that appears on the web page itself, and one that appears in the title bar of the browser. The title that appears in the title bar of the browser is the title that the web developer inserts in between <title> tags in the <head> of the HTML document. This title bar is very important because most search engines use those titles extensively. When a search engine provides a list of web pages, usually the first piece of data provided is the title of the web page, from the data provided by the <title> tags. The responses provided by the search engine Google show that the web page title is the first thing that the user sees (see Fig. 7.8). More information on submitting web pages to search engines is available in Chapter 11 on marketing your web site.

Figure 7.8

The Google search engine displays the web page title first

SUMMARY

Individual web pages should be designed with a number of user considerations in mind; the most important of these considerations is a fast download speed. This is not to say that all plug-ins, graphics, and Java Applets are bad; rather, before including any of these features, it is important to consider whether these extras will add value to the user experience. There is no need for a Java Applet that provides navigation, since it will not add anything to the user experience, and it will increase download time for a web page. On the other hand, if the Java applet does something outstanding that adds to the user experience, it might be worth the extra download time. When choosing the colors, page layouts, and graphics, the needs of the user should always come first.

Deliverables

At this point, you should have:

1. Determined what user factors are important to consider in the page layout
2. Chosen any graphics that will be included
3. Chosen clear page titles
4. Chosen a color scheme
5. Considered text layout and fonts

Discussion Questions

1. What is chunking and how does it relate to page layout on the web?
2. What factors influence download speed, and which of these factors can the web development team control?
3. What are three factors that influence the user's perception of quality content?
4. Why is it not a good idea to require that users download a plug-in application?
5. Why might animation be distracting, and where might animation be appropriate?
6. How is a web page like a newspaper, and why do you need to provide identifying and contact information on every page?
7. How do search engines use page titles?
8. What are the default colors for unvisited and visited links on web pages, and why should web designers use those default colors?

REFERENCES

1. Preece, J., Rogers, Y., Sharp, H., Benyon, D., Holland, S., & Carey, T. (1994). *Human-Computer Interaction*. Wokingham, England: Addison-Wesley.
2. Miller, G. (1956). The magical number seven, plus or minus two: Some limits on our capacity for processing information. *Psychological Review, 63*(2), 81–96.
3. Shneiderman, B. (1998). *Designing the User Interface: Strategies for Effective Human-Computer Interaction* (3rd ed.). Reading, MA: Addison-Wesley.
4. Nielsen, J. (2000). *Designing Web Usability: The Practice of Simplicity*. Indianapolis: New Riders Publishing.
5. Ramsay, J., Barbesi, A., & Preece, J. (1998). A psychological investigation of long retrieval times on the World Wide Web. *Interacting with Computers*, 10, 77–86.
6. Sears, A., Jacko, J., & Borella, M. (1997). *Internet delay effects: How users perceive quality, organization, and ease of use of information*. Proceedings of the CHI 97: Human Factors in Computing, 353–354.
7. Lazar, J., & Norcio, A. (1999). *To err or not to err, that is the question: Novice user perception of errors while surfing the web*. Proceedings of the Information Resource Management Association 1999 International Conference, 321–325.
8. Lazar, J., & Norcio, A. (2000). System and Training Design for End-User Error. In S. Clarke & B. Lehaney (Eds.), *Human-Centered Methods in Information Systems: Current Research and Practice* (pp. 76–90). Hershey, PA: Idea Group Publishing.

9. Tiller, W., & Green, P. (1999). *Web navigation: How to make your web site fast and usable*. Proceedings of the Human Factors and the Web. Available from:http://zing.ncsl.nist.gov/hfweb/index.html.

10. Huizingh, E. (2000). The content and design of web sites: An empirical study. *Information & Management*, 37, 123–134.

11. Zhang, X., Keeling, K., & Pavur, R. (2000). *Information quality of commercial web site home pages: An explorative analysis*. Proceedings of the International Conference on Information Systems, 164–175.

12. Davern, M., Te'eni, D., & Moon, J. (2000). *Content versus structure in information environments: A longitudinal analysis of website preferences*. Proceedings of the International Conference on Information Systems, 564–570.

13. Small, R., & Arnone, M. (2000). Evaluating the Effectiveness of Web Sites. In B. Clarke & S. Lehaney (Eds.), *Human-Centered Methods in Information Systems: Current Research and Practice* (pp. 91–101). Hershey, PA: Idea Group Publishing.

14. Zhang, P. (2000). The effects of animation on information seeking performance on the World Wide Web: Securing attention or interfering with primary tasks? *Journal of the Association for Information Systems*, 1(1). Available at: http://jais.aisnet.org/

15. Lynch, P., & Horton, S. (1999). *Web Style Guide: Basic Design Principles for Creating Web Sites*. New Haven: Yale University Press.

16. Chen, G., & Sturosta, W. (1998). *Foundations of Intercultural Communication*. Boston: Allyn and Bacon.

17. Dix, A., Finlay, J., Abowd, G., & Beale, R. (1998). *Human-Computer Interaction* (2nd ed.). London: Prentice Hall England.

18. Axtell, R. (1991). *The Do's and Taboos of International Trade*. New York: John Wiley & Sons.

19. DelGaldo, E., & Nielsen, J. (1996). *International User Interfaces*. New York: John Wiley & Sons.

20. Navarro, A., & Khan, T. (1998). *Effective Web Design*. San Francisco: Sybex.

21. Rosenfeld, L., & Morville, P. (1998). *Information architecture for the World Wide Web*. Sebastopol, CA: O'Reilly and Associates.

22. Niederst, J. (1999). *Web Design in a Nutshell*. Sebastopol, CA: O'Reilly and Associates.

CASE STUDY #1

▲ Best Buddies Maryland

Based on the requirements gathering, it was apparent that the Best Buddies Maryland web site would need to be designed for maximum flexibility. The requirements gathering phase of the development of the Best Buddies Maryland web site revealed a user group spread across a wide age range (10 to 65 years), with diverse levels of education (middle school to advanced degrees), using slow connections (primarily dial-up modems), and having limited computer skills. To avoid alienating any of these user populations, the development team planned to avoid complex terminology and to use simple language as much as possible. Any text on the site would need to be clear and straight to the point. The user population would be viewing the web site with a variety of browsers, so the site would be designed to ensure usability regardless of the browser used to view it. At a minimum, the web site had to look and perform the same on the latest two versions of the two most popular browsers, Netscape Navigator and Microsoft Internet Explorer. Additionally, <alt> tags would be included in the site to aid those accessing the site with Lynx or a "reader"-style browser.

To facilitate those users accessing the site by dial-up modem (a group that represents 90% of the user population surveyed), the web site would be designed to perform well when users had a slow connection speed. Users might become annoyed if a web site took much more than 10 seconds to download. The Web development team planned that graphics would be kept to a minimum number and have minimum file size. Pages would be short. Sound and animation would not be included on the site. Even though Best Buddies Maryland did not wish to alienate any of the visitors to its web site, the long-term success of the organization could be tied to not alienating potential donors of money. In general, the development team planned to meet the special needs of the Best Buddies Maryland web site's user base by designing an easy to use, easy to understand, quick downloading web site.

The web pages would be developed using the following colors: light sea green, orange, gold, lavender, black, white, and blue. These are the colors used in the Best Buddies' logo, except for blue, which is the standard link color. The team planned to use a white background with black text wherever possible, to aid in readability. The links would be blue in order not to confuse users, who were used to seeing blue for links. The other colors would be distributed throughout the web site to help give a clear presentation. These other colors would enhance the look of the web site, to avoid having it look too sedate, as quite a number of users are under eighteen years of age.

The survey results concerning the web preferences offered little information about users' preferences regarding frames and most users lacked knowledge about web page layouts. Nevertheless, the team believed that it was necessary to use a frame-like navigation system to promote ease of navigation. When frames are used, the designer has to make only one navigation document that is then used as a frame for every page. However, according to the article "Top Ten Mistakes in Web Design," appearing in Jakob Nielsen's Alertbox column (<http://www.useit.com>), frames have been and still are a problem for bookmarks and printing. On the other hand, tables are harder to setup, but cause no usability problems. After deliberating the pros and cons for both options the team decided to use tables for their usability virtues.

The team wanted to design the web site so it would appear within the boundaries of a 480 × 640 screen, to accommodate all users. The web site would have to be readable and usable by Lynx users as well as by all graphical browsers. To achieve compatibility with the Lynx browser, <alt> tags would be included in the HTML documents wherever necessary. A consistent and uniform layout between all pages of the web site was deemed necessary to reflect professionalism.

The overall layout of the web pages would be a table with three cells with the main navigation on the left column. The top right cell would contain the title. The bottom right cell would be used for the main content of the page. (An image displaying this layout is shown in Fig. 7.9. Note, this is merely an example of the layout, the end product may differ in its use of color, graphics, fonts, and content.)

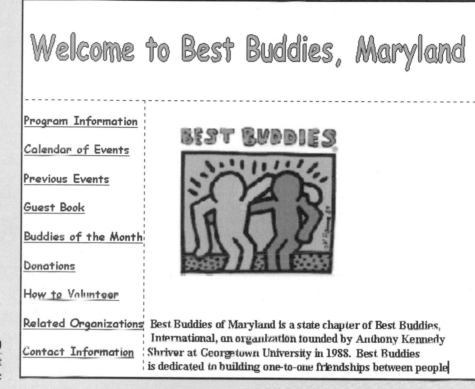

Figure 7.9

Layout for Best
Buddies web site

Because of the slow Internet connections of the majority of surveyed users, the graphical issue had to be considered carefully. Interviews with Best Buddies officials revealed that the logo of the organization should be included along with pictures taken by the development team at events organized by Best Buddies Maryland. These photographs would be placed on a separate page with a warning as part of the link to it informing users that the page contained several photographs and would take longer to download. The majority of the rest of the pages would have the Best Buddies' logo as the only graphic. Despite the desire of some users to see many animated graphics on the web site, the team ruled that such graphics would be of minimal benefit to the web site and could undermine the web site's usability and performance.

All pages on the Best Buddies Maryland web site would contain links to all of the web site's other pages. This would make navigating through the site easier for users because they would not have to return to the home page to view other pages. The links to different pages on the web site would be located on the left of each page and would remain the same throughout the web site. Although the links would all be in the same position on each page, the current page's link would be deactivated, which would aid users in recognizing their location within the web site. As was mentioned earlier, frames would not be used to navigate the site; rather, the upper-left cell of the table comprising each page would contain navigation links. The links would be in standard colors; they would originally be blue and change to purple when the user had viewed the page. For longer pages containing a large amount of text, links to navigate within the page would be located at the top of the page.

The design plan for the Best Buddies Maryland web site was conceived with the user as its central focus. Care was taken to ensure that users would not be frustrated by slow download speeds, confusing navigation, and language they did not understand. Additionally, the resources to be included on the web site would be based entirely on users' requirements. With this user-based approach, the Best Buddies of Maryland web site would have the best chance of serving as a beneficial resource to its entire user population.

 **CASE STUDY #2**

▲ Institute of Notre Dame

The Institute of Notre Dame (IND) web site is maintained by a single individual, Fred Germano. However, in the future, students might take over responsibility of maintaining the school web site. After a lot of debate, the web development team decided that a top priority would be to make the site as easy to maintain as possible. There are a lot of places throughout the web site that could be made interactive using JavaScript, DHTML, or some other new technology. However, the team decided that in the long run, IND would appreciate a site that was relatively easy to maintain rather than a site with new technology. Fred Germano mentioned that for the next year or so he would create most of the content for the web site. However, the long-term goal was to have the students place their own content on the site and maintain the web site. He believed it would be harder for students to maintain the web site if it contained a lot of advanced programming, such as JavaScript. Simplicity would be a key to successful maintenance. This expression of IND's long-term goals helped the team in their decision about not using new technologies, such as JavaScript.

Since IND is an educational institution, users might be accessing the web site using a number of different browsers, so the team wanted to make sure that the design of the web site would be compatible with most, if not all, browsers. The goal was to make sure that the web pages would appear properly in Microsoft Internet Explorer 4.0 and 5.0, Netscape Navigator 4.0, and Lynx. The web development team did not have access to Microsoft Internet Explorer 3.0, but because the site would not include JavaScript, the chance that the web pages would appear properly in these browsers is very good. In addition, since some users might be using Lynx or might have graphics turned off, the web development team would include <ALT> tags on all graphics. The <ALT> tags would appear if the browser did not support graphics or if the user had the graphics turned off. In addition, no browser-specific HTML tags would be used in designing the web sites.

One of the major issues with IND's current site was the lack of navigation. The web development team analyzed the data from the requirements gathering to find out what type of navigation would benefit IND the most. As they started drawing the navigation out on paper, they realized that the site would require two sets of navigation. After discussing ideas, the team decided to create a main navigation bar at the top of the page, which would allow users to jump quickly to other sections of the site. The navigation would include the user groups: Students, Faculty, Parents, and Alumnae. Once the web user is within one of these sections of the site, the development team implemented a section-specific navigation bar along the left-hand side of the page.

The problem with navigation on the left-hand side of a page becomes obvious when a user is browsing the site using Lynx, the text browser; Lynx does not handle tables well. When Lynx is parsing through the HTML, it displays the text in the order located in the file. However, when there are two columns within a table, the first column's table appears above the second column's content. In other words, in order to read the content of a page, users would have to scroll through the navigation on the page first. They will have to do this for every page they access. Understanding this flaw, and realizing that there isn't a perfect solution, the team decided to minimize the number of links in the left-hand navigation bar. This way, even if users had to scroll through the navigation to get to the content, they would not have to scroll too far. In addition, this same problem holds true for any web sites that use table-based navigation and are viewed in Lynx. Therefore, if users frequently used Lynx to view web pages, they should have become aware of the necessity of scrolling down on the web page to see the main content.

The main navigation bar would include IND's logo and name. The web development team created graphics so that the navigation bar would look beveled (three dimensional), and the IND logo would look engraved into the navigation bar. The graphics were made very small in size so that they would download very quickly. Furthermore, the same graphics were used on each page, so that the team could utilize the browser's cache to maximize response time. The graphics also would incorporate IND's colors of blue and white. In order for the links to appear on the blue background, the team changed the navigation link color to white. They felt that the main navigation bar provided all of the visual effects needed without being too overwhelming. See Fig. 7.10 to see the page layout for IND's web site.

After the team designed the main navigation bar, they worked on the sectional navigation bar. They wanted to incorporate the navy blue into the sectional navigation bar as well. However, after much debate, they decided against it. Once again, taking into consideration that students would maintain the web site in the near future, the team realized that if a student created a link in the sectional navigation bar and forgot to change the link's color to white, the web page would have a blue link on top of a blue background. They decided to choose a light gray color that worked with the wording "The Institute of Notre Dame" located in the main navigation bar.

Once again, navigation was the main focus for the development of the site. However, navigation encompasses more than the links that the users see on their screen. The di-

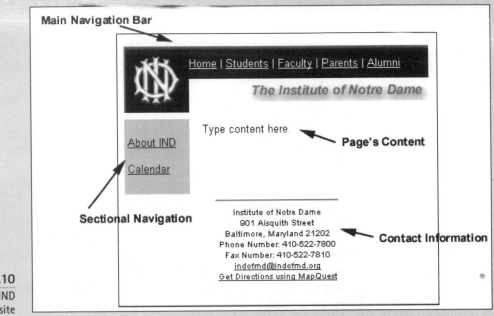

Figure 7.10

Layout for IND
web site

rectory or folder structure of a web site also plays a major role in navigation. There are many sites on the web that have their entire web site in one directory. They may have exceptional navigation on their site, but their navigational structure is less than desirable. Microsoft Corporation has an exceptional navigation structure. Each of their products has its own directory. For example, Windows can be located at http://www.microsoft.com/windows. The structure of the web files actually may provide some navigational information for the user. In practice, what this means is that a user might never have to go to Microsoft's homepage because the navigational structure is very easy to understand. The web site development team wanted to create a site based on Microsoft's navigational structure technique. They first created a directory for each of the main sections (students, parents, faculty, and alumnae). Any user could now access a specific section of the IND site, without ever going to the home page. Once they finished creating the main folders, they decided that it would also be beneficial to have other root folders, such as admissions and athletics. If users wanted information about admissions, they could go to www.indofmd.org/admissions. The navigational structure of the web site is as important to users as the navigational links.

IND's colors worked perfectly with the chosen site design. Navy blue and white are two colors within the 16-color palette offered by some older monitors and/or laptops. The light gray color for the sectional navigation bar was also chosen because it is another color in the palette. By using the 16-color palette, the team made the site much more accessible to people. When they visited IND, the team printed directions off the Internet using MapQuest.com. They figured that it would be very convenient for users to click on a Get Directions link, which would automatically link them over to MapQuest's site with IND's address in the destination fields already. A user would only have to type in their address to receive directions to IND. The user would not have to know IND's address, which would be very user friendly! The team contacted MapQuest and asked permission to link to their services.

After this project has been completed, the overall site design will allow IND to expand in many different ways. For instance, IND can choose a different color for each of the sections of the site. A user than would realize what section they were in based on the color of the sectional navigation bar. The team wanted to create something for IND that was truly scalable. The sectional navigation bar accomplished this goal. IND will be able to expand their site without worrying about navigation. The main navigation will remain constant, whereas the sectional navigation bar will grow with the site. Very scalable! Overall, the web development team believed the new design of IND's site to be very appealing, user-friendly, and scalable. Every user will hopefully enjoy visiting IND's web site and will eventually return.

CASE STUDY #3

▲ Eastman Kodak Company

Introduction

In addition to selecting the links that would appear on the home page and top-level pages, we needed to determine how these links would be laid out and presented on each page. These page layout decisions affected not only usability, but also each page's ability to convey the aesthetic and emotional qualities we desired.

Focus on Text

In contrast to our previous home page, which featured a large image map, we decided to make the new home page primarily textual. There were multiple reasons for this. The first reason was speed. Much existing research on Web usability points to greater speed and shorter download times as being of prime importance to users. Because text downloads faster than images, we chose to use textual links to enable users to navigate our site more quickly and without having to wait for images to download.

The second reason was flexibility. The previous home page and top-level pages consisted of large image maps with up to eight links, accompanied by text link equivalents. Consequently, changes to these pages were very infrequent and difficult to make. Usually, an existing item had to be removed in order to accommodate a new item. On rare occasions, new links were added without removing any of the existing ones, which was awkward in terms of visual design. As an example, the introduction of the "Kodak Picture Network" (an online picture management / sharing service) in 1997 required a home page link to learn about, join, and use the service. Of the existing home page links at the time, eight were gray buttons at the bottom of the image map, and one—"What's Hot"—was a graphical link in the upper right-hand corner. (Refer back to the figure in Chapter 3 showing the previous home page.) In order to provide a link to the "Kodak Picture Network," a ninth gray button was placed on top of the other eight—a solution that met the business requirements, but was not an elegant design solution. Because the new home page would be mostly textual, it could easily be modified to reflect the nature of the site. We could add, change, or remove links without much effort whenever necessary to accommodate new or changing content, address usability issues, and make special announcements.

The Look of the New Pages

Designing the look of the new home page proved to be a difficult task. We were dealing with several groups of links, and we wanted to present them in such a way that would not overwhelm the user. We also wanted to showcase photography and the great imagery that would be expected of Kodak. We tried an exercise in which each member of the multifunctional working team sketched his or her own concepts of what the new home page should look like, then laid the sketches out for all to see and from which to derive inspiration.

Ultimately, the duty of producing initial concept sketches of the new home page fell to our lead visual designer, who produced very basic layouts for us to show participants in our second set of usability tests, where users were presented with actual screen layouts (discussed in detail in Chapter 10). The layouts were similar, involving two alternative arrangements of the same components, and usability test participants were evenly split between which layout they preferred.

The designer proceeded to create several composites of new home page concepts, based on the layouts, with different color combinations and different uses of images. They were circulated among the kodak.com user experience group for comments. Many colleagues offered feedback, but they did not consistently favor any one concept over another.

After we had refined the links and groups to address the issues raised in the first usability test, the visual designer again developed a composite design, incorporating the color scheme and visual elements from one of the composites that had received a number of favorable comments, as shown in Fig. 7.11.

When the results of the second usability test (discussed in detail in Chapter 10) became available, required changes to the links and groups were minimal. All that remained at this point was to finalize the visual design of the home page. The visual designer worked with input from the rest of the team to develop the design that was presented to kodak.com users in the preview survey. (The details of the survey are discussed in Chapter 11.) After exmaining a few days' worth of survey respondents' comments, he made some final modifications to the design, which was used in the site launch (Fig. 7.12).

Figure 7.11
The composite design
presented by the
visual designer before
usability testing

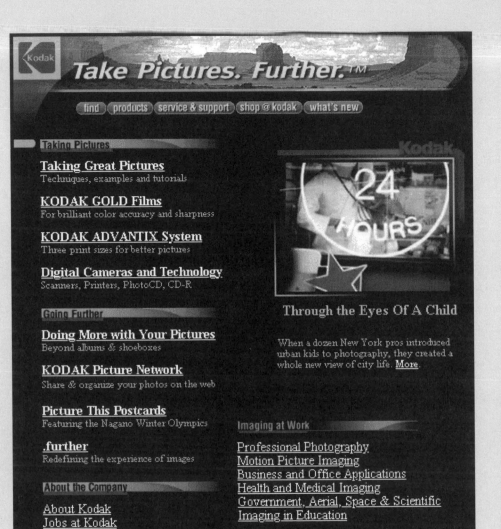

The other top-level pages were designed to follow the same groups of text links and visual design motif, as shown in Fig. 7.13.

Kodak

Digital Cameras and Technology

find | products | service & support | shop @ kodak | what's new

Digital Learning Center

A wealth of educational, information, resources, and course material

Sample Digital Pictures

An Overview of Digital Products and Solutions
A gateway into our digital offerings

Digital Cameras
Our complete line, for everyone from the casual snapshooter to the professional

Scanners
For getting your pictures and documents into your computer

FlashPix Format
A "smart" format for handling digital images

Photo CD
Store pictures on a CD for display on a computer or television

Writable CD
Recordable CD media and equipment for storing and sharing large amounts of data

Inkjet Media
Specially formulated paper and transparency film for your inkjet printer

Dye Sub Printers
For professional quality prints of your digital pictures

KODAK IMAGE MAGIC System
A family of products and services designed to help you go digital and do more with your pictures

Figure 7.13

An example of a top-level page

Conceptual Design
of the Web Site
Designing for All
Browsers

CHAPTER

8

One of the most frustrating challenges facing web designers is the
need to design for numerous browser platforms.[1] For traditional information systems, systems designers knew everything about the
user. For corporate information systems, designers knew exactly what computers, what processors, what monitors, and what locations they were designing for within a company. For mass-market software packages, designers
could specify a minimum setup, for example IBM-compatible with 100 MB
hard drive space, 32 MB RAM, and so on. Welcome to the future—now anyone can look at a web site, using any browser at hand!

▶ 8.1 THE BROWSER CHALLENGE

The web environment is quite unlike that of past information systems. Although the web development team can try to learn as much as possible about the target population of users, once the web pages are posted to the web, anyone around the world can view the web pages (unless they are password protected) using a browser. The two most popular browsers used in viewing web sites are Internet Explorer and Netscape Navigator. And there are a number of other browsers, such as Neoplanet, Opera, and Lynx that are used as well. This variety would not be a problem, except that these different browsers can interpret the HTML differently. The exact same web page can appear differently in different browsers because of the way the browsers read HTML. This is a problem. And to make it worse, different versions (3.0, 4.0, etc.) of each browser exist, and they can each respond to HTML differently. Moreover, the same version of the same browser on a different platform (Internet Explorer 4.0 on the PC vs. Internet Explorer 4.0 on the Macintosh) can act differently.[1]

The Challenge of Users with Disabilities

Not only do web sites need to be accessible to those using different browsers, but web sites need to support a wide variety of users, including those with disabilities, such as visual or hearing impairment. The browsers utilized by users with special needs might not be able to interpret graphics or sounds. Textual descriptions of these web site components need to be supplied. The World Wide Web Consortium has a set of guidelines related to web accessibility for those with disabilities. For instance, these guidelines state that web pages should be accessible even when graphics and Java applets are turned off. For more information on the Web Accessability Initiative go to http://www.w3.org/WAI/.

The Challenge of Browser Incompatibility

How different can a web page look when viewed in a different browser? A quick look at the web site for Michael English can serve as an introduction (see Figs. 8.1 and 8.2). The whole section of "Newsbytes" displays properly only in Internet Explorer, not Netscape Navigator. In Netscape Navigator, the section of "Newsbytes" does not appear at all.

The Michael English site does note that it is best viewed in Internet Explorer 4+ or Netscape 6+. However, it is unrealistic to assume that all users will have Netscape 6+. Although most browsers are available for no-cost

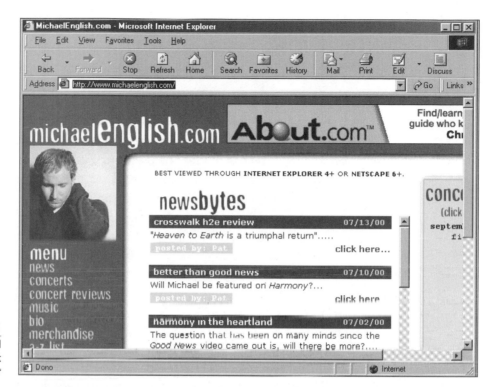

Figure 8.1
A web site displayed
using Internet
Explorer

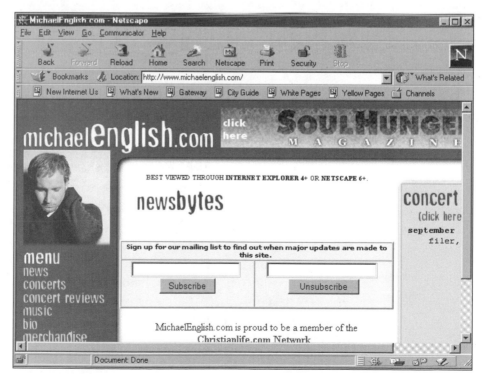

Figure 8.2
A web site displayed
using Netscape
Navigator

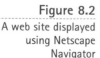

download, users do not frequently upgrade their browsers.[2] Most users do not install their own browsers; the browser is usually installed by either someone from the IT department, or a friend or colleague who enjoys using technology.[2] The user is therefore unlikely to be comfortable or familiar with how to install a browser. In fact, Jakob Nielsen estimates that it takes two years for an overwhelming majority of users to upgrade one browser version.[2] What this means is that once the browser is installed and working properly on a user's machine, the user is unlikely to change it. Furthermore, in many organizations (such as companies and universities), for security reasons, the users are not allowed to install their own software; they must use the software provided in the computer lab or installed on the departmental network. Therefore, it is unacceptable to require that the user has the latest browser, since (1) they might not know how to upgrade or change their browser, (2) they might not feel comfortable doing this, and (3) they might not be allowed to do any personal installation of software.

It is interesting to note that, at the time we accessed the Michael English web site, Netscape 6+ had already been unveiled to the press, but a full working version was not yet available for download at the Netscape web site. Since many universities and IT departments do not install the first release of any software and instead wait for a later version in which the bugs have been fixed, a large majority of users certainly were not using Netscape Navigator version 6 at that time even though the site notes that users should view the site with version 6.

▶ 8.2 STANDARDIZATION

It would seem that there is a need for standardization on the web. There should be one set of standards, and everyone should follow them, right? Well, a set of standards does exist. The World Wide Web Consortium has defined a set of standards for the languages and protocols used on the web. For instance, there is a standard for HTML, which is now at version 4.01. For more information on World Wide Web Consortium (also known as W3) standards, go to the web site <http://www.w3.org>. The W3 Consortium also offers a validator service at <http://validator.w3.org>. You can submit the URL of your web page to the validator, and it will check for compliance with HTML standards.

If you follow W3 HTML standards, however, it does not mean that your web page will appear correctly in all, or even any, of the browsers. The major browser companies design their browsers to be different. The browser companies try to win market share by adding new features that will work only in their browser.[3] These companies want to differentiate their product from their competitors', not to produce a standard browser. And unfortunately, it appears that the differences in browsers are only getting worse.[4] Therefore, when designing web pages, it is important to consider how the web pages will look in all browsers. It may be difficult to make the web pages appear exactly the same in all browsers, but a reasonable goal is to make sure that the web pages appear properly in all browsers.

Universal Usability

There is a current push for standards that will allow web sites to work properly, regardless of browser. This concept of making informational systems that anyone can use from any platform, any screen size, any browser, any location, and with any disability, is called *universal usability*.[5] Unfortunately, this movement is currently stronger in academic circles than it is in industrial circles. As we move forward, the need for universal usability, especially browser compatibility, will increase. Users will be viewing web sites not simply from a desktop computer. Instead, they will be accessing web sites from cell phones, palmtop computers, pagers, dashboard screens in cars, and other platforms that we probably have not even thought of at this point. E-mail and web content is already available on cell phones that use the *Wireless Access Protocol* (WAP). Web site design for all browsers and locations will be an increasingly important challenge. The first conference on universal usability (sponsored by the ACM) was held in November, 2000; for more information, go to <http://www.acm.org/sigs/sigchi/cuu/>.

Browser Usage Data

Since there is no definitive list of all web users, it is impossible to do either a census of users, or a strict random sampling of users, to determine what browser (and version) they are using.[6] A number of organizations have tried to estimate current browser usage. However, all of these estimates suffer from some bias. For instance, the most recent estimate of browser usage from BrowserWatch <http://browserwatch.internet.com> has 59% of users using Internet Explorer, 26% using Netscape Navigator, and the rest of users using 10 other browsers. However, these statistics are based on visitors to the BrowserWatch web site, which tends to be visited by computer professionals. Other estimates indicate that although Netscape Navigator had been the market leader, Internet Explorer has been gaining market share. It is also interesting to note that it has been estimated that 10% of users use neither Internet Explorer nor Netscape Navigator.[3] For more information on current browser releases, as well as statistics on browser usage, check the web site <http://browserwatch.internet.com>. Another great resource is CNET's browser reference, at <http://www.browser.com>, which has a lot of browser resources.

▶ 8.3 SOME COMMON BROWSER INCOMPATIBILITY PROBLEMS

There are a number of common browser incompatibility problems that tend to occur frequently and that require the attention of the web development team. The next sections will discuss some general and specific incompatibility problems. It is hoped that these common pitfalls can be avoided.

Missing End Tags

Internet Explorer tends to be more lenient when interpreting HTML tags than Netscape Navigator. For instance, if an end tag (such as </table>) is missing from a web page, Internet Explorer will assume that the end tag was supposed to be there, whereas Netscape Navigator will not display the table at all. This is a problem, but especially so when a web page uses tables for navigation. If a table is used as a container for the navigation and the content and if a </table> tag is missing, the entire web page will not appear in Netscape Navigator.

Consider the following HTML code:

```
<html>
<head></head>
<body>
A table will appear only in Internet Explorer <p>
<table border="2">
<tr><td>Name</td><td>Phone Number</td></tr>
<tr><td>Fred </td><td>434-555-2354</td></tr>
<tr><td>Ginger</td><td>654-555-1146</td></tr>
<tr><td>Larry</td><td>636-555-3234</td></tr>
<tr><td>Moe</td><td>565-555-3561</td></tr>
<tr><td>Curly</td><td>756-555-7453</td></tr>
<tr><td>Schemp</td><td>786-555-7654</td></tr>

</body>
</html>
```

The purpose of the preceding HTML code is to display a table, with a list of names and corresponding phone numbers. However, the </table> tag was left out. The table still appears correctly in Internet Explorer. However, this table does not appear at all in Netscape Navigator (see Figs. 8.3 and 8.4).

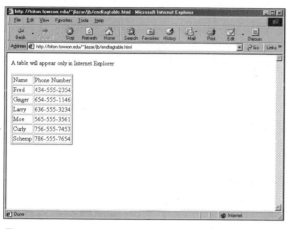

Figure 8.3
A table dislayed using Internet Explorer

Figure 8.4
A table dislayed using Netscape Navigator

An example of this problem can be seen in the web page for the Surry County Health and Nutrition Center. The home page appears normally in Internet Explorer, but does not appear properly in Netscape Navigator (see Figs. 8.5 and 8.6). This occurs because the "enter" text is included in a table, but the end </table> tag is missing.

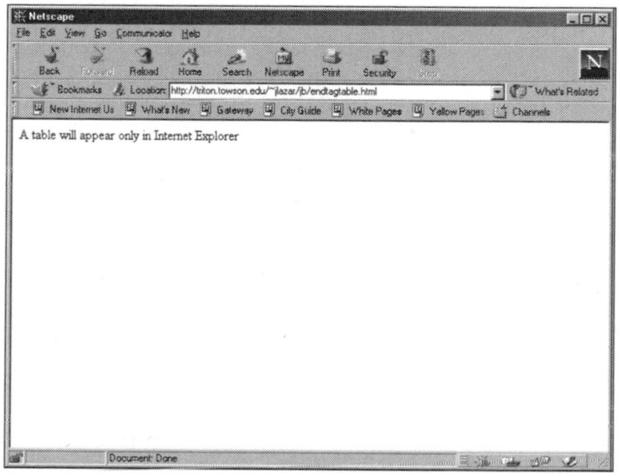

This problem of browser incompatibility can be fixed easily. All end tags should be included. This is not a browser problem as much as a problem

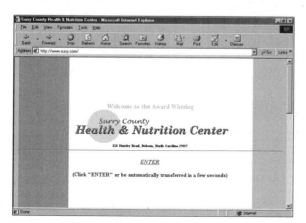

Figure 8.5
A web site displayed using Internet Explorer

Figure 8.6
A web site displayed using Netscape Navigator

with sloppy HTML.. Missing end tags can also cause problems with newer technologies such as cascading style sheets (CSS), so it is a good policy to always include the appropriate end tags.

Incorrect Nesting of Tags

HTML tags need to be nested in an appropriate manner. If a web designer incorrectly nests tags on a web page, Internet Explorer allows for more flexibility, but Netscape Navigator requires HTML formatting tags to be nested correctly.

In general, this is the correct way to nest HTML tags:

```
<tag 1><tag 2>Hello out there!</tag2></tag1> <tag2><tag3>Hello again!</tag3></tag2>
```

This example of nesting would be incorrect:

```
<tag 1><tag 2>Hello out there!</tag1><tag3>Hello again!</tag2></tag3>
```

Consider the following inappropriately nested HTML code:

```
<html>
<head>
</head>
<body>
This text should appear plain. <b>This text should appear to be bold. <i>This text should
appear to be bold and italicized</b>. This text should appear to be only italicized.</i>
</body>
</html>
```

Notice how the HTML tags are nested incorrectly. After the first sentence, the <b> tag makes the second sentence appear in bold. However, at the end of the second sentence, if a new style tag (such as <I>) is used, an end tag </b> should first be used, before the new style tag is used. Tags should be nested correctly, as in the following example:

```
<html>
<head>
</head>
<body>
This text should appear plain. <b>This text should appear to be bold.</b> <i><b>This text
should appear to be bold and italicized.</b></i><i> This text should appear to be only
italicized.</i>
</body>
</html>
```

Inappropriate nesting of HTML code can be a problem in different browsers, as Figs. 8.7 and 8.8 show.

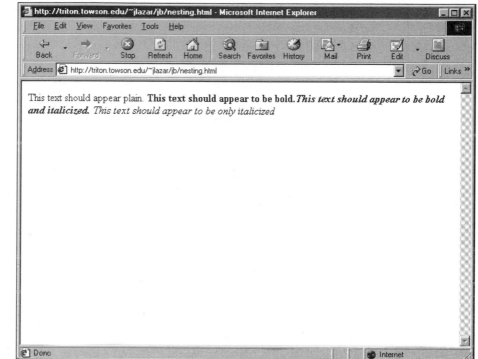

Figure 8.7
An innappropriately
nested HTML page
displayed using
Internet Explorer

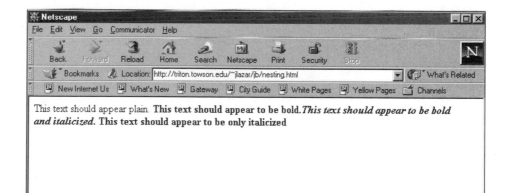

Figure 8.8
An innappropriately
nested HTML page
displayed using
Netscape Navigator

On Internet Explorer (Fig. 8.7), the first three sentences display correctly, and the fourth sentence displays in italic text. On Netscape Navigator (Fig. 8.8), the first three sentences display correctly, and the fourth sentence displays in bold (but not italicized) text.

Incorrect nesting can also be a problem if nested tables or frames are used for the overall layout of the browser window.

Link Titles

Link titles are an example of a feature that currently works in Internet Explorer, but not Netscape Navigator. Link titles are a part of the W3 HTML standard. A link title is a full description of a link on a web page. When a mouse pointer is placed over a link, a small bubble pops up, providing a fuller description of the link. This link title gives a fuller description of the link, giving the user more information and helping the user to determine link choices. A link title can be coded in the following manner:

```
<a href="http://www.towson.edu" title="The Home Page of Towson University in Towson,
MD"> Towson University</a>
```

In the above coding example, when the user places the mouse pointer over the link for Towson University, a link title bubble will appear, with the description "The Home Page of Towson University in Towson, MD."

An example of a link title in Internet Explorer is displayed in Fig. 8.9. When the mouse pointer is moved over the link for "Call for participation," a bubble pops up, describing the link in greater detail. The same web page in Netscape Navigator (see Fig. 8.10) shows that the link title does not appear. The <a> tag is still interpreted correctly by Netscape Navigator, but it ignores the link title attribute. Although Netscape Navigator does not offer the link title functionality, there is no functionality problem when the Netscape Navigator browser reads a web page with a link title. Netscape just ignores the link title, and its presence or absence does not cause any problems. Therefore, the web page designer should use link titles. Similarly, the hover feature of cascading style sheets works only in Internet Explorer, but it does not reduce the functionality or usability any in Netscape Navigator.

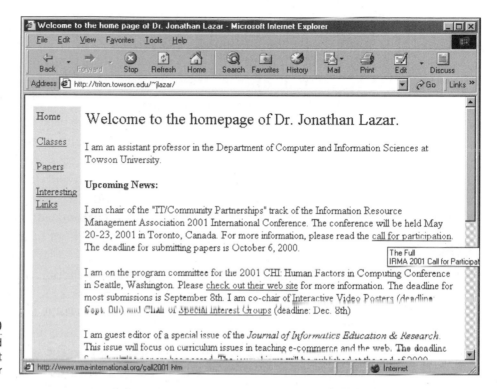

Figure 8.9

A web site displayed using Internet Explorer

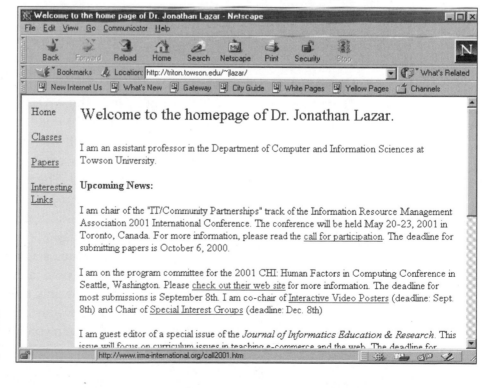

Figure 8.10

A web site displayed using Netscape Navigator

Browser Compatibility for Advanced Web Programming

Web pages can now be designed with more interactivity and more control over design by the use of JavaScript, cascading style sheets (CSS), and dynamic HTML (DHTML). Unfortunately, browser compatibility is also an issue with these newer technologies.

JavaScript is a scripting language that can be used to add interactivity to a web page by allowing the web page to respond to user actions, to detect conditions in the browser, and to respond accordingly.[1] Cascading style sheets (CSS) allow for more control over the presentation of content by providing for absolute positioning control and also allow for easier site maintenance.[1] DHTML also allows for a customized user experience by responding to user actions, using a combination of JavaScript, CSS, and the Document Object Model.[1]

Internet Explorer and Netscape Navigator support all of these technologies in a different manner. It is therefore necessary to check documentation for browser support for specific JavaScript, HTML, and CSS features, and then to test the web pages in a number of different browsers and browser versions. As long as the major browsers support the specific feature needed, the feature is safe to use. The user may disable the use of CSS or JavaScript (or it might not be available in the browser), so it is a good idea to check what a web page would look like if CSS and JavaScript features are not available at all. Since browsers allow the user to turn off these features, it is relatively easy to check for compatibility.

Unique Browser Features

There are some features that are not a part of the W3 HTML standards and are supported only by one browser. For instance, the <multicol> tag displays text in columns of equal width, but is supported only by Netscape Navigator, not by Internet Explorer. The <marquee> tag creates scrolling text, but works only in Internet Explorer, not in Netscape Navigator. There are also some HTML features that are supported by the W3 HTML standards, but are still not supported by both major browsers. The <iframe> tag creates a floating frame within a document, but is supported only by Internet Explorer. In most cases, if an HTML tag is not a part of the W3 Consortium standards, and is not supported by both major browsers, it should not be used in designing a web page, since doing so would be "asking for trouble." The only exception might be designing for a corporate intranet, if the web development team knows exactly what browser everyone will be using, and this is an enforced corporate policy.

The Customization Issue

In the web environment, the end user has ultimate control over how web pages are presented. The user can choose to use any browser and, in addition, can easily choose to turn off certain features. For instance, users may set their browser to reject all cookies. Users may set their browser to not display any graphics. Users may set their browsers not to download Java applets, not to run JavaScipt, or not to use CSS. See Fig. 8.11, which shows how users can do this.

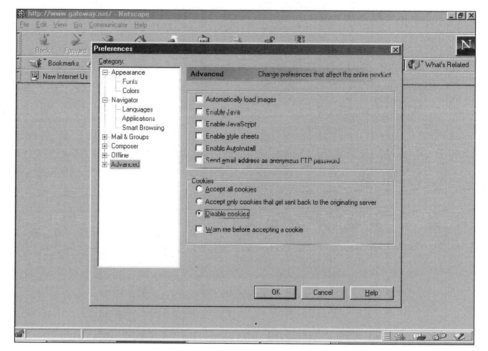

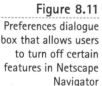

Figure 8.11

Preferences dialogue box that allows users to turn off certain features in Netscape Navigator

Because the user has ultimate control, ultimate flexibility should be planned into your web pages. In case the user turns off graphics, it is useful to provide ALT text (in the <IMG> tag) that will display text describing the picture. The screen shot in Fig. 8.12 shows that even though graphics are turned off, a description of the graphic still appears (see Fig. 8.12). This appearance also helps if someone has a disability and is using speech software to read their web pages aloud, because speech software cannot interpret a picture, but it can read the ALT text describing a picture. ALT text is an important part of the Web Accessibility Initiative <http://www.w3.org/wai>.

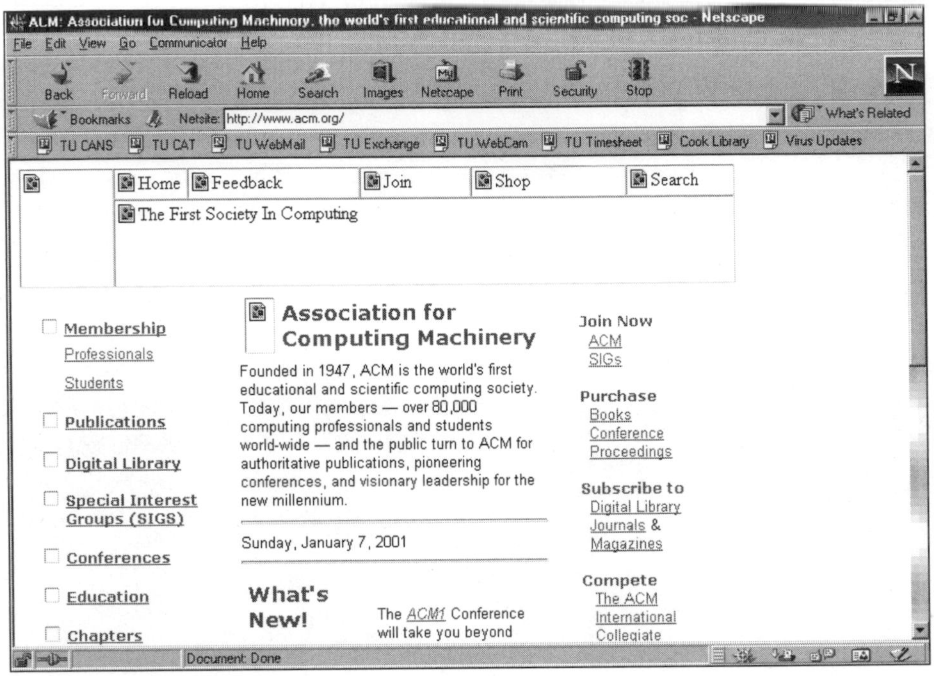

Figure 8.12

A description of a graphic appears when the Show Graphics option is turned off

Navigation should be provided for with text, not Java applets, so that if the user doesn't allow Java applets, that user will not be kept from navigating through the web site (see Chapter 6). If style sheets are turned off, the user should not receive a web page that is yellow text on a white background—a format that is nearly impossible to read. The web developer should consider all of these possibilities.

► 8.4 HOW TO DESIGN FOR DIFFERENT BROWSERS

It is important to consider that, in most cases, your users will be using a number of different browsers, as well as different versions of the browsers. A large number of people will not be using the latest browser version.[3] Generally, the best policy is to design web pages that will appear properly, regardless of browser, and will provide maximum flexibility to the user. By learning about the targeted user population's computing equipment in the requirements gathering, you can find that, say, 95% of the users are using a version 4.0 browser or higher. Even if a large majority of targeted users are using Internet Explorer 5.0, it is not a good idea to design a web page that will appear properly *only* in Internet Explorer 5.0. Although this is far from ideal, if you must use HTML tags that are specific to one browser, then it is suggested that you do one of the following.

1. Make very clear on the web site that for a maximum user experience, the user must use a specific browser. A strong statement such as "This web page will display properly *only* in Internet Explorer 5.0" should be included. A link to download the specific browser should be included. This is far from an ideal solution and should be used only in extreme circumstances, if at all. Not only could this hurt the user experience, but the web site will also appear to have been designed by an amateur.

2. You can ask people to click and select from two or three different web sites. One web site can be maximized for Netscape Navigator, and one can be maximized for Internet Explorer. It is also possible for users to select from a site that uses Flash, and one that does not. Some sites also offer users the choice of a web site that is maximized for those with text browsers or slow Internet connections.

3. You can write JavaScript code that will automatically deliver the appropriate web page to the user. If your content requires that you use browser-specific tags, then you will need to set up two different web sites, and create a JavaScript script that will automatically recognize the user's browser and then retrieve the web page that is appropriate for that browser.

The following JavaScript example will perform the task described in (3), above.

```
<script>
if (navigator.appName=="Netscape")
{
top.location.href='nnhome.html'
}
else
{
top.location.href='iehome.html'
}
</script>
```

The preceding JavaScript does the following:

1. It checks to see what browser is viewing the page.
2. If the browser is Netscape Navigator, the JavaScript will show the user the file nnhome.html, which is the web page appropriate for those using Netscape Navigator.

3. It the browser is not Netscape Navigator (usually meaning that it is Internet Explorer), the JavaScript will show the user the file iehome.html, which is the web page appropriate for those using Internet Explorer.

Of course, the filenames can be changed to anything that you desire.

► 8.5 THE NEED FOR TESTING

Since browser compatibility problems can ruin the entire user experience, it is important to address them during two stages of the web development life-cycle.

Avoid Browser Incompatibilities

During requirements gathering, the web development team collects some information on what browsers are being used by the target user population. However, it is still not safe to assume that everyone is using one particular browser. The cautious approach is to plan ahead; make sure that browser-specific features are not included in the conceptual design. It is better to have a less-striking web site and one that works equally in both browsers than a web site that is striking in one browser and unusable in the other browser.

Test for Browser Incompatibilities

The web development team also needs to *test* thoroughly for browser in-compatibilities! The team should view their web site in a number of differ-ent browsers and versions. Internet Explorer and Netscape Navigator, versions 4 and later, would be a good start. The web site should also be viewed in Opera (for compliance with W3 HTML standards) and Lynx. The web development team should ascertain whether the web site appears prop-erly in the different browsers, and whether all of the content, as well as any functionality, is available in the major browsers. There are a number of web sites and/or applications that can test for browser compatibility, such as Web Site Garage <http://websitegarage.netscape.com/>. Books such as Jennifer Niederst's *Web Design in a Nutshell* provide lists of HTML tags and their compatibility with different browsers and versions, as well as W3 HTML standards.

SUMMARY

Browser incompatibilities can negatively affect the experience of the user when viewing your web site. It is therefore necessary to plan in advance to consider browser incompatibilities in the web design process. Web developers should always include end tags, should nest their HTML tags appropriately, and should never use HTML tags that are supported by only one browser and are not a part of the W3 HTML standards. Web developers should check appropriate documentation to ensure that the tags and features being used are not limited in support to only one browser. Careful planning and thorough testing can ensure that users will be able to access the web site, regardless of which browser they are using.

Discussion Questions

1. Why do web pages appear differently in different browsers?
2. Why is it impossible to determine exactly what the browser usage is across the entire web user population?
3. What does universal usability mean?
4. Why is it unreasonable to require that all users upgrade to a specific browser and version?
5. What does the ALT attribute of a graphical tag do?

REFERENCES

1. Niederst, J. (1999). *Web Design in a Nutshell.* Sebastopol, CA: O'Reilly and Associates.
2. Nielsen, J. (2000). *Designing Web Usability: The Practice of Simplicity.* Indianapolis: New Riders Publishing.
3. Navarro, A., & Khan, T. (1998). *Effective Web Design.* San Francisco: Sybex.
4. Festa, P. (2000). IE 5.5 angers web standards advocates. *Cnet News,* July 13, 2000. Available at www.cnet.com
5. Shneiderman, B. (2000). Universal usability: Pushing human-computer interaction research to empower every citizen. *Communications of the ACM, 43*(5), 84–91.
6. Lazar, J., & Preece, J. (2001, in press). Using Electronic Surveys to Evaluate Networked Resources: From Idea to Implementation. In C. McClure & J. Bertot (Eds.), *Evaluating Networked Information Services: Techniques, Policy, and Issues.* Medford, NJ: Information Today.

Physical Design

This chapter discusses the subject of physical web site design. Physical web site design refers to the process of turning conceptual design requirements into a physical web site through developing the code. The conceptual requirements should clearly state the number of web pages, content, graphics, and navigation scheme. There are a number of different approaches to turning these conceptual requirements into coded web pages. Web developers might decide to write the code for the web pages by hand. Web developers might also use a number of software applications that assist them in writing the code. The idea behind these software applications is that they let the developer work in a WYSIWYG (what-you-see-is-what-you-get) environment, where the developer manipulates the layout on the screen, and the software application then creates the code. Word processing applications, such as Microsoft Word and Corel WordPerfect can provide basic web development features. Web development applications, such as FrontPage, Dreamweaver, and GoLive can provide a more advanced environment for creating web pages. A number of web sites also provide templates, graphics, and segments of code that can be downloaded and used in developing the web site.

► 9.1 DIFFERENT APPROACHES TO CODING WEB PAGES

Several methods exist for turning conceptual requirements into coded pages; hand coding is the most basic.

Coding by Hand

The most basic way of creating a web site is to code the web site by hand. This is especially appropriate for smaller-sized web sites. In such a situation, it is always a good idea to have a code reference book. Since the layout across the web pages on the site should ideally be similar, it is often a good idea to use a template. The web developer can create an HTML file that includes all of the page layout (color, style, etc.) and navigation information, without the content. That file can then be copied numerous times, and the content can simply be inserted into each web page. This way, the web developer does not have to retype the same code over and over. If possible, it is preferable to use cascading style sheets, because site maintenance becomes easier. A change in one file (the style sheet .css file) can immediately affect the style on all of the web pages on the site. If style sheets are used, the style sheet should be created first, so that all of the web pages are developed with the style sheet in mind.

When coding by hand, no special software tools are needed. The only requirement is to use a text editor. The text editor can be as simple as NotePad (on MS-Windows, see Fig. 9.1) or Pico (on Unix). The web developer can simply save the text file with the .html extension.

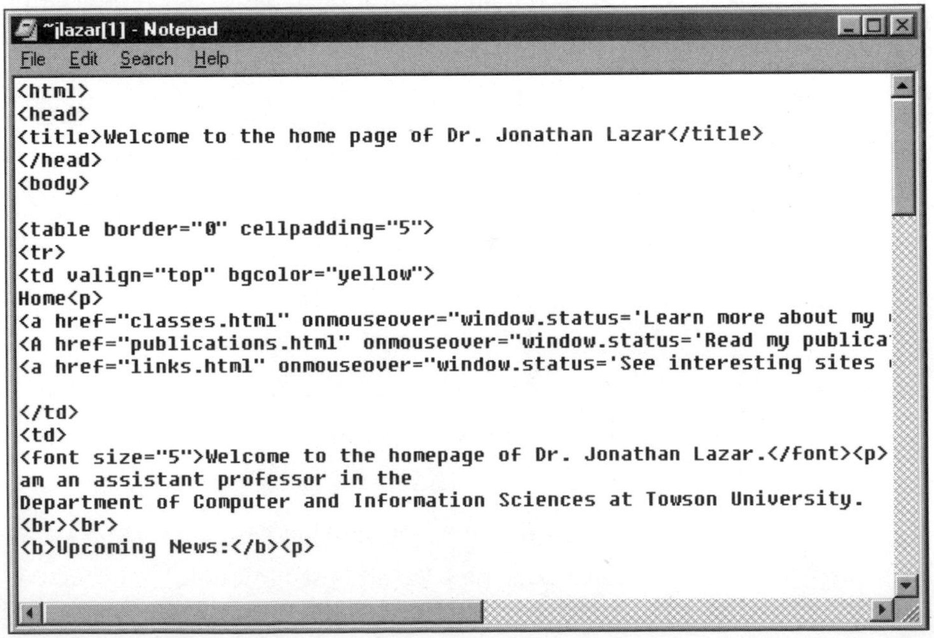

```
~jlazar[1] - Notepad
File  Edit  Search  Help
<html>
<head>
<title>Welcome to the home page of Dr. Jonathan Lazar</title>
</head>
<body>

<table border="0" cellpadding="5">
<tr>
<td valign="top" bgcolor="yellow">
Home<p>
<a href="classes.html" onmouseover="window.status='Learn more about my
<A href="publications.html" onmouseover="window.status='Read my publica
<a href="links.html" onmouseover="window.status='See interesting sites

</td>
<td>
<font size="5">Welcome to the homepage of Dr. Jonathan Lazar.</font><p>
am an assistant professor in the
Department of Computer and Information Sciences at Towson University.
<br><br>
<b>Upcoming News:</b><p>
```

Figure 9.1

An example of a text editor

Word Processing Applications

Word processing applications, such as Corel WordPerfect and Microsoft Word, can be used to develop web pages. When the web became popular, these manufacturers added basic web design capability to their word processing applications. Generally, these word processing applications can handle backgrounds, tables, font sizes and colors, text spacing, and creating links. Such applications can save a small amount of time, because the developer need not write the HTML code by hand. For instance, instead of writing out the HTML tags for a hyperlink, a web developer need only select the text, click on the "hyperlink" button, and type in the URL of the link (see Fig. 9.2). Tables can be created using only a few clicks, instead of typing in many <tr> and <td> tags. This can be a time saver. In addition, there are design templates set up for web pages in which a web developer can choose a design theme (as in MS-PowerPoint) that will specify font sizes and colors, background graphics, and bullet shapes. The web design functionality provided by these word processing applications is basic. However, if a web site is small, these word processing applications might be adequate for the job, and might save some time. The drawback to these word processing applications is that they can create only the simplest of web pages, and they tend to add a number of additional and unneeded HTML tags, which can increase download time.

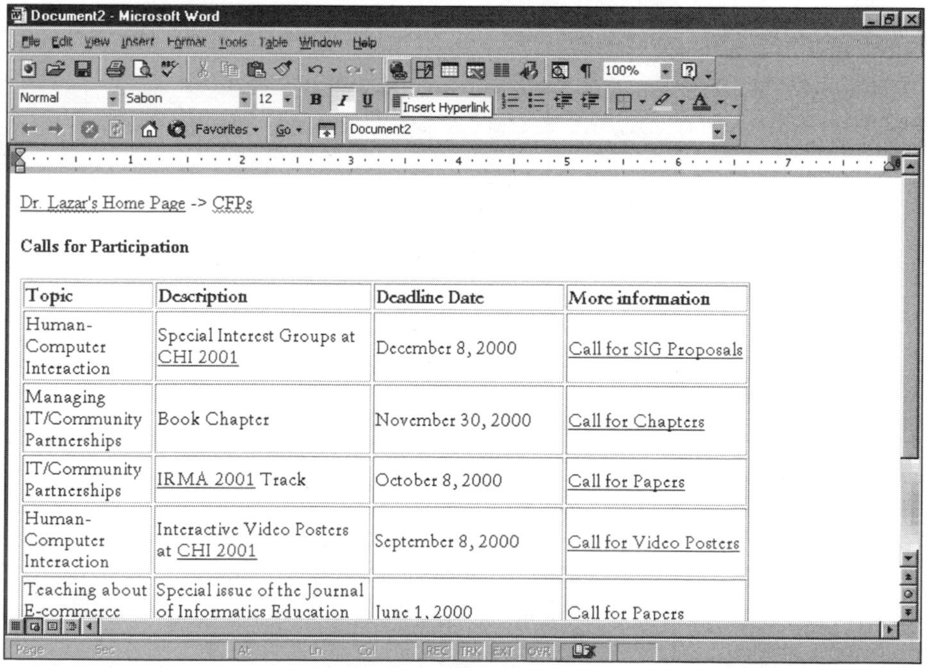

Figure 9.2

Basic web design capability in a word processing application

Web Design Applications

A number of software applications have been created specifically to assist in the process of web development. These applications can provide the web developer with advanced HTML functionality, and in many cases, can also create JavaScript and cascading style sheets. A number of helpful features, such as checking for linkrot, and estimating the download time using different connection speeds, can help the web developer with usability issues. Some of the leading web design applications include Microsoft FrontPage, Adobe GoLive, and Macromedia Dreamweaver. These web design applications work by letting web developers create their web pages in a WYSIWYG environment, in which the web developer describes how the web page should appear without specifying the HTML code. The web design application then creates the HTML (and in some cases, JavaScript) code "on the fly." See the screen shot of Microsoft FrontPage in Fig. 9.3 for an example. The web developer can then fine-tune the HTML code. A brief description of two of the major web development applications, Dreamweaver and FrontPage, follows.

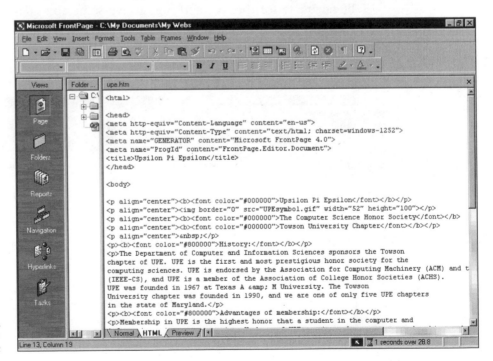

Figure 9.3

FrontPage creating HTML code

Macromedia Dreamweaver

Macromedia Dreamweaver provides advanced web design features that can save web developers time (see Fig. 9.4). Dreamweaver provides basic web

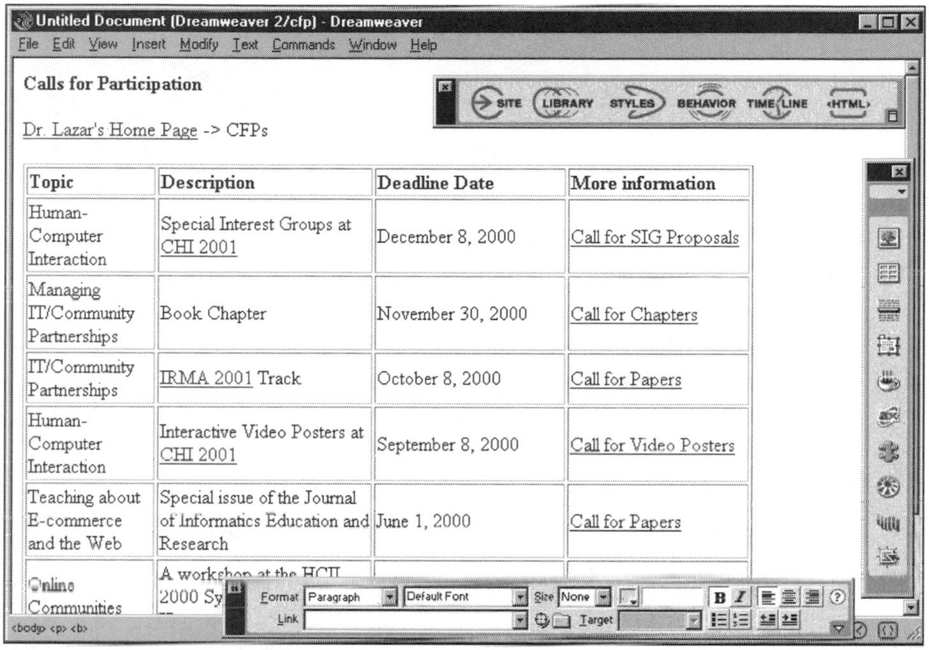

Figure 9.4
Macromedia
Dreamweaver

functionality, including text color and size, links, and bulleted lists. Dreamweaver also allows web developers to create web pages that incorporate tables, frames, forms, and JavaScript mouseovers, without writing any code. Dreamweaver has a number of nice features, including the ability to create cascading style sheets and clickable image maps. Compatibility is a major theme with Dreamweaver, which can convert web page files to be fully compatible with earlier browsers, and will not modify the code when HTML code originally created in another web design application is imported. A screenshot of Dreamweaver is shown in Fig. 9.4.

Microsoft FrontPage

Microsoft FrontPage is a part of the Microsoft Office package, and the interface layout is similar to those of the other Office applications, such as Word. Microsoft FrontPage has many of the same features as Dreamweaver, such as the ability to control text presentation, and create tables, frames, forms, and mouseovers. But FrontPage also has added features that allow the web developer to provide more powerful functionality without writing any extra code. These features are called FrontPage extensions, and these features only work if the web server (on which the web site will be hosted) is using the FrontPage server extensions. (Contact the ISP or webmaster to determine if the server is running FrontPage extensions.) The FrontPage extensions pro-

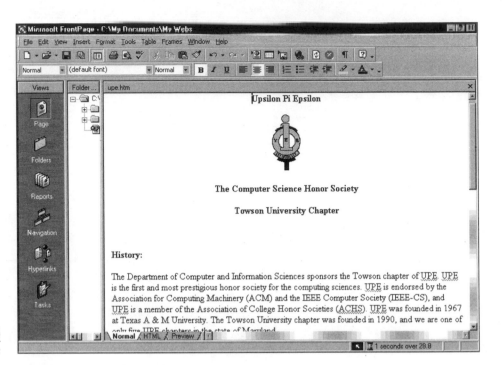

Figure 9.5
Microsoft FrontPage

vide a number of features without requiring the web developer to create or install CGI scripts. For instance, FrontPage extensions allow the web developer to insert search engines, time stamps, and form validation without writing any additional code. User responses to forms can automatically be saved in a web page or text file, again, without the web developer having to write any additional code. One drawback of FrontPage is that it tends to insert additional and redundant HTML tags, so some code clean-up might be required. A screenshot of FrontPage is shown in Fig. 9.5

Web Sites that Provide Assistance

In addition to software applications, a number of web sites can provide assistance in the physical design of a web site. Some web sites offer coding tips and/or code modules (in HTML, JavaScript, Java applets, and CGI Scripts) that can be downloaded and used in the development of a web site. For instance, it is possible to download a Java applet that will make text appear in flames without writing any Java code. Other web sites offer assistance in creating banners and buttons and other type of graphics. Most of these web sites offer these services for free. The following list provides a sample of these web sites.

▶ Web Sites that Offer Assistance with Physical Web Site Design:

ABC Banners   <http://www.abcbanners.com/>

ButtonMaker   <http://www.buttonmaker.com/>

FreeCode   <http://www.freecode.com/>

Java Boutique   <http://javaboutique.internet.com/>

Matt's Script Archive   <http://www.worldwidemart.com/scripts/>

WebMonkey   <http://hotwired.lycos.com/webmonkey/>

▶ 9.2 HOW TO CODE NAVIGATION

Navigation on the top or left side of web pages is frequently designed using tables or frames. The next few pages will discuss how to code these different approaches.

Table-Based Navigation

HTML provides support for tables, primarily for presenting rows and columns of data.[1] However, tables are frequently used to control the layout of the web page, providing an ideal manner for presenting navigation. The table serves as a "container" of sorts for the two main elements on the web page: (1) the navigation, and (2) the actual content itself. At a minimum, this means that the table has two cells. The cell on the left is for navigation, and the cell on the right is for the content (see Fig. 9.6).

▶ How to Code Table-Based Navigation

```
<html>
<head>
<title>An example of table-based navigation</title>
</head>
<body>
<table cellspacing="3">
<tr>
<td bgcolor="yellow">
Navigation<br>
Choice 1<br>
Choice 2<br>
Choice 3<br>
Choice 4<br>
</td>
<td valign="top">
Place all of your content here. In this second cell of the table, you can place all content, and the
navigation will remain in the first table cell on the left. More content. We want more content.
```

```
</td>
</tr>
</table>
</body>

</html>
```

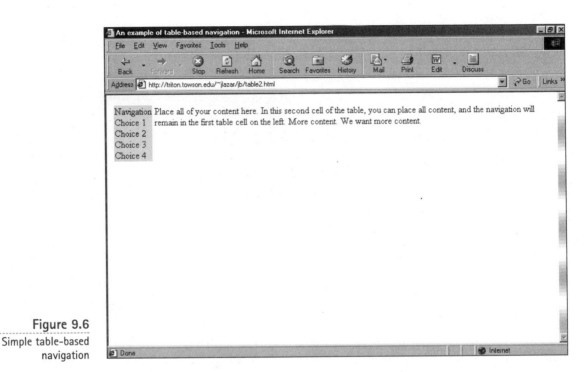

Figure 9.6
Simple table-based
navigation

What exactly is this code doing?

- The <table> tags are creating the table.
- Choice 1, Choice 2, Choice 3, and Choice 4 are items that represent links to the different sections of the web site. They can be replaced with something like <a href="history.html">History</a>, which would take the user to the web page on history when the user clicks on that link.
- The <td> tags are specifying the table cells.
- The first <td> tag is creating the table cell for the navigation, and the bg-color="yellow" is specifying that the table cell should have a yellow background, which will create the appearance of a separate navigation strip on the left side of the screen.

- The second <td> tag is creating the table cell for the content. The valign="top" serves to keep the content at the top of the table cell. The default is at the center, so without valign="top", the content would appear in the center of the screen.

Another way to provide table-based navigation is to place the navigation at the top of the screen, instead of at the left side. This could be done by creating two table rows. The first row could provide the navigation, and the second row could provide the content.

```
<html>
<head>
<title>An example of table-based navigation</title>
</head>
<body>
<table cellspacing="0">
<tr bgcolor="yellow">
<td>Choice 1</td>
<td>Choice 2</td>
<td>Choice 3</td>
<td>Choice 4</td>
</tr>
<tr>
<td colspan="4">
Place all of your content here. In this second cell of the table, you can place all content, and
the navigation will remain in the first table cell on the left. More content. We want more
content.
</td>
</tr>
</table>
</body>
</html>
```

How is this example different from having the navigation on the left side of the screen? In this example, we are creating two rows of data, not two data cells. The first row is specified to be yellow, marking it as our navigation bar. We split the first row into four separate cells, so that we have adequate space for each of our navigation choices. This is done by specifying four <td> tags within a table row. Since there are four table cells in the top table row, we will have four table cells in the second table row, unless we specify otherwise. By specifying <td colspan="4">, we indicate that our second table row should only consist of one table cell for our content (in other words, the table cell should span all four columns). Figure 9.7 shows table-based navigation with navigation at the top of the screen.

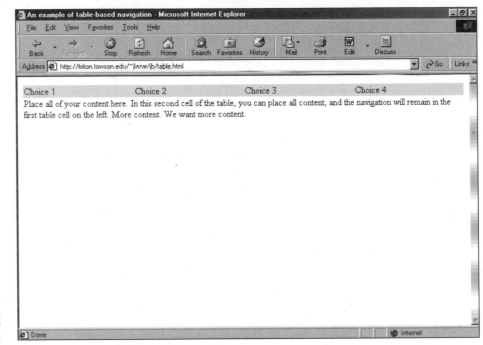

Figure 9.7

Table with top
navigation

There are a number of other possibilities for providing navigation through the use of tables on a web page. For instance, navigation bars on the left and the top could be provided simultaneously. However, all uses of tables for navigation are based on these two simple examples of using tables as "containers" for navigation and content.

Frame–Based Navigation

Frames can be used to implement navigation in web pages. A frame occurs when the browser window is divided, allowing more than one HTML document to be displayed in the window at a time. When setting up a framed document, there are a few different HTML documents involved. It is that combination of documents that makes up the framed window. Each document can be scrolled individually. For an example of this, see Fig. 9.8, a screen shot of the International Academy for Information Management.

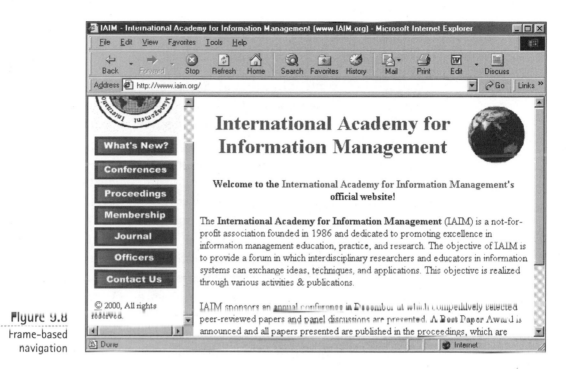

Figure 9.8
Frame-based
navigation

A framed document requires, at minimum, three HTML documents. There is the frameset document, which specifies what size the frames will be, and what the source documents will be. The frameset document will be the file that the user actually accesses with the URL. For instance, if a frameset document specifies that the browser window will consist of two frames, one frame that takes up 25% of the screen on the left, and the other frame that takes up the other 75% of the screen on the right, then there are actually three HTML documents involved: (1) The frameset document, which creates the frame layout, (2) the HTML document that will go into the left frame, and (3) the HTML document that will go into the right frame. Usually, navigation goes into the left frame and content goes into the right frame.

Here is an example of the code required to create a frameset document:

```
<html>
<head>
<frameset cols="25%,75%">
     <frame src="navigation.html" name="leftframe">
     <frame src="content.html" name="rightframe">
</frameset></head>
</html>
```

This code sets up a framed document with two frames in the document, one frame on the left side of the screen (25%) and one frame on the right side (75%). The documents that should go into each frame are stated (navigation.html, content.html), and names are given to each frame. These names will become important when we look at the code for our source documents. An example of frame-based navigation appears in Fig. 9.9.

We then need to create two other HTML documents, one for the navigation and one for the content. For the content, we just create a plain HTML document with our content. However, for the navigation, we need to pay careful attention to make sure that we create our navigation correctly. If we just place a list of links in the HTML document, then when the user clicks on a link, it will change the web page in the navigation frame, and the navigation will no longer be persistent for the user. We don't want this to happen because it ruins the purpose of the navigation. Instead, we want the navigation to function in the following manner: When the user clicks on the navigation in the left frame, the HTML document in the right frame changes, but the navigation stays in place. This can be done by placing the following code in the navigation document:

```
<html>
<head>
</head>
<body>
<a href="http://triton.towson.edu/~jlazar" target="rightframe">
Navigation choice 1</a><br>
<a href="http://triton.towson.edu/~jlazar/classes.html" target="rightframe">
Navigation choice 2</a><br>
</body>
</html>
```

Note the use of the *target* attribute. When the user clicks on the link for navigation choice 1, the default is that the document would change in the frame that the user clicked in, which is the navigation frame. But instead, the code listed above includes a *target*, which specifies that when the user clicks on the link, it should place the new document, not in the current frame, but instead in a different frame, the frame named *rightframe*. The main content frame was named *rightframe* in the frameset document. By targeting our frames correctly, we can use frames to keep our navigation consistent throughout the web site. It is important to note that frames can cause some confusion for users. Many users do not understand the concept of a frame, and therefore, may have problems printing framed documents and bookmarking framed documents. For instance, when the user is navigating through a frame-based site, the URL in the browser address bar does not change. Therefore, the URL can not easily be bookmarked (the user can bookmark the document frame, but not the entire frame layout, by right-clicking the mouse button on the frame), nor can it provide any location information for the user. Some authors even go as far to suggest that frames should not be used.[2] However, frames are just another tool in the toolbox of the web development team.

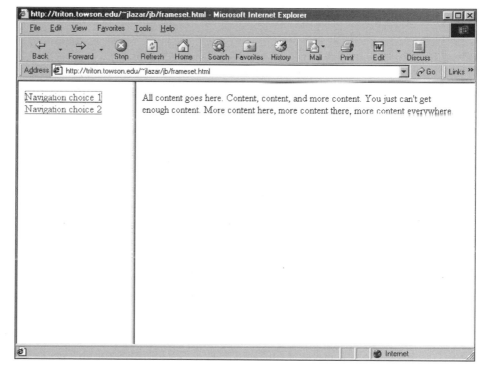

Figure 9.9
Frame-based
navigation

Navigation in Body of Document

Navigation can also be provided without any frames or tables. It is possible to place links to all important sections of the web site at the top of a web page. This is a simple way of providing navigation, but as long as the navigation stays present throughout the web site, this is an appropriate way of providing the user with navigation.

▶ 9.3 GATHERING CONTENT FOR THE PAGES

It is the responsibility of the client organization to provide the content for inclusion in the web site. Although the web development team is responsible for a number of tasks, it is generally not the responsibility of the web development team to create content. The web development team might, however, be provided with content on paper, which will need to be turned into an electronic format. The web development team might also be provided access to those who can verbally describe the content. If word processing files (or other data files) exist, it is an ideal situation for these files to be provided to the web development team. If data files exist, the web development team can simply cut-and-paste the content into the HTML files. If the web site is being redesigned, much of the content will already be contained within HTML files, so this content that will remain in the new site can simply be copied and pasted into the new HTML files. One note of caution: Unfortunately, in some situations, the web development team is forced to "sit on" the web site because the client organization has not delivered the content on time. This can be frustrating for all concerned.

▶ 9.4 TESTING THE PAGES

The pages must be tested for functionality and for browser compatibility.

Functionality Testing

Once the web pages are coded, it is important to test the web pages to determine whether they are functionally correct. The web pages should be accessed through a browser. At that time, the web developer can look to make sure that the text and layout appear appropriately. When problems occur, many times the problem is as simple as forgetting to include an end tag. For instance, if </a> is not included at the end of a link, all of the text after the link will appear underlined, as a link. Debugging a web page is relatively simple, because many problems on the web page are obvious to the eye. In addition, web development applications will generally detect any inappropriate code. Any advanced web programming, such as JavaScript, Java applets, or CGI scripts should also be tested to ensure that they work properly. All links should be tested to make sure that these links are taking the user to the appropriate page.

In addition, the World Wide Web Consortium provides a validator service that will check a web page for compliance with HTML standards. The validator service is available free-of-charge at <http://validator.w3.org/>. It is important to note that this service will not check whether a web site will appear properly in the different browsers. Remember that the major browsers are not in total compliance with the W3 HTML standards!

Testing for Browser Compatibility

Once the web pages are developed, it is important to test them to make sure that they appear appropriately in the major browsers. In theory, a web page should be designed to appear appropriately in any browser. This design is important because it is impossible to determine in advance what browser will be used to view a web page. But, the results of the requirements gathering should strongly influence this activity. If the target user population is relatively homogeneous in browser usage, then this should be a focus of the browser compatibility testing. If 90% of the target user population uses Internet Explorer 4.0 or higher (such as an organizational intranet), then this provides an important benchmark. However, the web pages should look appropriate in recent versions of Internet Explorer and Netscape Navigator, as well as Lynx. Many of the web design applications (such as Dreamweaver) provide the capability to automatically check for compatibility with different browsers and versions. For web developers not using a web design application, up-to-date browser versions can be downloaded from the Netscape <http://www.netscape.com> or Microsoft <http://www.microsoft.com> web sites. Older browser versions can be downloaded from a number of web sites, including: <http://www.cnet.com/internet/0-3773.html> and www.browser.com. If there is a web page that appears inappropriately in one of the major browsers, it is important to determine the cause of the incompatibility (some common problems are discussed in Chapter 8), and then to change the code so that it will appear appropriately in each browser.

SUMMARY

The major issues involved in the process of physical web design have been discussed in this chapter. Web developers may write code by hand, use a word processing application, or use a true web development application. A number of web sites also have code modules and graphics that can be downloaded and used to develop the web site. The content for the web site should be provided by the client organization. Once coded, the web site must be tested for functionality as well as browser compatibility.

Deliverables

At this point, you should have:

1. Written the code for the web pages
2. Tested the web pages to ensure that they work properly
3. Tested the web pages for browser compatibility

Discussion Questions

1. What are some advantages and disadvantages of using a web development application?
2. Why might tables be used, and how might tables be superior to frames?
3. When a team is creating a frame layout with three frames, how many HTML files are required?
4. Why is it important to test for browser compatibility?
5. What different types of currently existing web sites can assist with the physical design process?

REFERENCES

1. Niederst, J. (1999). *Web Design in a Nutshell.* Sebastopol, CA: O'Reilly and Associates.
2. Nielsen, J. (2000). *Designing Web Usability: The Practice of Simplicity.* Indianapolis: New Riders Publishing.

CASE STUDY #1

▲ Best Buddies Maryland

Based on the conceptual requirements, the web development team coded the web pages by hand. The content was provided by the employees of Best Buddies Maryland. After coding the web pages, the development team tested the Best Buddies Maryland site in Internet Explorer, Netscape Communicator, and Lynx. The web site looked exactly as planned by the development team when viewed in Internet Explorer (IE). An error in the code was found while browsing the site in IE, but it was not a browser-related error. It was discovered that the following line of code was left off the Affiliated Schools page: A:hover { background-color:white }. This error eliminated the effect of a change in background color when the mouse was dragged over a link in the navigation cell. In Netscape, errors relating to the font tags were found. The development team used "Comic Sans MS" as the font face throughout the site. When the Best Buddies Maryland web page was viewed in Netscape Communicator, however, the information in the lower left-hand section of each page reverted to the browser's font defaults (Times New Roman, in the case of the test browser). The development team discovered that adding font tags with the face attribute set to "Comic Sans MS" inside each <td> tag cleared up the problem. It is interesting to note, however, that the problem did not appear at all in Internet Explorer. The other browser compatibility issue associated with Netscape was that the background color of the links did not change when the tester moved his mouse over them. The cascading style sheets property "A: hover" is not supported in Netscape. This does not reduce the functionality of the site, but does make it less aesthetically pleasing. The Best Buddies Maryland web site was completely navigable in Lynx. The test revealed that <alt> tags were missing for the Best Buddies logo, but otherwise all links and information were viewable and appeared in a consistent order on all of the pages.

CASE STUDY #2

▲ Institute of Notre Dame

Because a large number of web pages had to be designed for the Institute of Notre Dame, it was decided that the web development team would first create a template that would include the basic layout, navigation, and graphics for each web page. This would not only allow the web development team members to create new web pages with ease, but it would also assist the Institute of Notre Dame in creating additional web pages at a later time. The team decided to hand code the template because most web development tools or word processors, such as FrontPage or Microsoft Word, tend to reformat the code to the way the program "thinks it should be done." In fact, some applications add numerous extra HTML tags. When all of the additional unnecessary tags are included in the web files, the file size grows, which leads to a longer download time. Since the template was a very important aspect of the design of the entire IND web site, the team wanted to make sure that the template included only the necessary HTML tags.

Once the team had a basic template for the web site, they tested the template in the different versions of browsers, Internet Explorer 3.0–5.0, Netscape 3–4, and Lynx. They discovered that Internet Explorer and Netscape interpreted HTML table tags differently. When the team opened the template within Internet Explorer, the web site looked exactly the way that was wanted. However, when the team opened the web site in Netscape, the table cell widths were completely "off." After testing a number of hypotheses with Netscape, the team determined that if enough content appeared within a cell to fill up one entire row, then Netscape would interpret the cell's widths correctly. Realizing this, the team decided to position a transparent image whose height was one pixel and whose width equaled the width of the cell. After they inserted the graphic into the cell, the template appeared the same within Internet Explorer and Netscape. Since some government agencies and schools still used the text-browser Lynx, the development team also viewed the template within Lynx. They discovered that even though the web page wasn't as pleasing without the colors and graphical layout, the web page was still completely usable.

After the team was satisfied with the results of the template, they then created numerous web pages (based on the template) and inserted the content. Since the IND web site was being redesigned, some of the content was already available in electronic format and simply needed to be pasted into the new web pages. To insert the content, some of the web development team members used Netscape Composer (a simpler web development application) to type in their content. Other team members inserted the content into the web page by using NotePad. Each member of the web development team was responsible for a "section" of the web site, such as Alumnae, Students, or Faculty. Since IND's web site contained a lot of information, breaking up the sections allowed each group member to concentrate on the content for one section only.

After the entire web site was finished, the web development team used Microsoft FrontPage's link checker to verify that there weren't any broken links. They also had team members check every link within their section. Most web users hate when they click on a link and they receive the famous "404—File not found" error. The team wanted to make sure that visitors to the IND web site did not experience the "404" error, but instead had a positive experience!

CASE STUDY #3

▲ Eastman Kodak Company

Developing Web Pages

The Web developers at kodak.com used and continue to use a variety of methods to implement Web pages. Most Web developers forgo so-called WYSIWYG ("What You See Is What You Get") authoring tools and instead hand-edit HTML with or without the help of HTML editing tools because of the ability to control exactly what elements are used and better understand how the underlying code will interact with various Web browsers. Because browser compatibility is always an important issue, the Web developers who created the actual pages that comprised this particular redesigned site hand-edited the HTML.

Web pages were constructed for use in the second usability test. This test was intended to require participants to actually use the page and follow links to existing sitelets in kodak.com. The site redesign did not include any changes in site functionality (e.g., development of new applications), nor did any of the redesigned pages contain scripts. Consequently, testing was limited to checking the new Web pages against different browser/platform combinations to ensure that the Web pages rendered as expected. There were no surprises uncovered during this stage of testing. The new home page designed at this stage appears in Fig. 9.10.

Take Pictures. Further.™

Taking Great Pictures
Techniques, examples and tutorials

Doing More with Your Pictures
Beyond albums and shoeboxes

KODAK Picture Network
Store and share your pictures on the web

Digital Cameras and Technology
Scanners, Printers, PhotoCD, CD-R

KODAK ADVANTIX System
Three print sizes for better pictures

KODAK GOLD Films

.Further

PictureThis Postcards

Shop at Kodak

About Kodak
Press Center
Investor's Center
What's New
Jobs at Kodak
Kodak Around the World
For Dealers and Developers

Large Fish Are Interesting!
This graphic and text is for position
the future it will link to a feature arti

Find | Products | Service & Support

Professional Photography

Motion Picture Imaging

Business and Office Applications

Health and Medical Imaging

Aerial, Space and Scientific Imaging

Government and Law Enforcement

Imaging in Education

FPO

Figure 9.10
The newly developed
home page

Usability Testing

One of the hallmarks of user-centered design is usability testing. Usability testing is different from functionality testing, or code walkthroughs, or any other type of testing that focuses on whether or not a technology actually works. Usability testing does not focus on whether the technology (hardware, software, web site) is functionally correct. Rather, it focuses on whether a specific technology is easy for the user to utilize. The theory behind usability testing is that although the system designers do the best that they can to create an easy-to-use system, the system designer is not the user. The system designer generally has more computer experience and is more technically knowledgeable than the user. However, the user has more experience with the specific task domain (the task that the computer will be used for). Even though system designers do their best to follow good principles for interface design, it is still impossible to predict how users will interact with a system. The only way to truly find out what works for users and what is frustrating is to actually have users test a system through the process of usability testing.

► 10.1 THE USABILITY MOVEMENT

Usability testing has been widely used in developing large-scale software applications, and, in general, has been popular for years with large-scale applications, because it generally saves money and makes for more satisfied users.[2] However, usability testing has not so far been a standard part of developing web sites; this situation is starting to change. In fact, usability testing of web sites is especially important. The web development design team has no control over what browser/version/download speed the user will have, and therefore, the web page not only has to be easy to use on one platform, but must be easy to use under many different circumstances. Because of this interesting situation, the web usability movement has been growing. A number of books on usability have been published,[2,3,4,5] and the National Institute of Standards and Technology of the U.S. government is currently working on developing measurable standards for usability (see http://zing.ncsl.nist.gov/iusr/ for more information).

When Is Usability Testing Done?

Usability testing is usually performed once a working system (or a prototype) has been created, but before the final working system (and interface) is delivered to the users and implemented. Periodic usability tests might be useful if systems (or users) change over time, to ensure that the information system remains easy to use. For a web site, this usually means that the coding for all (or most) of the web site has already been done. Some authors suggest first testing paper prototypes of what an interface could look like and testing those paper mock-ups with users, before any coding is done, and then re-testing the interface with users once it has actually been coded.[1] Although this is a great idea, in reality, many web development projects do not allow the time for this approach. In fact, many web sites are implemented without any usability testing at all.

Testing with Users vs Testing with Experts

Generally, usability testing can be done with two different groups of testers: either with users who accurately represent the target population, or with experts in interface design and usability, a process also known as an *expert review*.[6] Different testing methods are used for each group. In fact, some authors will call this process usability testing only if actual users are involved. However, both users and experts may have useful suggestions to improve the usability of a web site.

The Role of Usability Experts

Usability experts are experts in interface design, but not necessarily in the tasks that the users will perform. Usability experts tend to comment on problems that violate usability guidelines, such as problems in consistency of color or terminology across a set of web pages. Often the experts find the larger usability problems, and the actual users are then able to pin down smaller problems, more related to task concerns, which would not be as obvious to the experts.

Both Experts and Users in the Mix

Some researchers advocate testing with users only, their argument being that expert reviewers are not experts in the task domain that is represented in the interfaces, and being unrepresentative of the user population, cannot offer useful feedback. In reality, what usually happens is that both experts and users are used, depending on factors such as schedule pressures, costs, and the availability of users. For instance, one usability firm indicates that most of their clients first ask for a heuristic evaluation (see more on this technique later in the chapter) with a usability expert to root out any major usability problems. After the expert heuristic evaluation, the clients usually want user-based usability testing to be performed in a lab setting with 5–10 users.

▶ 10.2 SETTINGS AND PARTICIPANTS FOR USER–BASED USABILITY TESTING

For any usability testing that is user-based, a step-by-step process guides each stage from the initial selection of users to the final processing of testing results.

Select Representative Users

Users who truly represent the target user population must be recruited to take part in the testing. It is essential to have a representative set of users. Having users who are unrepresentative of the user population is like asking teenagers what they think of the AARP (American Association of Retired Persons), or asking senior citizens about the newest set of Pokeman cards. College students should not be performing usability testing on a management information system that will be used by senior executives.[2] Does the choice of users really make a difference? Would you want airline pilots to test an interface that will be used by doctors and nurses in a hospital? The airline pilots would not have the knowledge in the task domain to effectively use the hospital computer system. Most likely, the airline pilots would not have previously worked in a hospital, nor would they be working in a hospital in the future. They would not have experience using hospital computer systems, nor would they be expected to use such a system in the future. The feedback from airline pilots on what they thought of the hospital system interface would be worthless, much as the doctor's perceptions of an interface for piloting a jet would similarly be worthless.

How to Recruit Users

One of the first issues to address in user-based usability testing is how to recruit the users. This step can be harder for new web sites, but easier for web sites that have previously existed and are being redesigned. Hopefully, the client organization can provide a list of potential testers who accurately represent the target user population. Potential users should be contacted to find out (1) if they do accurately represent the target population of users, and (2) whether they would be willing to take part in usability testing. Much as with jury duty, users are usually compensated for taking part in usability testing. This compensation can be in the form of money, food, or a simple thank you. The level of compensation is related to how interested the users are in the web site, how important they feel the web site will be, and the monetary value of their time. Those who are very interested in using the web site under development might be willing to perform usability testing for free. Those who are not as enthusiastic about the web site might be willing to do the usability testing for $10–$30 an hour. On the other hand, to get medical doctors to usability test a web site might cost a few hundred dollars an hour per doctor. Again, it is important to have users who are representative of the target user population.

Select the Setting

Usability testing can take place almost anywhere. The location is influenced by the access that the web development team has to equipment and to the users themselves. Many large companies and governmental organizations (such as IBM and the National Institutes of Health) have in-house usability laboratories and teams of experienced usability professionals. Consulting firms can provide expertise in usability, and can therefore be hired to do usability testing. If you need to rent usability equipment, some companies will let you rent portable usability equipment, or an entire usability laboratory, by the hour.

A Usability Laboratory

Formal usability testing can take place in a usability laboratory in which there is special equipment, made especially for usability testing.[6] Usually, there will be a chair, and a computer at a desk. The user sits at the desk, with a camera mounted either on the wall or on top of the computer. The camera records the actions and/or facial expressions of the user. The actions on the screen of the computer are also recorded to see what the user is doing. These two views, one of the user, one of the screen, are recorded side-by-side or picture-in-picture, usually in digital format. The user wears a microphone to assist in recording comments. The observer (or usability professional, or web development team member) may sit next to the user.[6] Alternatively, many usability laboratories have a small room next door to the usability laboratory, and a one-way mirror separates the user from the observer.[2] The observer watches the user through the one-way mirror, but the user cannot see the observer. The one-way mirror makes the user more comfortable and reduces nervousness about being watched. An example of this usability layout is shown in Fig. 10.1. The user is on the left and is separated from the observer (on the right) by a one-way mirror.

Figure 10.1

An example of a usability lab

Photo courtesy of UserWorks, Inc., a usability consulting firm located in Silver Spring, MD. www.userworks.com

Workplace Testing

Another possible location for usability testing is the workplace. It is possible for the web development team member to go the user's workplace (or home) and observe an individual's interaction with the web site. The advantage of this approach is that the user is in his or her natural environment, and so hopefully will feel comfortable interacting with the computer. In addition, it might be easier to get access to users in their workplace environment, since they will not need to take out large amounts of time from their day to leave work and travel to the usability laboratory. Usability equipment that is portable is sold under such names as "lab-in-a-bag" and "lab-in-a-box" (see Fig. 10.2 for an example of a portable usability lab). This usability equipment can be brought to the user's place of work, and the

Figure 10.2

An example of a portable usability lab.
Photo courtesy of UserWorks, Inc., a usability consulting firm located in Silver Spring, MD.
www.userworks.com

equipment will record the user's actions, as well as the interaction on the screen, using portable recorders and cameras. However, this equipment is expensive and often is not appropriate for testing with small numbers of users. Another possibility is that the observer can simply watch what the user does, listen to what the user says, and make detailed notes.

Web-Based Usability Testing

A newer type of usability testing is web-based testing, also called remote usability testing.[7] In this type of usability testing, the user and the evaluator are not physically located in the same location; rather, they are connected via the Web. The user performs usability testing by accessing the web site via the Web itself. The evaluator might be communicating with the user in real-time, or the evaluator might talk with the user at a later time.

Web-based usability testing has several advantages. Generally, it allows more users to take part in the usability testing of a web site. Users might not be available to come to the usability lab, and the observers might not be able to go watch the users in their workplace setting. But with the Web, users can perform usability testing on a web site at any time of day or night. In addition, factors that are outside the web development team's control (such as download speed) do not appear in the usability lab, but they are apparent when the users performing usability testing are distributed across the country.[7] The web-based usability testing is a natural method in which to test a web site.

The main disadvantage of the web-based usability testing approach is that the observer cannot record every action, or be able to listen to what the user has to say. But there are a number of techniques that can be used to collect data through web-based usability testing. Videoconferencing could be used to allow the web team's developer (evaluator) to watch what the user is doing.[7,8] The user could talk over the phone to the evaluator as part of the think-aloud protocol (more information later in this chapter).[7] The evaluator could remotely view the user's screen using software such as PCAnywhere.[7,8] The user's system could provide some type of data logging, allowing for post-hoc review of statistical data.[9] If there are a large number of users performing remote usability testing, a chat room or bulletin board could be set up for these users to share their comments and discuss their suggestions.[9] After users have completed the tasks, they could be presented with a web-based questionnaire asking their opinions on the web site.[7,10]

▶ Usability Testing Can Take Place:
  • In a usability laboratory
  • In a workplace (or home) setting
  • Over the web
  • Anywhere

Testing Realities
In an ideal world, usability testing would be done with hundreds of users in an advanced usability laboratory. In the real world, usability is about trying to find and fix as many problems as possible, as quickly as possible, with as little cost as possible, and need not be done in an extensive laboratory setting. Most web development projects do not have the budget for renting a usability lab, nor do they have the time to test 100 users or even the access to 100 users. Any usability testing is better than no usability test-

ing. If all the project budget/timeline/access allows is testing with 5 users, then this is better than testing with no users. Testing with at least 5–10 users is desirable. Of course, the more users that can take part in usability testing, the better, because an increased number of users are more likely to find more usability problems. In addition, it is useful to see the patterns that occur over numerous users during usability testing. If one user has mistakenly looked in the "History" page of the web site for information on current events, this might be an aberration. On the other hand, if eight of the ten users all mistakenly looked in the "History" page for information on current events, this more than likely indicates a problem that might occur with additional users. More users are better, but some users are better than no users.

▶ 10.3 PROCESS OF USER–BASED TESTING

In usability testing, the users are asked to perform a set of tasks, and the web development team (or evaluator) learns about the usability problem of the system through this process. The tasks and instructions for performing the tasks should be given to the users on a sheet of paper. The tasks should represent common tasks that the users will be expected to perform. In requirements gathering, the users might have stated what they would like "to do" with the web site, or the clients might have indicated what tasks they expect users to perform. In the case of informational web sites, these tasks are usually related to information gathering.[1] Users should be sent on a "scavenger hunt" to find information on the web site. For an e-commerce site, users should attempt to find a product on the web site and purchase it. If any interactivity (a dynamic response to a user action) is included in the web site, then the users should also be requested to engage in those tasks. In most usability testing scenarios, the users will be asked to attempt the tasks without any outside assistance. This matches the user's natural environment, where the user would attempt tasks without assistance from anyone else. Since the test tasks should be representative of common user tasks, the computer equipment should also be representative of the common user computing equipment. If most users will be accessing a web site from a school with slow computers, small screens, and a slow Internet connection, then the usability testing should not be done on a high-end workstation with a 21" monitor and a cable modem.

Collect the Data

There are a number of different approaches for gathering data in a usability test:

Performance Measurement

In performance measurement, quantitative measures are taken of performance using the interface. This data can measure how many of the tasks were successfully completed (task performance), how long it took the user to complete a specific task (time performance), and the number of errors and time spent recovering from the errors.[2] This data can be manually recorded, or, like response time, can be logged by the computer.

Thinking Aloud Protocol

Users are encouraged to verbalize, out loud, their thoughts as they attempt to complete the set of tasks. The users may point out parts of the system that are satisfying, parts of the system that are confusing, or they may express satisfaction or frustration. These comments should be recorded on video or audio (with the user's prior permission, of course), or should be recorded by an individual whose purpose is to take notes of the session. Another possibility is to have two users working together, a process that helps increase the amount of discussion about the system. The technique of having two users test the system simultaneously is called codiscovery learning or constructive interaction.[2] Usability testers might also be asked to review a videotape of their actions at a later time, and provide retrospective comments.[2]

Coaching Method

In most of the usability testing methods, the user attempts to perform the tasks without outside help. In the coaching method, the user is assisted by the evaluator (a member of the web development team), who provides advice on how to use the system, along with asking many questions of the user. The user may also ask questions about the system, such as "What does that icon represent?"

Questionnaires

Users can be asked to answer questions while they are attempting the tasks. For instance, if a user is given a list of tasks, after each task there can be a question on their list such as "Were there any parts of that task that you found to be confusing?" Users can also be requested to fill out a questionnaire at the end of the usability session, with questions such as "What was the most confusing part of the web site?" and "What did you think of the color scheme?" It is especially important to ask the users questions about parts of the interface that might have been controversial during the web development process. If there were any components of the web site that were not requested by users, or any parts that the clients were specifically concerned about, it might be useful to solicit the users' opinions on these aspects of the interface. In addition, there are validated questionnaires, such as the Questionnaire for User Interaction Satisfaction (QUIS)[11] (see Chapter 12) that can be used to ascertain the user's overall satisfaction with the system.

Before and After the Test Session

Informed Consent

Before the usability testing session is about to begin, the user should be asked to fill out an informed consent form.[6] Such a form should provide information about the usability test, and inform the user that his or her participation is voluntary, confidential, and each person is free to end the session and leave at any time.[6] In addition, users should be reminded that they are not being tested. It is the *interface* that is being tested, and the user is simply the one testing the interface.[6] If the user is being videotaped or recorded, the user must be aware of this and agree to it.

Debriefing

After the user has performed the requested tasks, the user should be debriefed.[2] This debriefing should consist of asking the user for any final thoughts on their experience, and offering appreciation to the user for participating. After the usability test is completed, it is a good idea to make notes on all aspects of the usability session before these details are forgotten.[2] This protocol should be used, regardless of whether the usability testing is in a formal usability laboratory, a workplace setting, or over the web. The only difference is that, over the web, more time may elapse between the user being sent instructions, and the user actually performing the usability testing.

▶ Steps in User–Based Usability Testing:
1. Select representative users and set up time/location for usability testing.
2. Introduce the usability test, get informed consent form, and give users the tasks.

3. Ask users to attempt to perform tasks; collect data (via videotape, notes, data logging).
4. After the usability session, ask users to fill out a questionnaire.
5. Thank those tested for their participation and compensate them.

▶ 10.4 EXPERT REVIEWS

The term expert reviews refers to a process of getting people who are experts in the area of usability and interface design to look at the web site and offer feedback. Expert reviews have also been called usability inspections.[12] Although usability experts might be a part of the web development team, they should not be used for expert reviews. The idea behind an expert review is to get a different viewpoint from someone who is an expert in usability and interface design. An expert reviewer must be someone who was not involved in the actual web development project. If a member of the web development team is a usability expert, that person could not offer a separate viewpoint. Furthermore, if the member of the web development team had noticed a problem related to usability, the issue should have been pointed out earlier, not at this late date.

Expert reviews share some characteristics with user testing in that they can take place in any type of setting, such as a workplace, a usability lab, or over the Web. The reviewers themselves can come from consulting firms, usability labs, or universities. These expert reviewers, much like the users, normally expect to be paid for reviewing a web site. However, the expert reviewers are not representative users. Because of this difference, the techniques that expert reviewers use are different from user-based usability testing. There are a number of different types of expert reviews, described as follows.[6]

Heuristic Evaluation

In a heuristic evaluation, an expert checks a web site to see if it violates any rules contained in a short set of design heuristics. The heuristics are usually a list of approximately 6–12 design rules, and the expert reviewer checks the web site to see if it violates any of these general design rules. Two well-known examples of usability heuristics are Shneiderman's 8 Golden Rules[6] and Jakob Nielsen's Top 10 Mistakes in Web Design (available from http://www.useit.com/alertbox/9605.html). Heuristic evaluation is quite common since it is quick and does not require a large number of experts. For instance, the heuristic evaluation method was used in usability testing of the web site of the U.S. Bureau of Labor Statistics.[13]

Guidelines Review

A guidelines review is similar to a heuristic evaluation, except that the expert reviews a web site against a much larger list of design guidelines. Design guidelines for specific organizations or interfaces can contain hundreds of design rules, so this type of review takes a long time and is rarely performed in usability testing of web sites. However, efforts are underway to develop software that will automate the process of a guidelines review.[14] This software will scan a web page and look for usability guidelines or heuristics that are not being followed.[14] For example, the automated usability application might notify the designer that the graphics do not have any <alt> text, specifying what to display if the graphics are not being viewed.[14] This is not a violation of an HTML guideline, so an HTML validator would not find this, but since it would be a violation of a web usability guideline, the software could determine that a change was needed.[14]

Cognitive Walkthrough

In a cognitive walkthrough, the experts (it is usually a group of experts, not an individual) go through a series of tasks that the user would typically perform. The idea is that by performing typical user tasks, the experts would discover areas of the web site that could be confusing, unclear, or problematic. It is important to select tasks that are representative of common user tasks, and to have a good understanding of who the users are. Language and instructions that might be confusing to a usability expert might actually make sense to the targeted user.

Consistency Inspection

In a consistency inspection, an expert reviews all of the web pages on the web site to ensure that the layout, terminology, and color are the same. For instance, if most pages on a web site have navigation on the left, and the corporate logo at the top left-hand corner of the web page, then the user will expect to see this arrangement on every page. Users can become disconcerted or disoriented when similar pages do not appear to be consistent.[15] For instance, if most pages appear similar, but two pages are missing the common layout (different color scheme, no navigation on left or corporate logo), the user may mistakenly perceive that they have left the web site.

Formal Usability Inspection

In a formal usability inspection, the designers justify and defend their design choices to expert reviewers, screen by screen. This justification takes place in a process that is similar to the code inspection methods used by software designers.[12] A number of different roles, such as the designer, moderator, scribe, and inspector, are required.[12] The formal usability inspection is rarely performed in web design.

There are also a number of newer expert review methods, such as the pluralistic walkthrough. A good reference on expert reviews is the Nielsen and Mack book, *Usability Inspection Methods* (1994).

▶ 10.5 INCORPORATING TESTING FEEDBACK

After the usability testing has been completed, the members of the web development team should take some time to discuss what was learned. Were there any aspects of the web site that users consistently found to be frustrating? Was there language that was unclear to the users?[13] Did the users have to go through too many menus to find the information that they were looking for? Is the amount of screen scrolling overwhelming?[16] Was the navigation scheme confusing?[16] Did the web pages take too long to download?[16] Were there too many links or too many graphics?[1] Is too much mouse movement around the screen required?[9] These are common problems that have been found in the usability testing of major web sites. It is important for the web development team to determine, based on the usability tests, what the biggest usability problems were.

The web development team should decide what the major lessons learned from the usability testing were. If these were minor changes (such as changes in wording), then it is generally acceptable to go ahead and make those changes without consulting the client. If major changes need to be made, then it is important to consult with the client and discuss these changes with them. Although the client may not agree to the suggested changes, the client needs to be made aware of the usability problems discovered. Documentation of any changes, and the outcome of the usability testing, should be provided to the clients. Even if changes were only minor, documentation should still be provided to the clients, since they will want to know, "Why did we pay for usability testing?" The web development team should be prepared to answer this question, discussing what was learned from the usability test, what needs to be changed, and why this was an important step. In addition, it may sometimes be difficult to convince clients of the need for certain changes. The best way to convince a client of a severe usability problem is to provide data. This can mean a videotape of users having problems, written comments that show that the user found the site to be confusing, or summary data showing that 75% of users could not find the information that they were looking for. Any of these types of data will help to convince the client that there are serious usability problems that need to be addressed. If major design changes are in fact made based on findings from the usability testing, it may be necessary to do another round of usability tests to determine what problems exist with the new interface.

SUMMARY

Usability testing is an important part of the web development process. Usability testing ensures that there are no serious usability problems that will affect the ability of the users to successfully interact with the web site. There is no one specific method or technique that is right for all situations. Similarly, there is not a specific number of users that can discover all usability problems. The usability testing approach needs to be tailored to each specific web development project. Obviously, the more data that can be collected, the better. However, with the rapid development times for web development projects, it is unrealistic to test a web site with 200 users and four different types of usability testing. The important thing is to consider the need for usability testing, and implement some type of usability testing using users and/or experts.

Deliverables

At this point, you should have:
1. Decided on a plan for usability testing
2. Recruited experts and users to perform the usability testing
3. Executed the usability testing plan
4. Determined what was learned from usability testing, and what needs to be changed
5. Received client approval to make the changes, and then made the changes

Discussion Questions
1. Why is usability testing important?
2. What are the strengths and weaknesses of user-based usability testing versus expert-based usability testing?
3. Why is it important to have representative users testing the web site?
4. What is an appropriate setting for a usability test?

5. Describe the setup of a formal usability laboratory.
6. What is a heuristic evaluation, who uses it, and how is it used?
7. Discuss three methods of data collection in a usability test.
8. How should the user in a usability test be treated? What rights does the user have?
9. Why should the client be informed of the full results of the usability testing?

REFERENCES

1. Yu, J., Prabhu, P., & Neale, W. (1998). *A user-centered approach to designing a new top-level structure for a large and diverse corporate web site.* Proceedings of the 1998 Human Factors and the Web Conference. Available at: http://www.research.att.com/conf/hfweb/
2. Nielsen, J. (1994). *Usability Engineering.* Boston: Academic Press.
3. Nielsen, J. (2000). *Designing Web Usability: The Practice of Simplicity.* Indianapolis: New Riders Publishing.
4. Preece, J. (1990). *A Guide to Usability.* Milton Keynes, England: The Open University.
5. Spool, J., Scanlon, T., Schroeder, W., Snyder, C., & DeAngelo, T. (1999). *Web Site Usability: A Designer's Guide.* San Francisco: Morgan Kaufmann Publishers.
6. Shneiderman, B. (1998). *Designing the User Interface: Strategies for Effective Human-Computer Interaction* (3rd ed.). Reading, Massachusetts: Addison-Wesley.
7. Hartson, R., Castillo, J., Kelso, J., & Neale, W. (1996). *Remote evaluation: The network as an extension of the usability laboratory.* Proceedings of the CHI: Human Factors in Computing, 228–235.
8. Hammontree, M., Weiler, P., & Nayak, N. (1994). Remote usability testing. *Interactions, 1*(3), 21–25.
9. Millen, D. (1999). Remote usability evaluation: User participation in the design of a web-based email service. *SIGGROUP Bulletin, 20*(1), 40–44.
10. Lazar, J., & Preece, J. (1999). Designing and implementing web-based surveys. *Journal of Computer Information Systems, 39*(4), 63–67.
11. Norman, K., Shneiderman, B., Harper, B., & Slaughter, L. (1998). *Questionnaire for User Interaction Satisfaction.* College Park, MD: University of Maryland.
12. Nielsen, J., & Mack, R. (Eds.). (1994). *Usability Inspection Methods.* New York: John Wiley & Sons.
13. Levi, M., & Conrad, F. (1996). A heuristic evaluation of a World Wide Web prototype. *Interactions, 3*(4), 50–61.
14. Scholtz, J., Laskowski, S., & Downey, L. (1998). *Developing usability tools and technique for designing and testing web sites.* Proceedings of the Human Factors and the Web. Available at: http://www.research.att.com/conf/hfweb/
15. Tedeschi, B. (1999). Good web site design can lead to healthy sales. *The New York Times,* August 30, 1999.
16. Corry, M., Frick, T., & Hansen, L. (1997). User-centered design and usability testing of a web site: An illustrative case study. *Educational Technology Research and Development, 45*(4), 65–76.

▲ Best Buddies Maryland

Usability testing is an important part of the development process, ensuring that the web site is easy for the users to use. The web development team for Best Buddies Maryland chose 16 users to usability test the website. Two of the users are employees of Best Buddies Maryland: Michelle Biccochi and Jill Halbrecht. A third employee, Carri Cerri, was to have tested the site, but was unavailable due to illness. Four members of Best Buddies tested the site. Three of the members were college-age people with mental retardation. The fourth member was a volunteer who is also a college student. (Please note, aside from the main contact people at Best Buddies, the identity of the other usability testers will not be revealed.)

Two expert users participated in testing the Best Buddies Maryland web site. One expert is a computer lab manager, and the other is a web developer. Two professional librarians tested the site. The librarians were chosen because they are experts in the organization and retrieval of information. Two adult community members who would be likely to make donations to an organization such as Best Buddies both tested the site. Four college students also tested the web site. The users who tested the web site were a diverse group that represented the many possible users of the Best Buddies Maryland site.

Location

The development team used both workplace and remote usability testing. Two members of the development team visited Best Buddies Maryland offices to oversee testing with the organization's staff. Two other members of the development team supervised usability testing at the University campus, where a volunteer and two Best Buddies members with mental retardation tested the site. The expert users and the librarians tested the site with members of the development team present. The older users, and some of the college students, tested the site from a remote location and sent in the results of their tests via e-mail.

User Tasks

The development team divided the testing of the site into two sections. The first section, called User Tasks, consisted of ten tasks that would directly test the usability of the Best Buddies Maryland web site. The second section, called User Evaluation, included questions related to the colors used on the site, the layout of the site, and the users' general impressions of the web site. The tasks and questions given to the users for testing the site can be found in Best Buddies Maryland Form A (see Fig. 10.3).

Michelle Bicocchi, Best Buddies Maryland Program Manager

Ms. Bicocchi found an error that was repeated on every page of the web site. The title on each page reads Best Buddies of Maryland, when the name of the organization is Best Buddies Maryland.

Ms. Bicocchi easily navigated through the tasks presented on the usability handout with a few minor exceptions. She looked for the name of a high school participating in Best Buddies on the Program Information page instead of the Affiliated Schools page. Additionally, she was directed to the wrong site by the "Return to Best Buddies" link on the Guest Book. Otherwise, each task was accomplished very quickly and with little trouble.

Ms. Bicocchi had many positive comments to make about the site. She loved the color scheme, but worried that perhaps the purple visited links on a purple background might be difficult for some people to read. She was very happy with the font chosen for the site and found the navigation to be consistent and easy to follow throughout the site. She stated that she would change nothing about the site saying, "I thought it was well put together and informative."

Jill Halbrecht, Best Buddies Maryland Program Manager

Ms. Halbrecht had no difficulty in performing the tasks as set forth in the usability handout. She even managed, by accident, to avoid a problem with the Guest Book nearly every other user encountered. After she posted her message in the Guest Book, she returned to the Best Buddies Home page by repeatedly clicking the browser's back button. Using the back button seemed to be Ms. Halbrecht's preferred method of navigation.

During the testing, Ms. Halbrecht commented that the navigation links might be grouped in a more logical manner by topic (e.g., Affiliated Schools closer to Program Information) and that the address of Best Buddies should appear on the home page. Additionally, she said that she would like to see a few more graphics on the site. Overall, her appraisal of the site was very positive. She loved the Comic Sans MS font, thought the color scheme was very attractive, and found the site to be very user-friendly.

Librarian 1

This user is a librarian and director of a county law library. A member of the development team was present during testing. She found all of the tasks very easy to perform with the exception of being misdirected by the link meant to return users from the Guest Book. The only other correction that this user felt was necessary was placing the address of Best Buddies on the home page.

In her overall evaluation of the site, this user had very positive comments to make about the color scheme, font, and about the way in which the information was presented.

Librarian 2

This user is a librarian at a law firm. A member of the development team was present during testing. This user encountered difficulty only when performing the task associated with the Guest Book. She found the button labeled Preview Entry to be confusing and was expecting one that said Submit in its place. Additionally, she was misdirected by the link back to the Best Buddies home page from the Guest Book.

This user thought the Comic Sans MS font went well with the Best Buddies logo, was easy to read, and conveyed a friendly feeling. She found the color scheme appealing and felt that the site was very user-friendly.

Nurse

This user is a 69-year-old retired nurse who tested the site from a remote location. This user had very positive comments to make about the site. She reported that she frequently has difficulty finding the information she is looking for on web sites, but had no such problems with the Best Buddies Maryland site. She found each of the tasks very easy to complete, with the exception of the "Buddies of the Month" task, for which no information is presently posted on the site.

This user answered "yes" to questions about whether she liked the color scheme, whether she found the text easy to read, and if the layout of the site presented information in a clear manner. Even though this is taken as evidence that she liked the site, it is difficult to gauge the depth of her reaction from a distance. The only positive answer that was more expansive was to the question regarding what she liked best about the site. She replied, "I liked the fact that it is easy to go through and I can find the data in it. Most often I can't."

Retired Army Officer

This user is an 86-year-old retired Army Officer who tested the Best Buddies web site from a remote location. He reported that he found all of the tasks easy to complete, with the exception of finding information about the Buddies of the Month, which is not currently available. This user reported that the forms for volunteering did not print very well. Page breaks on the forms came at odd places.

This user liked the color scheme used on the site and found the text easy to read. This user did not respond favorably to the font face used on the site. When asked what he liked least about the site, he wrote "apparent hand-printed home page." What he liked most about the site was the "concise presentation of information, without undue puffery."

Computer Lab Manager

This user is a computer lab manager and is 28 years old. He could be considered an expert tester because he has web development experience and is a computer lab manager. He had no problem completing most of the tasks assigned by the development team. However, he could not find the Best Buddies of the Month. He found use of the Guest Book to be easy and clear. When asked where the featured previous event was held, he first looked into the calendar of events instead of the Previous Events page. It made more sense to him to try to locate the previous event in the calendar. This user liked the web site for its consistency and color scheme; however, he found the navigation difficult because the links were blue on a purple background. Meanwhile, the navigation was appreciated because it was always present and consistent throughout the site. When asked to give additional comments, he stated that the font used (Comic Sans MS) might not be displayed correctly on computers supporting the following operating systems: Linux, Unix, Sun OS, and SGI.

Web Developer

This user is a 26-year-old web developer. Apart from not being able to find the Best Buddies of the Month, this user had no problem completing most the tasks listed in the usability testing handout. This user liked the site for its fast loading, clear text, layout, and easy navigation. However, the color of the links wasn't agreeable, and she found the site too wordy. When asked if she would like to change something about the web site, she said that she would make it more graphical.

College Student

This user is a 23-year-old college student. This user encountered no problem completing the tasks presented to him, apart from locating the Best Buddies of the Month. He was not sure he was looking at the right information when he was asked to find when Best Buddies was founded. When asked what he liked the most about the site, he replied that he liked the fast loading speed, consistency, and clarity of the information presented. He also found the site very informative. He disliked the colors used for the links and was not really impressed by the color scheme. If he could change something about the web site, that would be the links color. He would also provide more external links.

Best Buddies Volunteer

This user is a 22-year-old volunteer for Best Buddies at Towson University. This user was able to easily complete most of the tasks requested by the development team, but opted not to print the form for volunteering because she would have had to pay for the printing. She commented that the names of the high schools that participate in Best Buddies Maryland were well organized and easy to locate. This user was not able to locate who the Buddies of the Month were.

The three aspects of the site that this user enjoyed most were the calendar of events, pictures of the Buddies at the events, and the links to other sites. She also mentioned that she liked the color scheme and the text size; she felt that the layout of the site presented the information in a clear manner. Although she enjoyed the web site, there was one problem that she pointed out. After she signed the Guest Book she clicked on the link to return back to Best Buddies Maryland and was directed to the wrong page. Other than that problem, she felt that the development team did a great job on the Best Buddies Maryland web site.

Member of Best Buddies

Another participant who took part in our usability testing was a member of the Best Buddies chapter at Towson University. He did experience some difficulties with navigating through the web site and understanding some of the links. The observer assisted this user with navigating through the site, and after the observer explained to him what each link was for, he was able to decipher if he needed to go to a certain page to find the answer to the questions. For example, after the observer explained each link to him, he was able to find the name of a high school that participates in Best Buddies Maryland. He also made reference to the fact that the high school he attended was not a participating school. He was able to locate the form for volunteering but because it would have cost money to print the form (in the computer labs at the university), he decided not the print the form.

The user liked the color scheme and enjoyed the pictures on the web site. He liked the Previous Events page the best. Even though the user liked the colors on the site, he did mention that the he found the text on the screen difficult to read. When asked would he change anything on the site, he said no.

Two Members of Best Buddies

These two users performed the testing of the site simultaneously. They are both members of Best Buddies with mental retardation. These users were not asked about their Internet browsing experience in advance; rather they were chosen at random from a group of members of Best Buddies with mental retardation. In order to conduct the test, each task and question on the usability form had to be explained and performed one at a time. Overall, both of the users were very pleased with the web site. As people familiar with the Best Buddies organization, they recognized much of the information offered on the site.

When possible, the development team tried not to guide them to the answers to the usability questions. Scrolling down screens seemed to present a problem for these testers when the desired information was not presented "above the fold." Both users said that they liked the color scheme and design of the web site. One member especially liked the calendar of events, but they both liked the pictures from Previous Events the best. They said that they would prefer more pictures than text. From the testing, the development team learned that for users with mental retardation, very simple, clear, concise language is best. Using graphics rather than text might make a web site easier for people with mental retardation.

College Student, age 23

This user is a student majoring in finance who tested the web site from a remote location. Unlike the previous users, her concerns were quite different. She could not locate where the next Best Buddies event was being held, the name of a high school that participates in Best Buddies Maryland, or the address of Best Buddies Maryland. Finally, while completing another task, the user found the address of Best Buddies on one of the forms for volunteering.

In addition to not being able to complete some of the tasks, she had several other concerns. On the forms for volunteering page it states that the printout will be three pages. In fact, there were only two pages and the second page had one line at the top. Navigation for the user was difficult. For example, when visiting Best Buddies International (which opens in another window) the user did not realize that she either had to minimize that window or close it to go back to the Best Buddies Maryland site. She felt that if there were a back button it would be easier. When trying to return to the home page of Best Buddies from the Guest Book, she was directed to a different web site.

Unfortunately, this user did not complete the question on what she liked most about Best Buddies Maryland web site. She mentioned that she did not like the color scheme and felt that navigation through the site was neither consistent nor easy to follow.

College Student, age 20

This user is a female student majoring in education. She helped to demonstrate for the development team that the preliminary Best Buddies Maryland web site is very user-friendly, but at the same time could be improved. This user had little background using computers and therefore was extremely valuable in the usability testing on the Best Buddies Maryland web site.

The user had no problem in finding where the next Best Buddies Maryland event was going to be held. She looked right at the navigation on the left and clicked calendar of events and proceeded to find the correct event. The user also had no problems in finding the volunteer forms and had no problems printing out the forms, but noticed slight errors in the text, which are from the conversion of a Microsoft Word document to an HTML document. This user, however, did, at first, question where to find the high schools that participate with Best Buddies Maryland. The user then located the Affiliated Schools link, and commented that the link should be higher on the navigation. She also mentioned that the information currently on the home page should probably be separated into a page titled Fast Facts or something similar. The user found it hard to find the address for Best Buddies, as well as when and where Best Buddies was founded.

Despite some content issues for the Best Buddies of the Month page, this user was able to locate the page and tell the development team where to find the Buddy of the Month. The user further continued to locate and post a message in the Guest Book with no problems, as well as find the Previous Events and pictures page of the site. Lastly, this user located the Special Olympics page from the site and was very pleased as to how the site opened in a new window.

Overall, this user enjoyed the color scheme of the site and also commented that it was a very user-friendly site. She found the content to be very useful, easy to read, and very understandable from an outsider's point of view. Lastly, this user felt that the navigation was excellent as it was always on the left and, when you were on a specific page, the link to that page was deactivated.

College Student, age 22

This user is a student majoring in business with a lot of Internet browsing experience. While the user quickly and easily navigated through most of the assigned questions and tasks, he pointed out a few minor issues that should be addressed.

First of all, while the user quickly found the Buddies of the Month page, he was disappointed to find that the information was not available. Also, he had some difficulty finding the Affiliated Schools page and felt that the information currently provided on the home page should be split between a home page and a Fast Facts page. He also stated that the address of the organization should appear on the home page rather than just on the Contact Information page.

This user enjoyed the site immensely and stated that it was very user-friendly, had a lot of information, and had an excellent color scheme. He felt that the visited links should be a different color than purple; however, he found the rest of the colors to be very appropriate. This user was able to find all of the information necessary and post to the Guest Book. This user stated that he looks forward to viewing the site in the future.

Changes Made as a Result of Testing

As has been detailed in the previous sections, the development team, after creating a preliminary web site for Best Buddies Maryland, tested the site with users from different age ranges in order to learn of any possible usability problems. Many minor problems and issues were addressed with respect to the usability of the web site. The problems and issues discovered during testing enabled the development team to build a site that a wide range of users will find informative and easy to use.

Minor spelling mistakes and misplaced words were found very quickly and were easily fixed. First of all, on the Previous Events page with the pictures, pic 2 was labeled pic 3. Secondly, Michelle Bicocchi of Best Buddies Maryland pointed out that the title of the web site should say Best Buddies Maryland instead of Best Buddies of Maryland. On the Related Organizations page of the site, one line had site misspelled to say "stie." Lastly, in the discussion of Best Buddies Maryland on the Contact Information page, the word "their" was used where "our" would have been more appropriate. All of these mistakes and misplaced words were brought to the development team's immediate attention and handled quickly.

To improve navigation through the web site, the development team switched the order of the links to make them more logically grouped. For example, the Affiliated Schools link was placed under the Program Information link after a couple of users mentioned that they would go to Program Information to look up the Affiliated Schools, but if they saw that the Affiliated Schools link followed the Program Information link immediately, they would understand where the information they needed was located. The Contact Information and the Guest Book links were placed at the end of the navigation, as users reported they are more accustomed to finding them towards the bottom of navigation on most web sites.

The development team discovered that some adjustments to the content on some of the pages were necessary. First of all, the links on the volunteer page were very large and wrapped around when viewed on smaller monitors with lower resolutions. Therefore, the development team reduced the size of the links to make them better fit the page. Secondly, an employee of Best Buddies Maryland suggested that the development team mention the name of the towing company (Millis Industries, Inc.) in the car donation page of the web site. Also, the Affiliated Schools page on the web site contained a dead link, and after research by the development team, it was determined that the school didn't even have a web site, so the link was taken off of the page. Lastly, Best Buddies Maryland has not yet selected the Buddies of the Month, so the page now states that the Best Buddy of the month will be available shortly.

After testing the site, changes were made to make it more aesthetically pleasing. These changes resulted from the development team's own assessment of the site rather than from user feedback. First, borders were placed around the pictures from Previous Events to help the pictures stand out with some depth behind them. Larger titles for certain pages were implemented to help remind users as to which page he or she is currently on, and the link for the current page was disabled. Additionally, a standard color (teal) was selected for the titles of the individual web pages throughout the site. Lastly, the color of the visited links was changed to yellow, because the original visited link color of purple did not stand out very well against a purple background.

As the result of user feedback, the home page of the site was changed to contain a brief explanation of the organization Best Buddies Maryland, a few facts about the international organization, and Contact Information. The original content on the home page was moved to a page called Fast Facts. Lastly, the Guest Book contained a button that said "preview entry" that users were supposed to click after signing the book. This button was very confusing to users, so the development team decided to change it to "send" to reduce the confusion.

As a result of user testing, Best Buddies Maryland now has a web site that is very user-friendly. By testing the site with users spanning a wide range of ages and web-browsing abilities, the development team was able to build a site that will best meet the needs of the diverse populations served by Best Buddies Maryland.

Usability Testing Questionnaire

Instructions: Thank you for helping the development team assess the usability of the Best Buddies Maryland web site. For each of the following statements and questions, please fill in either the appropriate answer, or, if you cannot successfully perform one of the tasks, indicate "Could not complete." In the case of uncompleted tasks, please note in the space provided below the task the reason why it could not be completed and any other relevant comments relating how easy or difficult the tasks were to complete. Begin by navigating to the web site http://triton.towson.edu/~kkapla1/BB/home.html.

1. Find where the next Best Buddies of Maryland event is being held.

2. Print and fill out a form for volunteering.

3. Locate the name of a high school that participates in Best Buddies Maryland.

4. What is Best Buddies of Maryland's street address?

5. Who are the Best Buddies of the Month?

6. Post a message in the Guest Book. Did you have any problems?

7. Where was the featured previous event held?

8. Go to (and then please come back from) an affiliated organization's web site (e.g., Special Olympics). Were you able to find one easily?

Figure 10.3
continued

After you have spent some time on the web site, please answer the following questions:

9. When and where was Best Buddies, International founded?

10. What did you like most about the Best Buddies Maryland web site?

11. What did you like least about the Best Buddies Maryland web site?

12. Do you like the color scheme used on the site?

13. Was all the text easy to read?

14. Did the layout of the site present information in a clear manner?

15. Was the navigation through the site consistent and easy to follow?

16. If there were anything about the site you would change, what would it (they) be?

17. Additional comments.

Thank you for helping to test the Best Buddies Maryland web site.

▲ Institute of Notre Dame

The main goal of the usability testing is to test the redesigned navigation through the IND site. The original IND web site had no coherent navigation scheme, and the web development team focused their redesign efforts primarily on improving this aspect of the web site. Thus, the usability test was designed to be oriented toward information retrieval.

The usability test was developed to be a series of questions that visitors might try to answer by visiting IND's web site. These questions covered all the major sections of the web site because this breadth of coverage could test navigation back and forth through all the sections of IND's site. If users had consistent problems answering any of the section's questions, it would point to a need to redesign the navigation to that section.

In addition to asking questions that required the user to find information on the site, the team asked a series of general, open-ended survey questions in order to allow for additional feedback from the testers. The main goal was to discover navigation issues; however the team also wanted to see if the test audience had any other comments about the site, such as color or content, that would be useful in completing the final site design. Please refer to IND Form A (Fig. 10.4) for a copy of the questionnaire used in the usability testing.

Test Audience and Methods

The test audience was divided into the user categories identified in our initial user requirements survey. These categories were: students, faculty, parents, alumnae, and prospective students. However, two of these categories were difficult to test: prospective users and parents. For example, it is difficult to get access to users who are currently considering enrollment in IND. If there are potential students, the school is more concerned with turning them into enrolling students, rather than having them perform usability testing on the web site. Similarly, the web development team discovered during our user requirements survey that the response rate from parents was rather low, and it was also relatively difficult to gain access to current parents through the school. Although ideally the team wanted to perform usability testing on the web site with all user groups, this was not feasible. Thus, the primary focus was on identifying a set of students, faculty, and alumnae to serve as the test audience.

The contact at the Institute of Notre Dame, Fred Germano, was willing to assist with the usability testing by identifying students and faculty who were available to assist us by testing the site. It might have been a problem to organize alumni for testing, but fortunately, a few alumni of IND were available and were asked to test the site. Since some alumni were also parents of IND students, the team hoped that their responses would also be representative of the parent population. The web development team hoped that the design of a questionnaire that requires the testers to visit all sections of the site would offset the lack of parents and prospective members in the test audience. The optimal mix would have been approximately five users in each of the three categories of students, faculty, and alumni, for a total of 15 usability testers. Unfortunately, the team was not able to reach this goal for a number of reasons discussed later.

Student and faculty testing occurred in IND's computer lab. This provided a controlled environment where individual user reactions could be observed. Due to the difficulty involved in accessing alumnae face-to-face, the team used remote testing with instructions provided in a questionnaire for the alumni testers. The remote users attempted to find the information requested and e-mailed the completed questionnaire back to us. Unfortunately, schedule conflicts made it impossible for the web development team to directly observe the student and faculty testing. This was not ideal; however, Fred Germano agreed to help administer the test to the students and faculty. The team coached him about the goals of the usability test and the types of observations being sought.

Usability Testing Results

Unfortunately, the team was not able to get as many users to usability test the IND web site as had been hoped for. The goal was five testers each from the students, faculty, and alumni categories. However, due to problems with time restrictions, only a few users participated. The team received three surveys from alumni, one from a student, and one from a faculty member. The academic year was coming to an end, and perhaps this fact might have played a role in the lack of responses.

Overall, most users answered the questions correctly. They were very pleased with the amount of content on the site and the navigation between the pages. After the users filled out the survey, they were asked if they were using Netscape Navigator or Internet Explorer. Regardless of the browser used, the results were the same—the users were pleased with the overall direction of the site.

Two of the surveys mentioned that these users would like to have a search engine on the web page. The web development team agreed that a search engine would be a very nice addition to the site, but that it was out of the scope of the current project. Instead of actually creating the search engine, the team designed the site so that the search engine could easily be added. The team mentioned to IND that for further development of the web site, they can use Microsoft Index Server as their search engine, and that Microsoft provides many examples on how to interact with Index Server. Another question that was raised was whether or not IND was going to have online applications. Many of the documents that IND provided had the potential of becoming online applications. However, once again, online forms were beyond the scope of the current project and timeline.

A Surprising Comment

Something came as a surprise to the web development team. The team had developed the site from the beginning for speed and ease of maintenance. To increase the speed, we reduced the number of graphics without reducing the "look" of the site. However, the surveys that were received mentioned that users would like to see *more* graphics and/or icons on the site. Previously the development team had asked IND to provide pictures of the school and IND had hired a photographer to take photographs of the school. Since the surveys mentioned that the users would like to see more graphics of the school, the team has now incorporated many of the photographs into the site.

Of course, we would like every user to say, "We didn't have any problems." However, this is the real world and that is just not going to happen. A good web developer is always looking for comments—good or bad—about the web site. Users will always point out the problematic areas of the site, but tend not to mention the strong points. If a web developer doesn't receive any comments about the site, either the site is perfect—unlikely—or people have not used it. In the web development world, bad comments are actually good suggestions for improvement.

Major Concerns: Graphics and Navigation

The most surprising comment, as mentioned before, was the fact that users wanted to see more graphics on the site. As more users buy faster computers and have faster Internet connections, they are shifting their wants to reflect the new speed. However, even with the new high-speed computers and connections, it is essential to remember the users who have slow connection speeds. The team decided to include at most three pictures per page. By including some pictures on each page, the overall "friendliness" of the site was enhanced, but the site still provided very fast download speeds. On the pages that contain a lot of information, the number of graphics was limited to one, preferably none.

There were no obvious problems navigating the site reported by any of the people who participated in the usability testing, and most rated the site as either 4 or 5 overall. In almost all cases, all the site navigation questions were answered correctly. Thus, we will not go into details here about how each question was answered. However, the team modified the navigation slightly to compensate for some of the comments about the navigation, and it appears that the changes to the navigation scheme in the IND web site have been successful. Now the content is divided according to the type of user, and internal navigation within each of these sections is organized in a navigation bar going down the left side of the screen. Thus, it is easy to switch between sections of the site, and navigation within each section is fairly smooth. No major problems with this navigation scheme were uncovered during the usability testing. However, there are a few minor changes that can still be made in response to user feedback about the site. For example, some testers attempted to find information about Back to School Day for Parents under the Parents section of IND's site. They also searched this section of the site for tuition information.

Additional Modifications

As mentioned above, based on user feedback there seem to be very few additional changes needed. Links were added to the Parent section to both the Calendar and Admissions sections of IND. This should help fill out the Parent section as well as improve cross-navigation from this section of the site. The team has also searched for and created clip art appropriate to different sections of the new IND web site. These should help give the individual pages character while still maintaining a strong sense of site branding due to the consistency in color scheme, navigation layout, and page element placement.

Overall, comments on the site have largely been very positive, and the overall rating by testers was very high. Three main areas were targeted when redesigning IND's site: navigation, page layout/color scheme, and content organization. The usability test focused primarily on navigation and content organization. Navigation was improved considerably, and the content currently on IND's web site was organized in a coherent manner, cross-linked between sections where appropriate, and reformatted to be more consistent and pleasing to view. Again, from the comments received from the testers, the team believed their efforts have been successful.

The next to the last step in the development of IND's new web site was to finish adding content to the site, a task for the team and for IND itself. Documentation was finished, and efforts were made to compile an "IND web site maintenance" user's guide so IND would have the information necessary to make changes to the site on their own. In this process, usability testing played a key role in the IND web site development.

Usability Testing Questionnaire

Instructions: Hello and thank you for taking the time to answer the usability questionnaire. We are currently in the process of recreating the IND web site. In order to make the site better for you and other users, we have developed this questionnaire. This questionnaire is about the web site only. All of the answers below can be found on the web site. However, if you do not find the information, please tell us so that we can improve the site for you. Thank you again for helping us to create a better web site.

1. How long ago was the Institute of Notre Dame founded?

2. What is IND's fax number?

3. When is "Back to School Day for Parents for the Fall 2000 Semester"?

4. Who is the Director of Admissions and what is her phone extension?

5. You want to send an e-mail to the Music Director. What is her e-mail address?

6. Who is the Department Chair of the Science Department?

7. How many courses are offered by the Science Department?

8. When was the Alumnae Association organized?

Figure 10.4
continued

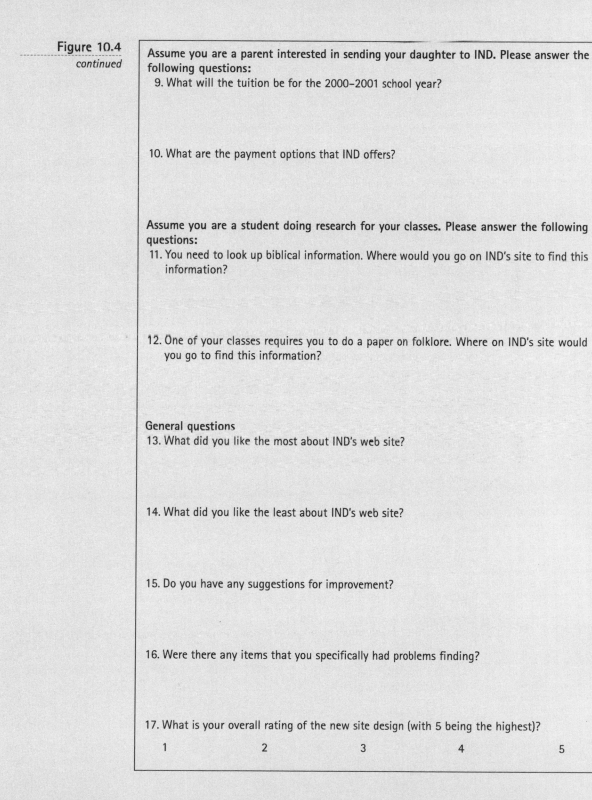

Assume you are a parent interested in sending your daughter to IND. Please answer the following questions:

9. What will the tuition be for the 2000–2001 school year?

10. What are the payment options that IND offers?

Assume you are a student doing research for your classes. Please answer the following questions:

11. You need to look up biblical information. Where would you go on IND's site to find this information?

12. One of your classes requires you to do a paper on folklore. Where on IND's site would you go to find this information?

General questions

13. What did you like the most about IND's web site?

14. What did you like the least about IND's web site?

15. Do you have any suggestions for improvement?

16. Were there any items that you specifically had problems finding?

17. What is your overall rating of the new site design (with 5 being the highest)?

| 1 | 2 | 3 | 4 | 5 |

CASE STUDY #3

▲ Eastman Kodak Company

Introduction

Two rounds of usability testing were conducted during the iterative refinement of the home page design. Chapter 6 discusses paper-based usability testing. This section discusses the computer-based usability test.

Computer-Based Usability Testing

In our second stage of usability testing, which was computer-based, we sought to validate the changes we had made to the top-level site structure and test the home page in actual usage situations. Thirty-three participants were recruited to complete ten information-seeking tasks each using a working prototype of the new site structure. The home page prototype (see Chapter 7) was used in this stage of usability testing.

Top-level pages were prototyped as simple textual listings and groupings of links, without visual design elements. All links were functional and pointed to the appropriate content on kodak.com. As in the earlier usability testing, tasks were designed to cover a broad range of content on kodak.com, but this time with emphasis on information popularly sought by users as identified by corporate customer support staff. Each participant was given three minutes to successfully complete each task. Table 10.1 shows the percentage of participants who were able to complete the tasks in the time given.

In addition to the task completion data, the usability test identified several specific potential improvements (based on feedback from test participants) to the home page to increase its usability, such as: labeling the major "chunks" of information, reducing the number of links, adding descriptors to more of the links, and removing the images along the left-hand side. These improvements were incorporated into the next and final iteration of the home page design.

All that remained at this point was to finalize the visual design of the home page. The visual designer worked with input from the rest of the team to develop the design that was presented to kodak.com users in the preview survey. (The details of the survey are discussed in Chapter 11.) After examining a few days' worth of survey respondents' comments, he made some final modifications to the design, which was used in the site launch (Fig. 10.5).

The other top-level pages were designed to follow the same groups of text links and visual design motif, as shown in Fig. 10.6.

TABLE 10-1	Phase II Usability Testing Results—Percentage of Participants Completing the Task Successfully within Three Minutes

Task	Percent completing	Number of participants
General PhotoCD information	100%	11
Job opportunities at Kodak	100%	22
Making gift items from pictures	95%	22
Business scanner	95%	22
Avoiding glowing or red eyes in pictures	91%	22
Using imaging in the classroom	91%	11
Learn about the technology behind digital cameras	91%	11
Online service to organize and share digital pictures	91%	33
General scanner information	86%	22
Inkjet papers	73%	22
Digital camera connectivity problem	73%	11
Discussion forums	64%	11
Gift items that can be bought over the Web	64%	11
Law enforcement imaging application	64%	11
Where to buy a digital camera	64%	11
E-mail Kodak	55%	11
DC50 camera FAQ	55%	11
Vacation photography tips	28%	11
Getting photographic quality prints from DC120 camera	18%	11
DC210 camera Windows compatibility question	18%	11
Thermal printer comparison	18%	11
Sample pictures	9%	11

Figure 10.5

The final design used
in the site launch

Figure 10.6

An example of a
top-level page

Implementation and Marketing

This chapter describes the process of implementing and marketing a web site. After the web site has been coded and the usability testing has been performed, then it is time to unveil the web site to the world. Many people refer to this step as "going live." However, before the web site can go live, a number of issues need to be decided, such as where the web site will be housed and what the URL will be. Once the site goes live, it must be marketed to the target population of users. The client organization is obviously interested in garnering high user traffic, so it is important to let the target user population know that the web site is there, waiting for them to come visit.

► 11.1 IMPLEMENTATION: HOUSING THE WEB SITE

Where do you house a web site? This may seem like an odd question, since a web site can be accessed from anywhere. However, a web site is based at a web server. Whenever a user requests a web page, the request is sent along to the web server where the actual web pages, the HTML files, are physically housed. The actual geographic location is relatively meaningless; however, there needs to be a "home" where these files reside. Usually, web sites are built and tested on accounts or servers that are owned by the web development team. When the web site is ready to go live, these files need to be moved from the web development team's server to the client's server.[1] If the web development team is not going to be involved in the ongoing maintenance of the web site, then the team should provide a backup copy of the web site files, as well as documentation on the files and on the overall structure of the web site, to the client.

A client organization may decide to set up their own web server with an internet connection and run it out of their organization. This is generally the solution for larger-scale web sites (such as e-commerce web sites), and this setup requires an intensive amount of work. However, smaller-to-medium sized web sites are usually housed on the web server at an Internet service provider. Internet service providers generally provide access to the Internet, as well as an e-mail account, for users for a monthly fee. Most ISPs also provide their users with web hosting space, where the user can post web pages in their account. Many universities also allow users to post web pages. In these situations, the URL for the web pages would be something along the lines of <http://www.towson.edu/~username> or <http://www.ispname.com/~username>.

Domain Name

The client organization needs to decide whether they want to reserve a domain name specifically for their web site. If an organization called the Singing Grillers (they are people who like to sing while making dinner on the barbeque grill!) chooses to purchase a domain name, the URL of the web site might be something like this: <http://www.singinggrillers.org>. On the other hand, if the client organization chooses just to use their ISP account for their web pages, without reserving a domain name, the URL will be: <http://www.ispname.com/~singinggrillers>. The second URL is obviously harder to remember, and it doesn't look as professional when you want to advertise your web site. In addition, if the client organization ever wants to move their web site to another ISP, the URL will change.[2] If you change ISPs and have to change your URL, the entire marketing process must start again. It's like moving from one house to another—everyone must be informed of the new address. If the client organization reserves a domain name, that domain name will stay constant and the users will always know where to find the web site.[2] Web developers can find out what domain names are still available by checking out the web site <http://www.internic.net/> or one of the domain name registrars, such as <http://www.register.com/>. It is important to remember that a domain name should not be very long, or include words that are commonly misspelled. A domain name that is short and easy to spell will help users remember. For instance, www.barnesandnoble.com was shortened to www.bn.com, which is much easier to remember.

ISP Services

In general, many ISPs have two separate levels of service, one level for residential customers and one for businesses. The residential customers will get Internet access, as well as the ability to post an estimated 10–30 MB of web pages, while the business customers will be able to post a minimum 40 MB of web pages. The ISP will register and manage a domain name, such as <http://www.singinggrillers.com>, for the business customer. The business customer will get also advanced features, such as FrontPage extensions, the ability to run CGI scripts, database connectivity, and access to server logs. If any feature (such as FrontPage extensions) is needed for the web site to run, the web development team should check that the ISP offers those features. The ISP will incrementally charge the business customer for larger amounts of web server space and more features. It is best to check the rates and services offered by a number of ISPs because these prices and features offered change rapidly. A current estimate of costs is $20 per month for a residential customer, and $50 for a basic-level business customer. This cost may be higher or lower, depending on how much ISP competition exists in your area. For a thorough list of Internet service providers, look at the following web sites:

http://dir.yahoo.com/Business_and_Economy/Business_to_Business/Communications_and_Networking/Internet_and_World_Wide_Web/Network_Service_Providers/Internet_Service_Providers__ISPs_>

or

<http://webservices.cnet.com/html/aisles/Internet_Access.asp>

The Contract for Web Hosting

The web development team can research and suggest appropriate choices for an Internet service provider, but if the team is not a part of the client organization, the actual contract for web hosting needs to be made between the client organization and the ISP. The web development team might be hired to continuously manage the web site. But in many cases, the web development team will end their involvement with the web site once the web site has been implemented and has been working for a few weeks. The client organization will either manage the web site themselves, or will hire someone else to manage the web site. Therefore, the contract for web hosting should be negotiated by the client organization, not the web development team. In fact, this arrangement should be clarified with the client organization, just to make sure that the client organization does not mistakenly assume that the web development team will manage the web site forever. The web development team should also provide the client organization with any information that is required for maintaining the web site.

The Final Test

When the actual HTML files are moved to the permanent home of the web pages, one final test should be done. The web pages should be examined by the web development team to make sure that the files are all in the correct directories, that all file protections are set correctly, and that no links are incorrect. It is possible that when the files were installed, some of the files were not placed into the correct subdirectories. When a user clicks on a link, it is possible that he or she will get an error message because the link is to a file that is in the wrong subdirectory. If there is any advanced functionality using CGI scripts, style sheets, or external JavaScript files, these should be tested to make sure that those files are in the correct location and are working properly. At this point, the site is live. People can access it from anywhere on the Internet. The question is, *will* anyone access your web site? This brings us to our next task, marketing the web site.

► 11.2 MARKETING THE WEB SITE

"If a tree falls in the woods, and no one is there, does it make a sound?" This is a common saying. In the web environment, this statement can be updated as, "If you create a web site, and no one visits the site, does the web site exist?" Coding is frequently viewed as the last major challenge to implementing a web site, but it is not. An important consideration is how to inform potential users about the existence of the web site. Think of the web site as a new product. Advertisements for cooking tools appear on the Food Network on cable television. Advertisements for clothing geared towards teenagers appear on MTV. When a new product is introduced, it must be marketed to the target audience. But Geritol commercials will probably not appear on MTV, and commercials for the new CD from the Backstreet Boys will probably not be seen on the Golf Channel. This same approach of marketing to a *target population of users* should be used when marketing a web site. The questions are: How can you reach those targeted users and will marketing be the responsibility of the web development team or will their responsibility end when the site goes live? A number of approaches for marketing a web site (such as letterhead and outgoing e-mails) are really outside of the control of the web development team, so these are naturally best handled by the client organizations themselves.

Large-Scale Traditional Marketing

A number of traditional marketing techniques can be used to market a web site. Most large organizations already use the traditional marketing techniques of television commercials, radio spots, and newspaper and magazine advertisements.[3] The URL of the organization's web site can be placed at the end of these media advertisements. Or, new advertisements can be created to grab the attention of potential users. For instance, William Shatner (Captain Kirk of *Star Trek* fame) did a number of commercials for the priceline.com web site. Television commercials for pets.com (now out of business) had a dog hand-puppet singing praises about the web site. Television commercials are expensive, and only large organizations and e-commerce sites tend to have large enough budgets to spend on this type of expensive mass media advertisement. An informational web site for a local school may not have a marketing budget at all, whereas a large e-commerce site may have millions of dollars to spend on advertising.

Small-Scale Traditional Marketing

Organizations with small marketing budgets (mostly informational web sites) can use smaller-scale marketing approaches. For instance, Pennsylvania was the first state to include the URL of their web site on their license plates.[4] Although most organizations cannot place their URL on a license plate, any organization can place their URL on a license plate frame.

Figure 11.1
A URL displayed on a tote bag

Figure 11.2
A URL displayed on a button

Figure 11.3
A URL displayed on a button

The URL can also be placed on various types of free "give-aways," such as t-shirts, tote bags, refrigerator magnets, buttons, lanyard key chains, mouse pads, pens, coffee mugs, frisbees, and leather portfolios.[2] These freebies should be distributed in places where many potential users of the web site are expected. Some examples are displayed on this page. The University of Maryland Human-Computer Interaction Lab places their URL on a tote bag (Fig. 11.1), which is distributed to those who attend their annual open house. Fool.com (a financial services company) places their URL on buttons (Figs. 11.2 and 11.3), which are passed out at parades and festivals. Ecampus.com places their URL on a t-shirt (Fig. 11.4), which is sent to those who purchase textbooks, and is likely to be worn by a college student on campus. TJ Maxx places their URL on plastic bags (Fig. 11.5), which are used to carry home purchases.

Other marketing methods can be used at minimal cost. An important way of marketing a web site is to include the URL on all related organizational materials. These materials include letterheads, business cards, newsletters, and promotional fliers.[3] These materials are already budgeted, so usually no added cost is involved. Many organizations have guidelines for any materials (such as press releases, newsletters, and fliers) that are sent outside of the organization. For instance, a policy

Figure 11.4
A URL displayed on a t-shirt

Figure 11.5
A URL displayed on a shopping bag

might specify that the organizational logo must be included in the upper right-hand corner, in red, and the organizational motto ("We're number 5—and improving!") must be included. These guidelines can simply be modified to require that the organizational URL be included on all publications released for distribution outside of the organization.

Computer-Based Marketing

Marketing a web site is not limited to advertisements or freebie giveaways. If you want users to go to a web site, you can reach them online. There are a number of different ways to reach potential users online.

Online Communities

Many online communities exist on the web, where users who share similar interests and hobbies gather to communicate and share resources.[5,6] These online communities consist of communication tools, such as listservers, newsgroups, and chat rooms, as well as shared resources, such as web pages and searchable databases.[5,6] Online communities provide a gold mine of marketing opportunities because they offer a concentrated, dedicated group of users who have a shared interest. Many e-commerce companies are getting involved in building online communities for this very reason.[6] It is very helpful to find an online community that relates to the topic of your web site, and where members of the target user population would be easy to reach. Information about the new web site can be posted on listservers, newsgroups, and mentioned in chat rooms. A link to the new web site can be added to the online community's web pages. Common sense is a good guide in finding appropriate communities, for instance. It would not be wise to post a message about a new web site for college students majoring in chemistry to the newsgroup alt.fan.seinfeld (which is for fans of the sitcom "Seinfeld"). Information about the many topical listservers is available at <http://www.liszt.com>. Similar information about topical newsgroups is available at <http://www.deja.com/usenet>.

Reciprocal Links

Even if an online community does not exist, you can still try to determine what web sites should provide a link to your new web site. First, determine what web sites your targeted population of users are likely to visit. This type of information might have been collected during the requirements gathering. Ask those related web sites to provide a link to your web site. You can offer to reciprocate by providing a link back to their web site. This would obviously not be feasible for e-commerce sites, which would not want to help bring customers to their competitors. But this is a very appropriate approach for informational web sites. If the client organization is a local or regional chapter of a national organization, or is affiliated in any way with a national professional organization, these partnerships should be utilized to direct traffic to the web site by providing reciprocal links.

In addition, if a web site already exists and is simply being redesigned, you can find out who is already linking to the web site. Many search engines (such as http://www.hotbot.com) allow users to do a search for web pages that link to a certain URL. As an example, one could use the search engine <http://www.hotbot.com> to find out which web pages provide a link to the web site for the Archdiocese of Baltimore <http://www.archbalt.org>. An example of this can be seen in Fig. 11.6.

Web Rings

Another possibility is to join a web ring.[2,7] A web ring is an agreement between web sites that allows the user to be taken on a virtual tour of related web sites,

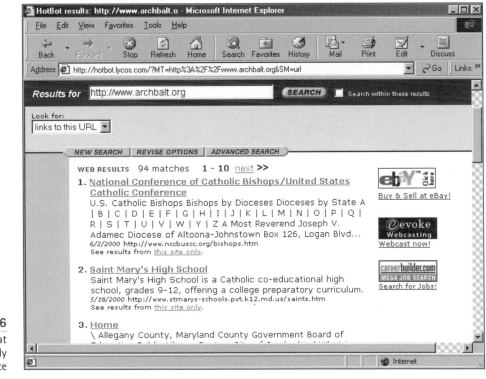

Figure 11.6

Finding out what web pages already link to your site

by linking together web sites of similar topics into a ring.[7] The user clicks on a link on each web site that will take them to the next web site in the ring.[2] To find web rings that are appropriate to reach the target population of users, go to <http://www.webring.com/> or <http://www.ringsurf.com>.

Banner Ads

In another method, the client organization can pay for banner advertisements.[7] A banner advertisement usually appears at the top or bottom of a web page so that it captures the user's attention.[7] If users click on the banner advertisement, they are directed to a new web site, usually the site of the organization that paid for the banner advertisement.[7] This is called a click-through.

Geographic Targets

If your web site is targeted towards a specific geographic area (such as school or a neighborhood club), it is possible to find other web sites that will also be targeted towards that geographic area. For instance, many newspaper web sites (such as *The Baltimore Sun* and *The Washington Post*) and city-based online communities (such as the Blacksburg Electronic Village and Seattle Community Network) have a section for local organizations, providing links to organizations in that geographic area.

E-mail

One additional way of marketing a web site is to add the URL to all outgoing e-mails from the client organization.[2] Most e-mail programs allow a user to specify a signature file that appears at the bottom of all outgoing e-mail messages. Many users include a signature file that basically replicates a business card, with the postal address, phone, fax, and e-mail address. The URL for the client organization's web site should also be included in all outgoing e-mail messages. Although this is not something that is within the control of the web development team, they certainly can encourage the client organization to use this opportunity to let users know about the organization's web site.

Search Engines

A majority of web users have used a search engine when they are looking for web pages that relate to a specific topic. The users know the topic that they want, but they do not know what web pages exist related to this topic. Because users go to a search engine looking for web sites, search engines are important places for marketing a web site. There are a number of ways to make sure that the web site is included in the search engine:

1. Go to the search engine and register the web page yourself. Some of the search engines (such as http://www.hotbot.com) allow users to manually add information on a web site to the search engine (see Fig. 11.7). Other web sites, such as Yahoo.com, provide subject catalogs, where web sites are organized by category. These web sites also allow you to request that a web site be added to the subject catalog (see Fig. 11.8).

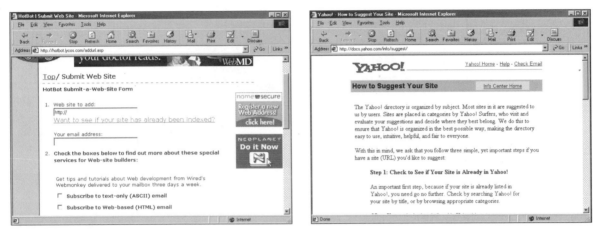

Figure 11.7

Adding a web site manually on hotbot.com

Figure 11.8

Adding a web site manually on Yahoo.com

2. A number of services will automatically submit your web site to search engines. You submit the URL of the web site, and the service will submit the web site to 50–400 search engines (Fig. 11.9). Some, such as <http://www.addme.com>, are free and some, such as <http://www.submit-it.com> and <http://www.world-submit.com>, charge a fee for this service.

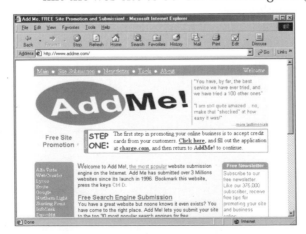

Figure 11.9

An example of a service that submits web sites to multiple search engines

3. Many search engines add web sites to their databases by using "spiders" or "robots" to find sites on the web. You can increase the likelihood that a search engine will "find" your web site by adding some extra code in the HTML document.[2,8] Meta tags can be used to assist the search engines. Using <meta> tags, you can specify a brief description of the web page, as well as appropriate keywords. <meta> tags should be placed in between the <head> tags in an HTML document. The following code[2,8] provides an example of how to do this:

```
<meta name="description" content="Dr. Jonathan Lazar's Classes and Research and Guitar Chords and Tofu Recipes">
<meta name="keywords" content="Lazar, User Error, Tofu, Guitar, Vegetarian, Baltimore">
```

Not all search engines will utilize these meta tags, but on the other hand, they will not really hurt your download speed, so there is no downside to including them.[8]

▶ 11.3 CONSIDERATIONS FOR SITE REDESIGN

Most of this chapter is not of great concern to those who are redesigning a currently existing web site. Implementation is a relatively simple step for those who are redesigning a web site. In designing a web site for the first time, the web development team and the client have to grapple with the issue of where to host the web site and whether to purchase a domain name. For those who are redesigning a web site, however, these decisions have likely already been made. It is certainly possible that the client organization has decided, as a part of the site redesign, that they want to change their ISP, or purchase a domain name for use in the new site. In most cases, the new web site will remain in the same location as the old web site.

Having the redesigned web site in the same URL location as the old web site is important, because this directly relates to the marketing of the web site. If the web site already exists, there are a certain number of people who visit the site, who have links on their web pages to the site, and who have the site bookmarked in their browser. Hopefully, through previous marketing, the web site is receiving user traffic. In that case, you do *not* want to move the web site to another URL location. The worst thing is for users to attempt to visit a web site and find that it is no longer there.

When implementing a site redesign, it might be useful to place a small message on the web site saying, "We hope you like our new web site design. Here's why we did it. . . . Contact us if you have any suggestions." It would be useful to do a small marketing campaign to the target population when a site redesign has been completed. E-mail messages can be sent out over listservers or newsgroups to let users know that the web site has changed, and to encourage them to come back and visit the web site again. The marketing should provide a good reason why users should revisit the site, such as: "Because we care about you, the user, we have made the web site easier to use, and we now offer more content!"

If users have specific pages bookmarked, they should be able to continue finding the same content at the same URLs. No user wants to see a "404-file not found" in their browser window.[9] However, if the client organization feels strongly about changing the URL, then it is important to market this fact. A great deal of marketing (as described earlier in this chapter) should be done to let the users know that the web site is moving. In addition, information about the new web site and the new URL should appear when a user requests the old URL. Also, when a user requests the old URL, <meta> tags can be placed on the web page to "pull" the user to the new web page.[8] These <meta> tags can be used in the following way:

```
<meta http-equiv= "refresh" content="5; url=http://www.newurl.org">
```

where http://www.newurl.org is the new web site that users should be directed to, and 5 is the number of seconds between the time the page is loaded and when the new web page will be requested. Although this is not a perfect solution, this is better than not directing the user to the new web site.

SUMMARY

The implementation stage of web development is exciting. At this stage, the web site has been coded and has gone through both functionality and usability testing. HTML files are then transferred to the permanent host, and the web site "goes live." The whole world can see the web site that the development team has worked hard to create. Marketing of the web site to the target user population must be done to let users know about the existence of the web site. After all, the web site can be a success only if users visit it.

Deliverables

At this point, you should have:
1. Determined where the web site will be hosted, and at what URL
2. Transferred the HTML files to the hosting server
3. Determined a date for having the web site "go live"
4. Designed and implemented a marketing plan

Discussion Questions

1. Why is it useful to have a domain name for the web site?
2. What qualities make up a good domain name?
3. What does it mean to "go live"?
4. What is an online community, and why might it be useful for marketing a web site?
5. What are some traditional, low-cost methods of marketing that are appropriate for web sites?
6. What are some methods of marketing a web site that will not incur any additional expenses?
7. What are two different methods of marketing a web site through a search engine?
8. How is marketing a new web site different from marketing a redesigned web site?

REFERENCES

1. Burdman, J. (1999). *Collaborative Web Development*. Reading, MA: Addison-Wesley.
2. Sweeney, S. (1999). *101 Ways to Promote Your Web Site*. Gulf Breeze, Fl : Maximum Press.
3. Powell, T., Jones, D., & Cutts, D. (1998). *Web Site Engineering: Beyond Web Page Design*. Upper Saddle River, NJ: Prentice Hall.
4. Eggen, D. (2000). States' plates say it. *The Washington Post*, July 23, 2000.
5. Lazar, J., & Preece, J. (1998). *Classification schema for online communities*. Proceedings of the 1998 Association for Information Systems Americas Conference, 84–86.
6. Preece, J. (2000). *Online Communities: Designing Usability, Supporting Sociability*. New York: John Wiley & Sons.
7. Navarro, A., & Khan, T. (1998). *Effective Web Design*. San Francisco: Sybex.
8. Niederst, J. (1999). *Web Design in a Nutshell*. Sebastopol, CA: O'Reilly and Associates.
9. Lazar, J., & Norcio, A. (2000). *Intelligent error message design for the Internet*. Proceedings of the 2000 World Multiconference on Systemics, Cybernetics and Informatics, 532–535.

CASE STUDY #1

▲ Best Buddies Maryland

Hosting

The web development team was very excited to have reached the implementation stage. One of the first issues they investigated in this stage was where the Best Buddies Maryland web site should be hosted. Some of the options that were explored included using a "free" hosting company, paying for server space from a hosting company, and attempting to get disk space on a server at a local university. Early in the development process, the client reported that they had very few funds available for paying for hosting of their web site. Additionally, they preferred to have an easy-to-remember domain name. Because of these constraints, the development team worked hard to find an attractive solution. After dismissing the possibility of free hosting because the domain name needed to be easy to remember (many of these services also required placing banner ads on the site, which was unattractive to the client), the development team found a local hosting company that offered special pricing to nonprofit organizations. Unfortunately, the Chapter Director of Best Buddies Maryland fell ill soon after this and the hosting decision was delayed.

After discussing the issue at length with the Program Manager of Best Buddies Maryland on two separate occasions, the development team was referred to an employee within the Best Buddies International office. After several attempts to reach this employee failed, the development team received an e-mail message from Best Buddies International very late in the project. In the message, the international organization volunteered to handle the registering of the Best Buddies Maryland domain name. At the time of implementation, www.bestbuddiesmd.org was the client organization's leading choice for a domain name. Best Buddies International took over hosting tasks through the director of their E-Buddies program. E-Buddies is a virtual community that connects buddy pairs through the Internet. In addition to facilitating these friendships, E-Buddies has recently taken on the tasks of helping with domain name registration and providing web site hosting space to the state chapters. Although a separate domain name is planned for the future, in the meantime, the web site of Best Buddies Maryland will be located at the URL: http://www.bestbuddies.org/md. The final web site is displayed in Fig. 11.10.

Marketing

It was decided that the marketing of the Best Buddies Maryland web site would be handled by Best Buddies International, who would market the web site in a variety of ways. First, the Best Buddies Maryland web site would be registered with several search engines. Presently, Best Buddies International registers their web sites with at least a dozen search engines including Yahoo, AltaVista, and Hotbot. Second, the Best Buddies Maryland web site would have a link from the Best Buddies International web site. The

Figure 11.10

Final web site for
Best Buddies
Maryland

international organization has a web page that lists all of the state chapters and provides links to those who have a web site. Third, the Best Buddies Maryland web site would trade reciprocal links with related organizations. These organizations include those that help people with special needs, such as Special Olympics and the Association for Retarded Citizens (ARC). The web site development team expected that these web sites would have target user populations that are similar to that of Best Buddies. Fourth, Best Buddies International would post the addresses of chapter web sites on listservers that focus on people with mental retardation. In addition, the Best Buddies Maryland Home Page would have keywords in its meta tags to help people find the site when searching the Internet. These meta tag keywords would include those found on the Best Buddies International site, which primarily relate to mental retardation, and also terms such as Maryland, Baltimore, Montgomery County, and Annapolis to bring in local traffic. The keywords would be added to the site prior to sending the files to E-Buddies. Finally, future mailings from Best Buddies Maryland would include the Uniform Resource Locator (URL) for the web site.

Management

The topic of management is divided into the following two categories: who should serve as webmaster and how often should the site be updated. A member of the development team offered to manage the Best Buddies Maryland web site for the next year, free of charge. His management of the site is pending the approval of Best Buddies International, which, as mentioned above, has taken on the responsibility of hosting the site and registering the domain name. After the year is up, a decision will need to be made on whether or not the team member will continue to be the webmaster, or if the international organization will take on that responsibility.

The Best Buddies Maryland web site contains several pages that need to be updated at least once a month. A brief description of each of these follows. The Previous Events page will be updated more often than the other pages. Best Buddies Maryland usually has several events going on each month; therefore, this page will need to be updated often. The Guest Book will also need to be updated often. The Guest Book itself will not change but the messages posted in it will need to be monitored closely and frequently. All improper messages or messages showing a lack of sensitivity will need to be deleted as quickly as possible. Each month, a new Buddies of the Month friendship pair will be chosen by Best Buddies Maryland, so this page will need to be updated monthly. As Best Buddies Maryland trades web site links with other organizations involved in helping people with disabilities, the Related Organizations page will need to be updated. The affiliated schools page will be updated when new schools join Best Buddies, when they provide a web site link for Best Buddies, or when they are no longer affiliated with the organization. The Calendar of Events page, is, perhaps, the most obvious section of the Best Buddies Maryland web site that will need regular updating. This page will be updated every month and pages with additional event information will be added as links from within the calendar. Were this page not to be updated it would be the most obvious evidence that the site was not being properly managed. Additionally, people will rely on this site for information as to when and where events are being held, so even last minute changes in these events should be reflected on this page. The other pages on Best Buddies Maryland may not need to be updated every month.

Summary

The web development team has been privileged to work with such an enthusiastic client. At the very end of the project, Best Buddies International handled any remaining issues about registering, hosting, and marketing the site. From the beginning, however, Best Buddies Maryland has been extremely cooperative. They were always willing to meet with the team whenever necessary and tried to provide access to any information needed for the web site. The Best Buddies Maryland staff of Carri Cerri, Michelle Bicocchi, and Jill Halbrecht deserve much of the credit for making their web site the useful and attractive information tool it is. The client was also very patient throughout the development life cycle and this patience paid off in the resulting site. By following this methodology of first gathering user requirements, then building the web site, then having users test the site, then implementing user-suggested improvements, the development team was able to create what is truly a user-centered web site.

CASE STUDY #2

▲ Institute of Notre Dame

Because IND had an already-existing web site and that web site was being redesigned, the implementation and marketing stage of the development process was relatively easy. Most of the decisions had been previously made by the IND staff, including Fred Germano.

Hosting

The web site development team and IND agreed that the redesigned web site would continue to be housed on IND's own web server. IND does not have the most powerful web server, but Mr. Germano did not expect a very large increase in the site traffic due to the redesign of the web site, so the current server should be sufficient. Mr. Germano also mentioned that he would upgrade the server if necessary at a future time. IND had previously reserved the indofmd.org domain name, and Fred will continue to use the URL <http://www.indofmd.org> for the IND web site. The redesigned web site is displayed in Fig. 11.11.

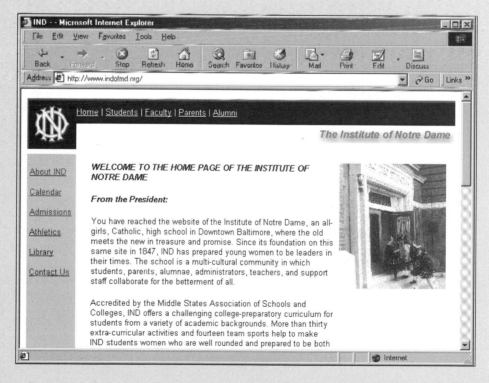

Figure 11.11

Final web site for IND

Marketing

The IND web site had already been on the web a while, and so there were a number of web sites that already provided links to the IND web site. However, the web site development team would get the word out about its "facelift" through an announcement made to teachers and students at IND. Also, the team expected to notify alumnae about the site redesign through the alumnae newsletter, and notify parents through the parent newsletter. Fred Germano indicated that he would register the IND web site with various search engines. The site was already registered, but since it had received a redesign, the team believed that it would be a good idea to reregister it.

Management

To start with, Fred Germano would manage the web site himself. However, later he would like to have the students and faculty be able to create and post their own pages. The web site development team would provide IND with templates for the site, so that IND could create new pages easily. Currently, IND uses many of Microsoft's products; they already had purchased Microsoft FrontPage and they were now trying to learn how to use it. After the students and faculty have been trained to use FrontPage, IND did not anticipate having any problems creating new pages with the templates that the team would provide. As more users are trained to create web pages, it is expected that there would be an increased number of web pages. At that time, the faculty and staff would themselves be responsible for keeping the web pages up to date. In the meantime, most web pages would not need to be updated frequently. Only the Calendar of Events pages would need to be updated frequently. The other web pages, such as the list of teachers in the school, the alumnae reunions, and the admission information, would require infrequent—perhaps once a year—updates. According to Fred Germano, as the number of web pages increases, a search engine might be added to the IND web site. This would be relatively easy to do, since IND already uses Microsoft Internet Information Server (IIS), which provides services for search engines.

Summary

Overall the web site development team's experience with this project has been very pleasant. The most difficult aspect of the project was getting information from the users at IND. Although Fred Germano was very helpful, many times the team had trouble getting feedback from the users themselves. As the academic year came to an end, everyone involved with the school (teachers, students, parents, and Fred Germano himself) became busier and less available to the development team. For the future, it might be good to attempt a site redesign when the users themselves are more accessible and less busy. But everyone at IND was always friendly, the facilities of the school were beautiful, and the team enjoyed working with IND.

CASE STUDY #3

▲ Eastman Kodak Company

Previewing the New Design with Users

Before the launch of the new Web page design, visitors to the kodak.com Web site were given a chance to preview the new site design and offer their feedback. At the end of many Kodak Web pages, a link was provided where users who followed the link could view an HTML prototype of the new home page. The links, while functional, pointed to "dead-end" pages that described the content to which each link would point. We did not link to the actual content in kodak.com because we didn't want users to navigate any more deeply than the new home page and either get sidetracked or provide comments that were not about the new home page. Users then had a chance to fill out a short Web-based survey. The survey was linked from the footer of every page of the site.

The survey was not intended to be a representative sampling of all kodak.com users. Because we placed the link on every page and invited users to come and comment, we were not randomly sampling within a defined population and could not make any claims regarding the generalizability of the results. Instead, we were simply trying to get as many opinions as we could get on the new design. In this sense, the survey was quite successful, yielding opinions and comments from over 800 visitors of kodak.com. Respondents to the survey answered two questions: "How appealing is the overall design of the new Kodak home page?" and "Overall, how does the new Kodak home page compare with the current Kodak home page?" The responses are listed in Tables 11.1 and 11.2.

TABLE 11-1	Results of Preview Survey: Overall Appeal

How appealing is the overall design of the new Kodak home page?

Response	% Respondents
Wow!!!	14.36%
Very appealing	48.51%
Appealing	25.87%
Neither appealing nor unappealing	5.43%
Unappealing	3.49%
Very unappealing	0.65%
Ugh!!!	1.68%
Number of Respondents = 773	

TABLE 11-2	Results of Preview Survey: Comparing Current and New

Overall, how does the new Kodak home page compare with the current Kodal home page?

Response	% Respondents
Much better	48.29%
Better	31.10%
Somewhat better	9.97%
Neither better nor worse	5.51%
Somewhat worse	2.89%
Worse	1.05%
Much worse	1.18%
Number of Respondents = 762	

We carefully read each of the 710 open-ended comments offered by survey respondents, and separated them into three categories: positive (total 338 comments), negative (total 162), and neutral or both positive and negative (total 210). Below is a sampling of positive comments. The fact that the results were so positive gave us confidence that the design would be well-received by users.

A Sampling of the Best

- I really like it! I didn't know all this cool content was under the current home page.
- This is one of the best homepage sites that I have visited. I hope you'll let me know when it's ready for use.
- Color scheme is excellent. Shows great definition and makes sense in that it corresponds well with the Kodak image. Much improvement for the consumer who had to search for info in the previous version. Much more consumer friendly. Why not make picture network more accessible? Perhaps try framing at the top for quick reference to consumer pages, like picture network and postcard page. Overall, loads up nicely, which isn't always the case today on the Net.
- It looks as though you've done your homework on what people are looking for on your site. Very nice. Clean, visually appealing, not distracting.
- The colors seem to say "Kodak!" Nice design and it makes it easy for users to find what they need.
- Very well thought out!—It appears that Kodak is a company that is very customer oriented and will be supporting our needs for years to come.
- This page makes going around the Web site a great deal easier. I was able to figure out more of where I needed to go. On the current page, I found it hard and unsure of the exact link I needed.
- I look to Kodak for info on how to make better pictures and how to use your products to achieve this. My impression is that the new home page will make it easier to get the information I need.
- It is neat, very "crisp," uncluttered. It is object-oriented, which will be a tremendous assist in navigation. I really like the features presented on the page and will definitely bookmark so I can return to peruse when it is finished. I like the colors, which are traditional for Kodak products. It seems to be "quick" to respond, but the pages are not yet loaded in for testing out that component. (I hate waiting forever for a page to load.) It seems representative of the trademark Kodak quality.
- Like Kodak products, it is excellent.
- Having been a proponent of Kodak merchandise for the past forty years, I think this Web site only fortifies my belief in Kodak's commitment to quality consumer products. MAGNIFICENTLY DONE!

A Sampling of the Worst

- It is a "muddled" list of things with little focus; neither aesthetic nor efficient. I find it disturbing that a corporate giant like Kodak, whose business is largely "visuals," cannot put a decent, simple, clever, attractive homepage up on the Web. Of course, this is just my opinion.

- Too busy. Does not make a single, powerful statement. Confusing or at least not easy to grab at once.

- While every element of the page is gorgeous, they are in violent competition for attention. Brilliant color is visual chocolate—too much can make you sick.

- Please leave the old home page if you not coming up with something better than that. It is cluttered hard to read and the selection of colors does not account for Kodak's image at all. Why change something good just for the sake of changes?

- I think you need to simplify the page even more. The viewer is hit with a very dense set of options made worse by the use of the black background. Also, avoid scrolling. Many viewers may not realize more is below. Alternatively, decide that the information contained below is not important. It's better to lead people to another page than to try to put everything on the first page. Use cookies to find out what is most interesting for the viewer and give it to them again when they come back to the site. Usually a viewer will be coming back for similar information based on products they own or use. "Hot info" can be placed in a text area on the viewers screen in case they want to jump-start the process.

- The new home page might be somewhat "busy," I tend to prefer fewer links per page, afraid that I'll overlook what I'm looking for, or miss links that might interest me because of the visual overload from many links.

Based on the results of the survey, we felt comfortable moving ahead with launching the redesigned top level as planned.

Marketing

Kodak issued press releases on the new site design. The teamwork and process that went into the new site design was featured in a local business publication. Because kodak.com was a Web site that had already existed, it was not necessary to address issues such as domain name registration, search engine registration, or marketing. Users already knew about kodak.com and how to access the site.

After the Launch

Surprisingly enough, we received very little feedback on the new site design. Because the change in the site design from old to new was so drastic, we were expecting to be inundated with user comments through the kodak.com "Guest book." In fact, we received no more "Guest book" messages pertaining to site design after the launch of the redesign than before it—around one percent of the messages daily.

Because of the need to reassign resources to other work immediately following the site redesign launch, kodak.com did not have the luxury of thoroughly studying the effects of the new design. Instead, we relied on the knowledge that we had developed the design based on a rigorous user-centered design approach, using various techniques for requirements gathering and thorough usability testing. The endorsement of hundreds of kodak.com users who rated the new design favorably in the prelaunch survey confirmed that the new design was a success.

Ongoing Maintenance

The new design was based on text links organized into logical groups. No limit was set on how many links could appear in a group or how many groups could appear on a page. As such, it became much easier to add links, change links, or remove links without significantly affecting the overall look of the page. Change requests became much more frequent, although it is unclear whether this was the result of the fact that changes were now easier to make, or that Kodak as a company was doing more that required changes to be made, or both. Consequently, change requests needed to be addressed much more frequently than with the previous design—both for the home page and for top-level pages.

The responsibility of handling change requests became the joint responsibility of three individuals—the site editor, the visual design director, and the user interaction design lead. These three worked together to determine the best way to accommodate requests through adding, modifying, or removing links and changing groups, wording, and/or labels. The actual development of kodak.com content was, and continues to be, a responsibility distributed among Kodak's various business units and corporate groups.

In 2000, kodak.com expanded its emphasis from being primarily an informational and product sales Web site to include a focus on being the Web's premier photo community, offering users a variety of interactive picture enhancement, printing, storage, sharing, and learning opportunities online. Subsequent redesigns of the kodak.com home page have reflected the ways in which Kodak's business has and continues to grow and change.

Maintenance and Evaluation

After a web site has been implemented, a periodic evaluation must be performed to determine if there are any problems and to see whether the web site continues to meet the needs of the users. If the web development life cycle has been followed properly, the web site will meet the needs of the targeted users at the time of the site's implementation. But over time, this situation may change. Content might become outdated, users might desire new types of content and features, and competition might increase. Over time, the technology might change as well. Outside factors such as newer browser versions, or changing HTML standards, might cause a web site redesign to be necessary. Many large-scale traditional informational systems have been running 15–20 years. Although this longevity is admirable, it is impossible to predict what the Web will be like 10 years from a given date. The technical foundations for the Web have only been around since 1990, and at that time, it would have been impossible to predict what the Web looks like today. Guidelines on how to evaluate and maintain a web site can be given, but it is truly impossible to predict what the Web will look like in the future; evaluation techniques, technologies, and the need for redesign might be substantially different in the future.

▶ 12.1 MAINTENANCE OF WEB SITES

The information and content on a web site must be continuously updated. If the information on a web site is stale and out of date, users will not continue to visit the web site.[1,2,3,4] Powell et al. refer to this process as content maintenance.[3] There should be a clear process for determining what needs to be updated, who has the responsibility for updates, and how frequently the web site will be updated.[3] Although it is possible that the client organization may hire someone to perform the actual content maintenance, the responsibility for providing the content ultimately belongs to the client organization.[3] During conceptual design, it should have been noted which web pages will need to be updated most frequently. For instance, a calendar or a web page that describes current events will need to be updated on a very frequent basis. However, all web pages should be updated frequently enough so that the information presented on the web page is current. In addition, web pages should note the date on which they were last updated. The date alone provides reassurance to the user that the information on the page is up to date. If any web pages change location, meaning that the same content is now located at a different URL, the old URL should provide information on where the content is currently located for at least one year after the content has moved.[5]

Another type of maintenance involves making sure that all of the links on the web site still lead to active sites.[2] Linked web sites are outside of the client organization's control. These outside sites may change URLs, or simply may "disappear" off the Web. Users can become frustrated if they receive a lot of "404–File not found" error messages,[6] and if a web site has a lot of dead links, it can lower the user's perception of the quality of the web site. Links can be checked by hand, but there are also a number of web sites that will check for dead links, such as <http://watson.addy.com/> and <http://websitegarage.netscape.com/>.

▶ 12.2 EVALUATION OF WEB SITES

Evaluation is an important aspect of maintenance activities in traditional information systems.[7,8] Without evaluation, it is impossible to know whether users are still happy with the system, whether changes need to be made, or even if a new system needs to be developed.[9] A periodic evaluation of the web site should be done to ensure that the web site is meeting the needs of the users, and that there are no functionality or usability problems. Although the web site originally might have met the needs of the users, those needs might have changed since the original launch date of the web site.

How do you periodically check on whether user needs have changed? As a start, users should be encouraged to e-mail their feedback related to the web site. This feedback might contain a user's opinion of the web site or a notification of a problem with the web site: content is old, links are incorrect, or there is a technical problem. This feedback is an informal type of evaluation. Feedback from users should get attention! It is likely that if there is a problem with the web site, for every user who e-mails about the problem, there are a number of users who experienced the same problem but did not send an e-mail about it. The idea is that users shouldn't get frustrated and leave, never to visit the web site again. Instead, the user should be encouraged to e-mail the web site manager (also called the webmaster), describing the problem or suggestion. A link (or a web-based form) should be provided on the web site so that users can easily make suggestions or provide feedback. In addition, it might be helpful to provide customized server error messages (when users select the correct web server but the wrong file name), so that users are provided information on how to find the correct HTML file.[6]

▶ Some Maintenance Tasks Include:
1. Keeping content up-to-date
2. Adding new content
3. Trimming old links
4. Performing periodic evaluations

Evaluation Surveys

One technique for performing an evaluation is to ask users to fill out surveys, providing their opinion about the current web site, and discussing their needs. These surveys are easier to implement than the initial surveys that were used to collect requirements for a new web site because there should now be an established population of users. When users access the currently existing web site, they can be asked to fill out a short list of questions, usually implemented using HTML forms. These questions can relate to user content needs, user computing environment, or any of the other important topics discussed in Chapter 4. Those responses can then be used to determine whether changes need to be made in the web site. In addition, if users are readily accessible, all of the requirements gathering techniques used in Chapter 5 can also be used as a part of evaluation. For example, as IBM updates and improves their ease-of-use web site <http://www.ibm.com/easy>, customer satisfaction surveys are used to determine if the web site is still meeting the needs of the targeted user populations.[1] Users of the IBM ease-of-use web site are asked questions related to navigation, task efficiency, consistency, and overall user satisfaction.[1] If users are available for taking part in focus groups, interviews, or phone interviews, then these are also appropriate techniques for evaluating a web site.

For larger-scale evaluations, a number of standardized surveys have been developed for determining user satisfaction with information systems. These surveys include the Questionnaire for User Interaction Satisfaction (QUIS),[10,11] which is one of the most widely used satisfaction surveys. This survey addresses users' satisfaction with their computer interaction. The QUIS is a multipart questionnaire that includes 12 different sections for topics such as screen layout, use of appropriate terminology, and multimedia.[10] The QUIS has been tested and validated in the research literature.[10,12,13] The QUIS is designed so that the different sections can be used individually to meet the specific needs of the evaluation.[10] A sample of the types of questions included on the QUIS are included in Figure 12.1. More information about the QUIS is available at http://lap.umd.edu/quis.

Because the need for evaluating web sites is relatively new, there is no one standardized evaluation tool (such as the QUIS for satisfaction with the user interaction experience), and some of these evaluation surveys are still in development and testing. These evaluation surveys include the WebMAC survey, the Information Quality survey by Zhang and colleagues, and the Web Analysis and MeasureMent Inventory (WAMMI).

WebMAC Survey

The WebMAC is a set of surveys to evaluate the motivational quality of web sites. Motivational quality is the concept of determining which features motivate users to spend time on a web site and return to that web site at a later time.[14] The WebMAC survey includes several different surveys related to different types of web sites, such as business and education, to assist in determining where web sites may need improvement. A sample of questions from the WebMAC is shown in Figure 12.2. For more information about the WebMAC surveys, go to <http://istweb.syr.edu/~digital/CDC/Resources/resources.htm>.

Figure 12.1

Sample questions
from the
Questionnaire for
User Interaction
Satisfaction (QUIS)
survey

Please circle the numbers that most appropriately reflect your impressions about using this computer system. Not applicable = NA.

Part 3: Overall User Reactions

Overall reactions to the system

Terrible   Wonderful
1   2   3   4   5   6   7   8   9   NA

Frustrating   Satisfying
1   2   3   4   5   6   7   8   9   NA

Dull   Stimulating
1   2   3   4   5   6   7   8   9   NA

Difficult   Easy
1   2   3   4   5   6   7   8   9   NA

Inadequate power   Adequate power
1   2   3   4   5   6   7   8   9   NA

Rigid   Flexible
1   2   3   4   5   6   /   8   9   NA

Part 10: Multimedia

Overall quality of still pictures/photographs
Bad   Good
1   2   3   4   5   6   7   8   9   NA

Picture/photo clarity
Fuzzy   Clear
1   2   3   4   5   6   7   8   9   NA

Picture/photo brightness
Dim   Bright
1   2   3   4   5   6   7   8   9   NA

Overall quality of movies
Bad   Good
1   2   3   4   5   6   7   8   9   NA

Focus of movie images
Fuzzy   Clear
1   2   3   4   5   6   7   8   9   NA

Brightness of movie images
Dim   Bright
1   2   3   4   5   6   7   8   9   NA

Figure 12.1

continued

Adequacy of movie window size
Never adequate   Always adequate
1   2   3   4   5   6   7   8   9   NA

Overall quality of sound output
Inaudible   Audible
1   2   3   4   5   6   7   8   9   NA

Smoothness of sound output
Choppy   Smooth
1   2   3   4   5   6   7   8   9   NA

Clarity of sound output
Garbled   Clear
1   2   3   4   5   6   7   8   9   NA

Overall quality of colors
Unnatural   Natural
1   2   3   4   5   6   7   8   9   NA

Number of available colors
Inadequate   Adequate
1   2   3   4   5   6   7   8   9   NA

Please write your comments about multimedia here:

_____

_____

_____

_____

_____

_____

_____

Figure 12.2

Sample questions
from the WebMAC
E-Business survey

Place the appropriate number about this web site on the line preceding each item.

3 = strongly agree
2 = somewhat agree
1 = somewhat disagree
0 = strongly disagree
NA = not applicable

_____ 1. The home page of this web site is eye-catching and visually interesting.
_____ 2. The information at this web site is accurate and unbiased (or the bias is properly identified).
_____ 3. The visuals (e.g., videos, photographs) and audio included in this web site enhance the presentation of service(s) and information offered.
_____ 4. The screen layout makes the site easy to navigate.
_____ 5. There are incentives at this site that motivate me to explore it.
_____ 6. This web site provides links to other relevant web sites.
_____ 7. This web site provides enough information about the services offered.
_____ 8. This web site has a help function that I can use at any time.
_____ 9. The screen layout of this web site is attractive.
_____ 10. This web site provides information that allows me to judge the company's credibility.
_____ 11. There is a menu or site map that helps me understand how this web site is organized.
_____ 12. I can control how fast I move through this web site at all times.
_____ 13. The information at this web site is written in an interesting manner.
_____ 14. The information at this web site appears to be current and up to date.
_____ 15. The purpose of this web site is always clear to me.

(Questions used with permission of Dr. Ruth Small. For more information about the WebMAC surveys, go to <http://istweb.syr.edu/~digital/CDC/Resources/resources.htm>.)

Information Quality Survey

An Information Quality survey is currently being developed by Zhang, Keeling, and Pavur.[15] This focuses on user perceptions of the quality of a web site based on the home page.[15] The argument is that, if the user does not perceive the home page to be of high quality, then the user will not go any farther in the web site. This survey focuses on evaluation of the presentation, navigation, and quality of a web site.[15] Sample questions are included in Figure 12.3. (For more information about this survey, see Zhang, Keeling, and Pavur, 2000.)

Figure 12.3

Sample questions
from the Information
Quality survey

Presentation

1. The use of graphics is very appropriate for this site.

1	2	3	4	5	6	7
Strongly disagree			Neutral			Strongly agree

2. The design elements are not annoying or distracting.

1	2	3	4	5	6	7
Strongly disagree			Neutral			Strongly agree

3. The amount of information displayed is just right.

1	2	3	4	5	6	7
Strongly disagree			Neutral			Strongly agree

4. The colors in this web site are pleasant.

1	2	3	4	5	6	7
Strongly disagree			Neutral			Strongly agree

5. This site organized its information in a way that is easy for me to understand.

1	2	3	4	5	6	7
Strongly disagree			Neutral			Strongly agree

6. This site's attractiveness invites me to go further into this site.

1	2	3	4	5	6	7
Strongly disagree			Neutral			Strongly agree

WAMMI

Another survey developed for evaluating web sites is the WAMMI (Web Analysis and Measurement Inventory). The WAMMI focuses on user satisfaction with web sites.[16] The WAMMI was developed based on feedback from a large number of users, developers, and webmasters as to what makes a positive or negative experience on a web site. WAMMI focuses on the major issues of the attractiveness of a web site, whether users feel in control, whether users can complete their tasks in an efficient manner, whether help or information is easily available, and whether the site is easy to learn.[16] The WAMMI can be used only by paying a fee; more information about the WAMMI is available at <http://www.wammi.com/>.

All of these survey tools have a slightly different focus, but some of them require a fee for use. For most smaller-scale evaluations, it is not necessary to purchase one of these survey tools. Instead, survey questions can be developed that relate to the specific concerns on a web site.

Web Site Logs

Web site logs provide yet another useful technique for evaluation. When a user requests a web page, that request is sent to a web server, which responds to the request. When responding to the user's request, the web server records data about the request such as the time of the request, the IP address of the user making the request, and the file that was requested.[2] From the data provided by web site logs, it is possible to get a rough estimate of important information, such as how many users visit a web site, what web pages are most popular, and what types of users are viewing the web site.

How the server records the data is partially dependent on web server software, and the web developer (or webmaster) can also specify what is to be recorded.[17] The data can be recorded in a number of separate log files, or it can be recorded together. There can be as many as four separate log files—the transfer log, the error log, the referrer log, and the agent log—or this same data can be concentrated in fewer log files.[17]

- The *transfer log* records the file requested, the time of the request, and the IP address of the user making the request.[17] This data can help determine who is accessing the web site, and which pages are most popular. An example of this is shown in Fig. 12.4.

- The *error log* records requests that were not able to be successfully fulfilled because the user entered the incorrect file name, or tried to retrieve a file for which file permission was lacking.[17] This data can help determine where users frequently made errors. (For example, another web site might be providing a link to an incorrect URL on the client's web site.) It can show where there are problems that need to be corrected.[17]

- The *referrer log* records the URL of the web page that the user was viewing when they sent a request for the web page.[17] This data is useful because it can help spotlight which web sites are driving user traffic to the client's web site.[17]

- The *agent log* records the name and version of the user agent (the browser) that is sending the request for the web page.[17] This data can assist in determining what browser is being used.

Figure 12.4

Transfer logs for
triton.towson.edu on
December 1, 2000.

```
> 172.132.226.130 - - [01/Dec/2000:08:00:11 -0500] "GET /~jkemp1/
> HTTP/1.1" 304 -
> 172.132.226.130 - - [01/Dec/2000:08:00:14 -0500] "GET
> /~jkemp1/advertising/metallic.jpg HTTP/1.1" 304 -
> 136.160.177.185 - - [01/Dec/2000:08:00:29 -0500] "GET /~schmitt/311/
> HTTP/1.1" 200 2061
> 136.160.177.185 - - [01/Dec/2000:08:00:29 -0500] "GET
> /~schmitt/311/images/tucosc.gif HTTP/1.1" 304 -
> 136.160.177.185 - - [01/Dec/2000:08:00:29 -0500] "GET
> /~schmitt/311/images/quiz.gif HTTP/1.1" 304 -
> 136.160.177.185 - - [01/Dec/2000:08:00:29 -0500] "GET
> /~schmitt/311/images/present.gif HTTP/1.1" 304 -
> 136.160.177.185 - - [01/Dec/2000:08:00:29 -0500] "GET
> /~schmitt/311/images/discuss.gif HTTP/1.1" 304 -
> 136.160.177.185 - - [01/Dec/2000:08:00:29 -0500] "GET
> /~schmitt/311/images/journal.gif HTTP/1.1" 304 -
> 136.160.177.185 - - [01/Dec/2000:08:00:29 -0500] "GET
> /~schmitt/311/images/assignment.gif HTTP/1.1" 304 -
> 157.2.21.248 - - [01/Dec/2000:08:04:50 -0500] "GET
> /~schmitt/server/servlet/bookstore/src HTTP/1.0" 301 267
> 136.160.177.164 - - [01/Dec/2000:08:05:07 -0500] "GET /~schmitt/311/
> HTTP/1.0" 200 2061
> 136.160.177.164 - - [01/Dec/2000:08:05:07 -0500] "GET
> /~schmitt/311/images/tucosc.gif HTTP/1.0" 200 5905
> 136.160.177.164 - - [01/Dec/2000:08:05:07 -0500] "GET
> /~schmitt/311/images/quiz.gif HTTP/1.0" 200 885
> 136.160.177.164 - - [01/Dec/2000:08:05:08 -0500] "GET
> /~schmitt/311/images/assignment.gif HTTP/1.0" 200 1560
> 136.160.177.164 - - [01/Dec/2000:08:05:08 -0500] "GET
> /~schmitt/311/images/discuss.gif HTTP/1.0" 200 1592
> 136.160.177.164 - - [01/Dec/2000:08:05:08 -0500] "GET
> /~schmitt/311/images/journal.gif HTTP/1.0" 200 1778
> 136.160.177.164 - - [01/Dec/2000:08:05:08 -0500] "GET
> /~schmitt/311/images/present.gif HTTP/1.0" 200 1054
> 136.160.177.164 - - [01/Dec/2000:08:05:09 -0500] "GET
> /~schmitt/311/01.html HTTP/1.0" 200 2155
> 136.160.177.164 - - [01/Dec/2000:08:05:10 -0500] "GET
> /~schmitt/311/images/tulogo2.gif HTTP/1.0" 200 1712
> 136.160.177.164 - - [01/Dec/2000:08:05:10 -0500] "GET
> /~schmitt/311/images/info.gif HTTP/1.0" 200 436
> 136.160.177.164 - - [01/Dec/2000:08:05:11 -0500] "GET
> /~schmitt/311/schedule.html HTTP/1.0" 200 2103
> 152.15.63.197 - - [01/Dec/2000:08:05:15 -0500] "GET /~stripl1/scorp1.gif
> HTTP/1.1" 200 29112
> 196.34.250.8 - - [01/Dec/2000:08:05:22 -0500] "GET
> /users/tparke2/list.html HTTP/1.1" 200 159748
>
```

All of this data is recorded in log files, which can be long and difficult to read. Summary data and trend analyses can be difficult to determine by eyeballing the data; therefore, a software program, such as Analog <http://www.statslab.cam.ac.uk/~sret1/analog/> can provide more accurate statistical analyses on web site logs.

It is important to note that counting a web "hit" is not equivalent to counting a user. If a web page includes five objects—the HTML file and four graphics—this will be a total of five hits, but this is actually only one page viewed by one user.[17] When that same user views other pages on the web site, these page views are recorded in the web site logs, but this is still only one user. So, it is very possible that a web site claiming to have one million hits might have only 10,000 users. In addition, it is sometimes hard to identify a unique user, because some ISPs do not provide users with a unique and permanent IP address, but rather, reassign users an IP address from a pool of IP addresses each time they log on.[2]

Those operating their own web server have access to the data in web site logs. Most business customers who have an account with an ISP will also have access to web site logs, and possibly to free software to analyze the web site logs.[2] Many ISPs, however, do not provide access to web site logs for their residential customers. In addition, most universities and organizations do not allow standard users to access the web site logs for their HTML files. However, web site log analysis is a growing field, and there are a number of consulting firms that can assist in the analysis.

▶ 12.3 WHEN TO REDESIGN A WEB SITE

A site redesign may become necessary when the current design of the web site no longer meets the needs of the user. The old cliché "If it ain't broke, don't fix it" remains true.[18] If there is nothing wrong with a web site, if it is meeting the needs of the users, and if it is providing the functionality desired by the client organization, there is no need to redesign it.[18] A site redesign is not the same as adding new content because new content should be added whenever appropriate. A site redesign is appropriate only when improvement is needed in the overall structure, navigation, and interface of the web site. A site redesign may mean that users might need to relearn the navigational structure of the web site, and this can actually harm the user's performance, so a site redesign should be done only when necessary.

A number of factors can trigger the need for a new site design: (1) when user feedback indicates that there are some usability problems with the web site, (2) when the number of pages (or the changing content) is starting to outgrow the current navigation scheme, or (3) when the client organization wants to offer new content or functionality on the web site. If this functionality can simply be offered by adding a few web pages and incorporating them into the overall structure of the web site, then a site redesign would not be needed. On the other hand, if a web site is moving from a 10-page informational site to a database-driven e-commerce site, a redesign would be necessary. Two other factors might trigger a new design: the client organization might have a changed mission or the client organization might want to expand the target user population for the web site, and therefore, the services offered need to be increased.

When a web site needs to be redesigned, the web development life cycle begins again. The target user population and the mission of the web site should be revisited with the client organization to determine whether these are still appropriate. A requirements gathering should be done to determine what the current needs of the users are. In summary, the web developer returns to Chapter 2 and starts the whole process again!

SUMMARY

Web site maintenance involves a number of different tasks. Content must be continuously updated. Old and outdated links need to be trimmed. Periodic evaluations should be performed to determine if the web site is still meeting the needs of the users. Satisfaction surveys and web site logs can be used to assist in the periodic evaluations. If the evaluation determines that the web site is no longer meeting the needs of the users, then it might be time to redesign the web site. At that point, the web development life cycle starts again.

Discussion Questions

1. How is updating content different from redesigning a web site?
2. When is it appropriate to redesign a web site?
3. What are four major maintenance tasks, and what does each entail?
4. What are some of the different evaluation surveys available, and how do they differ?
5. What are web site logs, and how can they be useful in evaluation of a web site?

REFERENCES

1. Dong, J., & Martin, S. (2000). *Iterative usage of customer satisfaction surveys to assess an evolving web site.* Proceedings of the Human Factors and the Web. Available at: http://www.tri.sbc.com/hfweb/

2. Navarro, A., & Khan, T. (1998). *Effective Web Design.* San Francisco: Sybex.

3. Powell, T., Jones, D., & Cutts, D. (1998). *Web Site Engineering: Beyond Web Page Design.* Upper Saddle River, NJ: Prentice Hall.

4. Zeff, R., & Aronson, B. (1999). *Advertising on the Internet.* New York: John Wiley & Sons.

5. Larsen, L., & Henry, D. (1998). *Nightmare on webstreet.* Proceedings of the ACM SIGUCCS Conference on User Services, 157–162.

6. Lazar, J., & Norcio, A. (2000). *Intelligent Error Message Design for the Internet.* Proceedings of the 2000 World Multiconference on Systemics, Cybernetics and Informatics, 532–535.

7. Hoffer, J., George, J., & Valacich, J. (1999). *Modern Systems Analysis and Design.* Reading, MA: Addison-Wesley.

8. Preece, J., Rogers, Y., Sharp, H., Benyon, D., Holland, S., & Carey, T. (1994). *Human-Computer Interaction.* Wokingham, England: Addison-Wesley.

9. Stewart, C., Grover, D., & Vernon, R. (1998). Changing almost everything and keeping almost everyone happy. *CAUSE/EFFECT, 21*(3), 39–46.

10. Norman, K., Shneiderman, B., Harper, B., & Slaughter, L. (1998). *Questionnaire for User Interaction Satisfaction.* College Park, MD: University of Maryland.

11. Shneiderman, B. (1998). *Designing the User Interface: Strategies for Effective Human-Computer Interaction* (3rd ed.). Reading, MA: Addison-Wesley.

12. Chin, J., Diehl, V., & Norman, K. (1988). *Development of an instrument measuring user satisfaction of the human-computer interface.* Proceedings of the CHI: Human Factors in Computing Systems, 213–218.

13. Harper, B., Slaughter, L., & Norman, K. (1997). *Questionnaire administration via the WWW: A validation and reliability study for a user satisfaction questionnaire.* Paper presented at WebNet 97 Conference. Available at http://lap.umd.edu/quis.

14. Small, R., & Arnone, M. (2000). Evaluating the Effectiveness of Web Sites. In B. Clarke & S. Lehaney (Eds.), *Human-Centered Methods in Information Systems: Current Research and Practice* (pp. 91–101). Hershey, PA: Idea Group Publishing.

15. Zhang, X., Keeling, K., & Pavur, R. (2000). *Information quality of commercial web site home pages: An explorative analysis.* Proceedings of the International Conference on Information Systems, 164–175.

16. Kirakowski, J., Claridge, N., & Whitehand, R. (1998). *Human centered measures of success in web site design.* Proceedings of the Human Factors and the Web. Available at: http://www.research.att.com/conf/hfweb/

17. Stout, R. (1997). *Web site stats.* Berkeley, CA: Osborne McGraw Hill.

18. Selingo, J. (2000). A message to web designers: If it ain't broke, don't fix it. *The New York Times,* August 3, 2000

Index